LATIN AMERICAN HISTORY

A Teaching Atlas

Published in Honor of
Howard F. Cline

Conference on Latin American History
Tinker Foundation

Latin American History: A Teaching Atlas

Latin American History
A Teaching Atlas

Cathryn L. Lombardi
John V. Lombardi
with
K. Lynn Stoner

Published for
The Conference on Latin American History
by
The University of Wisconsin Press

Preparation of this atlas has been
assisted by generous support from
The Tinker Foundation, Inc.

The University of Wisconsin Press
114 North Murray Street
Madison, Wisconsin 53715

3 Henrietta Street
London WC2E 8LU, England

10 9 8 7 6 5 4 3

Printed in the United States of America

Library of Congress Cataloging in Publication Data
Lombardi, Cathryn L.
Latin American history, a teaching atlas.
Includes index.
Bibliography: pp. xiv-xvi.
Contents: The Latin American environment—
The colonial period—The modern period.
1. Latin America—History—Maps. 2. Latin America—
Historical geography—Maps. 3. Latin America—Maps.
I. Lombardi, John V. II. Stoner, K. Lynn.
III. Conference on Latin American History. IV. Title.
G1541.S1L6 1983 911'.8 83-675775
ISBN 0-299-09710-2
ISBN 0-299-09714-5 (pbk.)

For

Clyde F. Lee
H. Lorene Lee

Contents

THE LATIN AMERICAN ENVIRONMENT

THE COLONIAL PERIOD
The Iberian Background

The Amerindian Background

THE MODERN PERIOD
Latin American Boundaries

Latin American International Relations

Latin American Countries ca 1975

Latin American Population

Latin American Economies and Society

INDEX

Introduction

LATIN AMERICAN HISTORY: A Teaching Atlas is the result of the cooperation, enthusiasm, and vision of many people and institutions. Most of them are mentioned in the Acknowledgments, but it is important to emphasize the vision of Howard Cline whose interest in Latin American maps was long, enduring, and profound. The extensive collection of published maps accumulated during his dynamic leadership of the Hispanic Foundation of the Library of Congress proved to be one of the important resources for this *Teaching Atlas.*

Designed to provide students and teachers of Latin American subjects with a set of useful cartographic materials, *Latin American History: A Teaching Atlas* emphasizes themes and topics appropriate for undergraduate courses in Latin American affairs. Although the main audience for this *Atlas* is, of course, composed of history students, the thematic approach is broad enough for the materials to be useful for politics, geography, and culture and civilization students as well. No collection of maps of this size can hope to be complete, and many important themes and topics had to be omitted for the lack of space or the absence of adequate, comparable information. Reflecting the historical approach taken by the *Teaching Atlas,* the material follows in basically chronological order.

After an introductory section that displays the basic physical features of the Latin American landscape in terms of geography, vegetation, and climate, the *Atlas* contains twelve parts covering the colonial period into the last quarter of the twentieth century. Although the maps themselves are self-explanatory, some comments about the rationale for thematic selection and organization may be appropriate.

Latin American history, for the purposes of this *Atlas,* begins with the discovery and conquest of America. The pre-conquest Indian civilizations and the history of Iberia before 1492 serve primarily as background for understanding the post-discovery history of Latin America. For this reason, the treatment of pre-conquest Indian civilizations is less than complete, and the same can be said of the maps on the Iberian background.

The discovery and conquest periods have traditionally attracted great interest in courses on Latin American culture and civilization. As a result, this part of the *Atlas* includes a number of maps with some emphasis on the conquest of Mexico.

Most courses on Latin America in the colonial period spend considerable time on the formal organization of government in order to explain the development and management of colonial economies and society. This part of the *Atlas* displays the general outlines of the captaincies, audiences, viceroyalties, and other jurisdictions at several points in the colonial period.

Although the mapping of commerce and trade is at best difficult, the *Atlas* includes a set of maps focused on trade, resources, and the competition for them. Special emphasis on the slave trade was made possible by the availability of Philip Curtin's *The Atlantic Slave Trade: A Census.* The maps on pirates, privateers, and interlopers illustrate the international competition for the domination of trade to and from Spanish America. The importance of mining in colonial Spanish America required an indication of the location of mining sites throughout the region, and the section on the colonial period ends, appropriately enough, with some maps of the independence-era military campaigns in South America.

The modern period of Latin American history, taken to begin after 1830, provides a wealth of more or less complete data suitable for mapping. However, this *Teaching Atlas* focuses on themes that are either difficult to discuss without maps or lend themselves to cartographic presentations.

Boundary disputes, almost impossible to discuss without maps, constitute a significant part of this category. Although not all the boundary disputes in Latin America could be accommodated, many of the more prominent controversies are included. Nothing mapped here should, of course, be taken as a judgment on the relative merits of any country's claims.

The international involvement of Latin America in the world wars and the League of Nations is included along with a display of United States interventions in Central America and the Caribbean.

No *Teaching Atlas* would be complete without a set of reasonably current maps for each of the countries of Latin America. The set included here is based on the *Britannica Atlas* which is current to about 1975. They provide a ready reference for instructors who want to discuss themes not included in this *Atlas.*

The final maps of the *Atlas* display a selection of data on modern Latin America focusing on population, economics, and society. Naturally, there is much more information available than could be included in this publication. Not all of it is usefully displayed on maps while other data are of primarily specialized interest. The maps included here illustrate some major characteristics of modern Latin America useful in classroom instruction. The population maps show relative changes in recent years, including urbanization. The economic maps show the dramatic contrasts within the Latin American region on a wide variety of indicators such as gross domestic product, investment, labor force, inflation, and public debt. In addition, a map on energy consumption is included as a surrogate for a standard of living index and a map on primary school students serves as an indicator of basic literacy and schooling.

The last section of the *Atlas* is a complete index of names and topics included on the maps. Place names in Latin America cause innumerable problems. We have followed the *Britannica Atlas* and *Webster's New Geographical Dictionary,* unless one of our advisors indicated a persuasive case for some other spelling.

This, then, is the general pattern of *Latin American History: A Teaching Atlas.* If these maps help students understand the complex environment and history that is Latin America, they will have realized the Conference of Latin American History and the Tinker Foundation's vision in sponsoring this publication.

Acknowledgments

LATIN AMERICAN HISTORY: A Teaching Atlas exists thanks to the cooperation and support of many individuals and institutions. Although it is only possible to acknowledge them briefly here, we are forever in their debt for all the generous assistance provided us throughout the process of preparing this publication. In every case, we received excellent advice and counsel. Although we could not always adopt the suggestions or implement the recommendations we received, the *Atlas* is a much improved document because of the help of many people.

From the members of the Editorial Board, listed above, came consistent advice and counsel throughout the design and preparation of this publication. Their advice, coming from experts in a wide range of disciplines related to Latin American studies, provided the principal reference for decisions related to content and style. Frederick M. Nunn chaired the Editorial Board with tact, efficiency, and wisdom. His skillful coordination of editorial advice kept our communications with the Editorial Board clear and productive.

Of course, this publication could not have happened without the strong support and encouragement of the Tinker Foundation. Ms. Martha Twitchell Muse, President of The Tinker Foundation, took an active interest in the project, and continued the Tinker Foundation's strong support for Latin American projects. Dr. Kenneth Maxwell, Program Director of The Tinker Foundation, also encouraged and supported all our efforts, and his suggestions proved most helpful.

At the University of Wisconsin Press we have been fortunate to work with a number of individuals whose interest in this project dates from the first tentative proposals. At the beginning of the project, Thompson Webb and Irving E. Rockwood offered excellent advice on the design and style of the *Atlas.* Over the course of this project we have greatly benefited from communications with Peter Givler, and Julie Kinney. All have been helpful and encouraging.

Most of the research for the maps during the first two years of this project was the responsibility of K. Lynn Stoner whose contribution to the *Atlas* is substantial. Without her commitment, energy, and knowledge we would have been hard pressed to develop the materials necessary for this work.

In addition to these individuals, we have received advice and assistance from many other people. While it is not possible to clearly indicate the importance of each of their contributions to the success of this project, their expertise in many fields proved indispensable in our work. G. Micheal Riley, one of the promotors and developers of this project as Executive Secretary for CLAH during the first years of the project, deserves much of the credit for getting the *Atlas* organized and launched, and he has remained an important contributor to our work throughout the project. Thomas M. Davies, Jr., the current Executive Secretary of CLAH, has maintained this high level of interest and commitment to the project and made our work smooth and efficient. The successive chairmen of CLAH during the lifetime of the project have also strongly supported our work and offered many helpful comments and suggestions. We are most grateful to Stanley J. Stein, Richard E. Greenleaf, James R. Scobie, Charles A. Hale, Dauril Alden, John J. TePaske, and Herbert S. Klein for all their help.

The *Atlas* is a project of the Projects and Publications Committee of CLAH. Under the chairmanships of Murdo J. MacLeod and Frederick M. Nunn, the committee has consistently provided strong support and valuable advice. Two other scholars gave important assistance to the project by sharing their extensive knowledge of Latin American historical cartography. Francisco Morales Padrón spent time in Bloomington sharing his draft maps from a forthcoming major cartographic publication, and Frederic Engle sent us copies of very useful maps with early Peruvian historical material.

As is usual in these projects, we have mercilessly exploited our friends and associates in search of material, data, and advice. Dauril Alden has heard a great deal about this project and contributed much more than his share. At Indiana University, Ronald R. Royce, Anya P. Royce, Glenn F. Read, Wesley R. Hurt, and Cathy Lebo gave us good advice and assistance. And our special thanks go to John Michael Hollingsworth of the IU Cartographic Laboratory who frequently found the essential base map, the required lettering style, or the necessary piece of equipment to make a difficult problem become a modest obstacle.

All of these people have helped in so many ways that it is impossible to catalog them all. We did not always accept their advice and suggestions. We probably should have. This *Atlas* reflects on every page their experience and knowledge, although we, of course, are responsible for the final content of the *Atlas.*

We also owe a great debt to the many scholars who have prepared the maps and atlases and done the research on which this synthetic work is based. The first collection of materials came from the Conference on Latin American History which is the custodian of a massive collection of photocopies of maps accumulated under the supervision of Howard Cline. These materials come from every possible printed source, but especially from monographs and texts in the field of Latin American Studies. The bibliography of these items alone runs to twenty pages.

The maps in this *Atlas* come from many sources. In most cases, we combined information from published maps, atlases, monographs, and any other source that seemed appropriate. In a few instances, such as the slave trade maps, we could find a complete set of maps and data that served as the basis for our presentation. These cases are indicated on the maps. Most of the difficulty encountered in preparing the maps came from conflicts among authorities either about what ought to be considered essential data for a map or where specific sites should be located. Often, information on one part of the Americas could not be easily combined with information on another part of the region. However, thanks to the many scholars whose works we consulted, most of these conflicts could be resolved.

While a complete catalog of every source, reference, or map consulted for this project would be more extensive than useful, the following list will give an indication of the range of material used. In some cases, we found that the most current research did not always provide the best maps or offer the clearest representation of places and events on maps. Earlier works frequently offered better maps than more recent scholarship. In any event, an item is included in the following list if it is representative of a category of material, if it served as a major source for one or several maps, or if it contained unique information. The list is not, of course, complete for any of these categories.

The items are organized into five general groups. General Atlases include some of the very useful large-scale collections of maps. Such atlases provide excellent coverage of many topics, although given their wide scope they tend to slight Latin America. A number of Specialized Atlases give highly detailed treatment to a variety of topics. The two items published by the University of Texas Press, Austin, on Mexico and Central America, and the item on Venezuela, show this category at its best. Geographies, it goes without saying, are essential, and several of those consulted appear here. We also found useful synthetic maps in many texts and other general treatments of Latin America. Some of these are included under General Works. The largest category, Specialized Works, represents but a small number of the many items consulted to resolve disputed points, to clarify geographic descriptions, and to identify essential materials.

General Atlases

Britannica Atlas. Chicago, 1974.

Goode's World Atlas. 15th ed. Chicago, 1978.

Hammond's New World Atlas. Garden City, New York, 1947.

Hammond Ambassador World Atlas. New York, 1966.

National Geographic Atlas of the World. 5th ed. Washington, D.C., 1981.

Oxford World Atlas. New York, 1973.

The Times Atlas of World History. Maplewood, New Jersey, 1978.

Specialized Atlases

Amaya Topete, Jesús. *Atlas mexicano de la conquista.* Mexico, 1958.

Arbingast, Stanley A., et al. *Atlas of Mexico.* Austin, 1975.

Arbingast, Stanley A., et al. *Atlas of Central America.* Austin, 1979.

Atlas Amèrica Latina. New York, 1919.

Atlas de Venezuela. Caracas, 1971.

Atlas histórico geográfico y de paisajes peruanos. Lima, 1969.

Miller, Theodore R. *Graphic History of The Americas.* New York, 1969.

Morales y Eloy, Juan. *Ecuador. Atlas histórico-geográfico.* Quito, 1942.

Paz y Miño, Luis T. *Atlas histórico-geográfico de los límites del Ecuador.* Primera parte. Quito, 1936.

Thrower, Norman J.W., ed. *A Thematic Atlas of the World.* 3rd ed. New York, 1975.

United States History Atlas. Maplewood, New Jersey, 1979.

World Atlas of the Child. Washington, D.C., 1979.

World Bank Atlas, 1978. Washington, D.C., 1978.

Geographies

Agricultural Geography of Latin America. Washington, D.C., 1958.

Butlands, Gilbert J. *Latin America. A Regional Geography.* London, 1960.

Geografía de América Latina. Métodos y temas monográficos. Barcelona, 1975.
James, Preston E. *Latin America.* 3rd ed. New York, 1959.
Webb, Kempton E. *Geography of Latin America. A Regional Analysis.* Englewood Cliffs, N.J., 1972.
West, Robert C., and John P. Augelli. *Middle America: Its Lands and Peoples.* Englewood Cliffs, New Jersey, 1966.

General Works

Bailey, Helen Miller, and Abraham P. Nasatir. *Latin America: The Development of Its Civilization.* Englewood Cliffs, New Jersey, 1960.
Bannon, John Francis. *History of the Americas. The Colonial Americas.* 2nd ed. New York, 1963.
Bannon, John Francis. *Latin America.* Encino, California, 1977.
Bernstein, Harry. *Modern and Contemporary Latin America.* New York, 1965.
Bolton, Herbert E. *History of the Americas.* Boston, 1935.
Diffie, Bailey W. *Latin-American Civilization. Colonial Period.* New York, 1967.
Dozer, Donald Marquand. *Latin America: An Interpretive History.* San Francisco, 1962.
Fagg, John E. *Latin America: A General History.* New York, 1963.
Herring, Hubert. *A History of Latin America from the Beginnings to the Present.* New York, 1967.
Historia de España. Barcelona, 1975.
Holmes, Vera Lee Brown. *A History of the Americas: From Nationhood to World Status.* Vol. II. New York, 1964.
Rippy, James Fred. *Latin America: A Modern History.* Ann Arbor, 1958.
Robertson, William Spence. *History of the Latin-American Nations.* New York, 1943.
Shafer, Robert Jones. *A History of Latin America.* Lexington, Mass., 1978.
Wilgus, A. Curtis, et al. *Outline History of Latin America.* New York, 1939.
Williams, Mary Wilhelmine, et al. *The People and Politics of Latin America.* Boston, 1955.
Worcester, Donald E., and Wendell G. Schaeffer. *The Growth and Culture of Latin America.* New York, 1956.

Specialized Works

Adams, Richard E. W. *Prehistoric Mesoamerica.* Boston, 1977.
Bargalló, Modesto. *La minería y la metalúrgia en la América española durante la época colonial.* Mexico, 1955.
Boxer, Charles R. *The Golden Age of Brazil, 1695-1750.* Berkeley, 1962.
Bushnell, G. H. S. *Ancient Arts of the Americas.* New York, 1965.
Clissold, Stephen. *The Seven Cities of Cíbola.* New York, 1962.
Coe, Michael D. *Ancient Peoples and Places: Mexico.* New York, 1962.
Curtin, Philip D. *The Atlantic Slave Trade. A Census.* Madison, 1969.
Driver, Harold E. *Indians of North America.* 2nd ed. rev. Chicago, 1969.
Exquemelin, Alexandre O. *The Buccaneers of America.* London, 1972.
Gandia, Enrique de. *Historia de los piratas en el Rio de la Plata.* Buenos Aires, 1936.
Gerhard, Peter. *The Guide to Historical Geography of New Spain.* Cambridge, 1972.
Gosse, Philip. *The History of Piracy.* New York, 1934.
Henige, David P. *Colonial Governors from the Fifteenth Century to the Present.* Madison, 1970.
Herrmann, Paul. *The Great Age of Discovery.* New York, 1958.
Hockett, Homer Carey. *Political and Social Growth of the United States, 1492–1852.* New York, 1933.
Humphreys, R. A. *Liberation in South America, 1806–1827: The Career of James Paroissien.* London, 1952.
Hussey, Roland D. *The Caracas Company, 1728–1781.* Cambridge, Mass., 1934.
Informationen zur politischen Bildung. "Lateinamerika Geschichte" (Mar/May 1967); and "Mittelamerika Land und Wirtschaft" (Oct/Dec 1967).
Ireland, Gordon. *Boundaries, Possessions, and Conflicts in South America.* Cambridge, Mass., 1938.
Josephy, Alvin M., Jr. *The American Heritage Book of Indians.* New York, 1961.
Kirkpatrick, F. A. *The Spanish Conquistadores.* Cleveland, 1946.
Lahmeyer Lobo, Eulalia Maria. *Administração colonial luso-espanhola nas américas.* Rio de Janeiro, 1952.
Lanning, Edward P. *Peru Before the Incas.* Englewood Cliffs, New Jersey, 1967.
Lecuna, Vicente. *Bolívar y el arte militar.* New York, 1955.

Lynch, John. *Spanish Colonial Administration, 1782–1810: The Intendant System in the Viceroyalty of the Rio de la Plata.* London, 1958.
Mason, J. Allen. *The Ancient Civilizations of Peru.* Middlesex, England, 1957.
McIntyre, L. "Lost Empire of the Incas," *National Geographic,* 6:144, 1973.
Menzel, Dorothy. *The Archaeology of Ancient Peru and the Work of Max Uhle.* Berkeley, 1977.
Metraux, Alfred. *The Incas.* London, 1965.
Navarro García, Luis. *Intendencias en Indias.* Seville, 1959.
Nowell, Charles E. *The Great Discoveries and the First Colonial Empires.* Ithaca, New York, 1954.
Parry, J. H. *The Spanish Seaborne Empire.* New York, 1972.
Penrose, Boies. *Travel and Discovery in the Renaissance, 1420–1620.* New York, 1962.
Pérez Valenzuela, Pedro. *Historias de piratas.* Guatemala, 1934.
Peterson, Frederick A. *Ancient Mexico. An Introduction to the Pre-Hispanic Cultures.* New York, 1959.
Peterson, Mendel. *The Tunnel of Gold.* Boston, 1975.
Priestley, Herbert Ingram. *José de Gálvez. Visitor-General of New Spain (1765–1771).* Berkeley, 1916.
Rowe, John H. "Inca Culture at the Time of the Spanish Conquest," *Handbook of South American Indians: The Andean Civilizations.* Vol. 2, ed. Julian H. Steward. Washington, D.C., 1946.
Sauer, Carl O. *The Early Spanish Main.* Berkeley, 1966.
Schneider, Ronald M., and Robert C. Kingsbury. *An Atlas of Latin American Affairs.* London, 1966.
Scientific American. Pre-Columbian Archaeology. Readings from Scientific American. San Francisco, 1980.
Scobie, James R. *Argentina: A City and a Nation.* New York, 1964.
Stone, Doris. *Pre-Columbian Man Finds Central America.* Cambridge, Mass., 1972.
Time. May 31, 1982.
Vianna, Helio. *História do Brasil. Tomo I–II. Período colonial.* São Paulo, 1961.
Vivo, Jorge Abilio. *Geografía humana de México: estudio de la integración territorial y nacional de México.* Mexico, 1958.
Webster's New Geographical Dictionary. Springfield, Mass., 1980.
West, Robert C. *Colonial Placer Mining in Colombia.* Baton Rouge, 1952.
Wilgus, A. Curtis, and Raul d'Eça. *Latin American History.* New York, 1963.
Wilkie, James W., ed. *Statistical Abstract of Latin America.* Vol. 20. Los Angeles, 1980.
Willey, Gordon R. *An Introduction to American Archeology.* Vol. 1. *North and Middle America.* Englewood Cliffs, New Jersey, 1966.
World Development Report 1981. New York, 1981.
Wycherley, George. *Buccaneers of the Pacific.* Indianapolis, 1928.

Clearly, then, this teaching atlas exists only because of the work and knowledge of many people. It has been a privilege and an experience to participate in this effort, and we thank everyone who helped in so many different ways to make this publication possible.

Cathryn L. Lombardi
John V. Lombardi

Bloomington, Indiana
December 1982

THE LATIN AMERICAN ENVIRONMENT

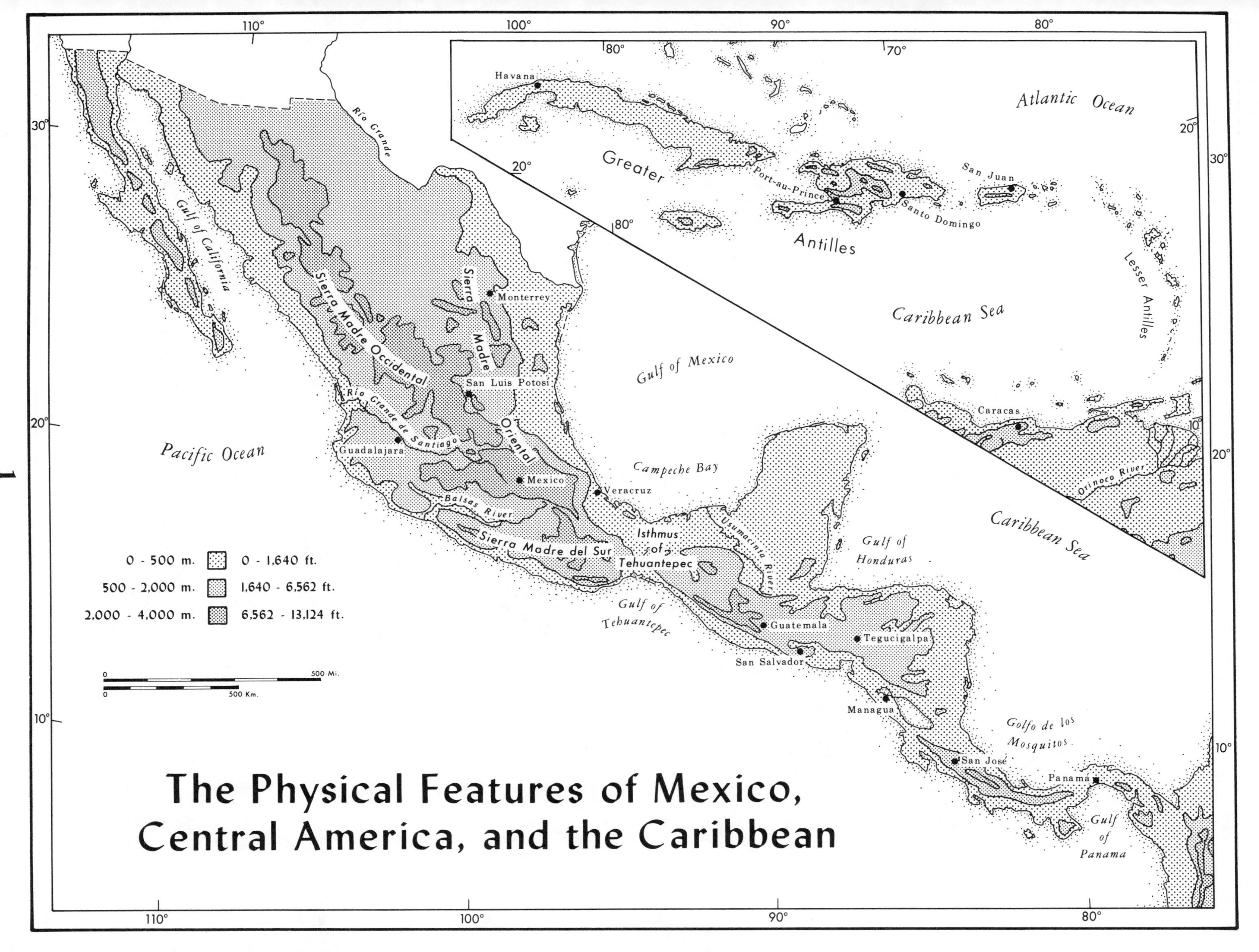
The Physical Features of Mexico, Central America, and the Caribbean
0 - 500 m.
0 - 1,640 ft.
500 - 2,000 m.
1,640 - 6,562 ft.
2,000 - 4,000 m.
6,562 - 13,124 ft.
0
500 Mi.
0
500 Km.
Pacific Ocean
Gulf of California
Río Grande
Sierra Madre Occidental
Sierra Madre Oriental
Monterrey
San Luis Potosí
Río Grande de Santiago
Guadalajara
Mexico
Balsas River
Sierra Madre del Sur
Veracruz
Gulf of Mexico
Campeche Bay
Isthmus of Tehuantepec
Gulf of Tehuantepec
Usumacinta River
Gulf of Honduras
Guatemala
San Salvador
Tegucigalpa
Managua
Golfo de los Mosquitos
San José
Panama
Gulf of Panama
Caribbean Sea
Havana
Greater Antilles
Port-au-Prince
Santo Domingo
San Juan
Atlantic Ocean
Lesser Antilles
Caracas
Orinoco River
110°
100°
90°
80°
70°
30°
20°
10°

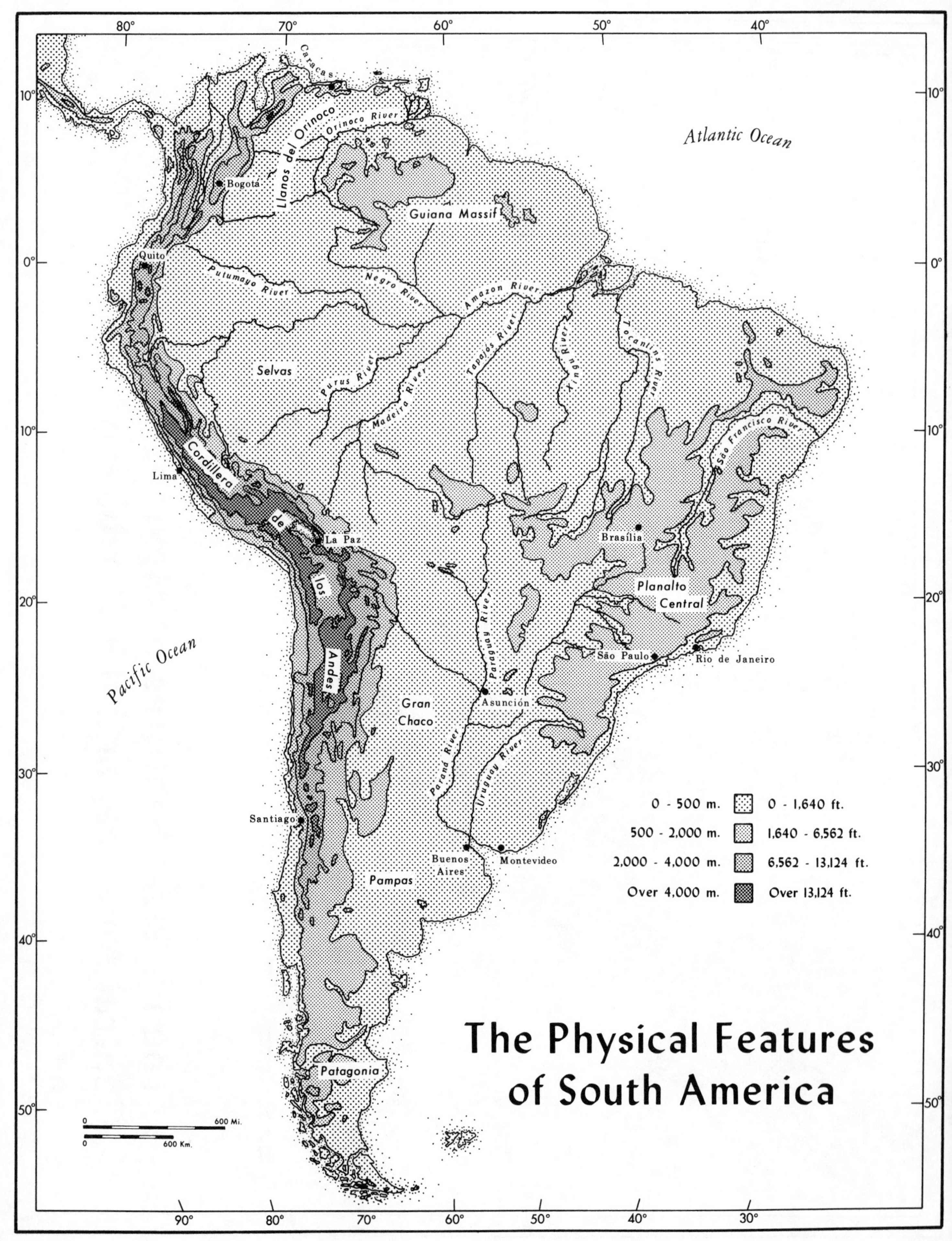

Caracas
Llanos del Orinoco
Orinoco River
Bogotá
Guiana Massif
Atlantic Ocean
Quito
Putumayo River
Negro River
Amazon River
Selvas
Purus River
Madeira River
Tapajós River
Xingu River
Tocantins River
São Francisco River
Lima
Cordillera de los Andes
La Paz
Brasília
Planalto Central
Pacific Ocean
Paraguay River
São Paulo
Rio de Janeiro
Gran Chaco
Asunción
Paraná River
Uruguay River
Santiago
Buenos Aires
Montevideo
Pampas
Patagonia
0 - 500 m.
0 - 1,640 ft.
500 - 2,000 m.
1,640 - 6,562 ft.
2,000 - 4,000 m.
6,562 - 13,124 ft.
Over 4,000 m.
Over 13,124 ft.
0 600 Mi.
0 600 Km.

The Physical Features of South America

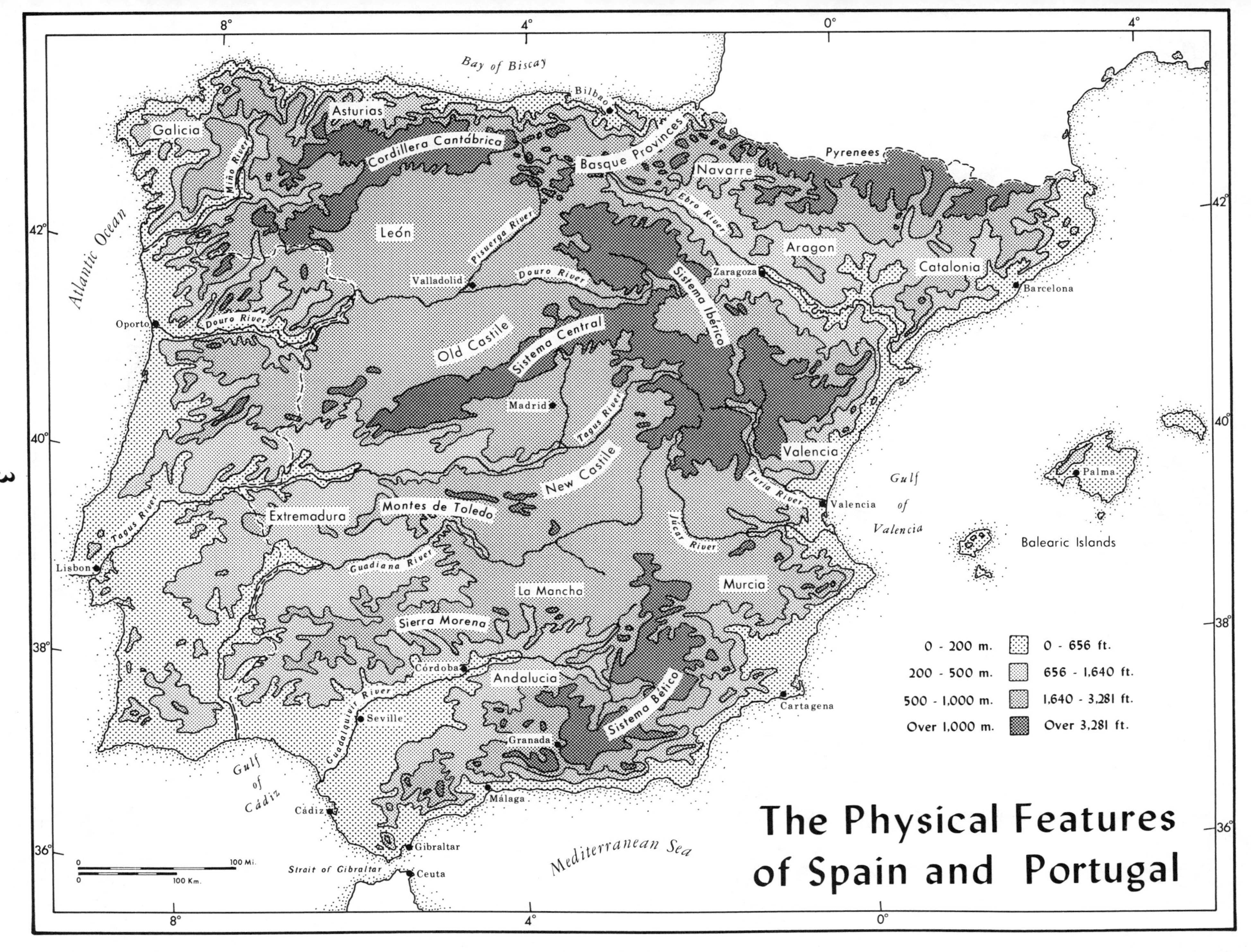
The Physical Features of Spain and Portugal
0 - 200 m. 0 - 656 ft.
200 - 500 m. 656 - 1,640 ft.
500 - 1,000 m. 1,640 - 3,281 ft.
Over 1,000 m. Over 3,281 ft.
Bay of Biscay
Atlantic Ocean
Mediterranean Sea
Gulf of Valencia
Gulf of Cádiz
Strait of Gibraltar
Balearic Islands
Palma
Pyrenees
Catalonia
Barcelona
Aragon
Zaragoza
Navarre
Ebro River
Basque Provinces
Bilbao
Asturias
Cordillera Cantábrica
Galicia
Miño River
León
Pisuerga River
Valladolid
Douro River
Douro River
Oporto
Old Castile
Sistema Central
Sistema Ibérico
Madrid
Tagus River
New Castile
Valencia
Turia River
Valencia
Júcar River
Murcia
Cartagena
La Mancha
Montes de Toledo
Extremadura
Tagus River
Lisbon
Guadiana River
Sierra Morena
Córdoba
Andalucia
Sistema Bético
Granada
Málaga
Guadalquivir River
Seville
Cádiz
Gibraltar
Ceuta
0 100 Mi.
0 100 Km.
8°
4°
0°
4°
42°
40°
38°
36°

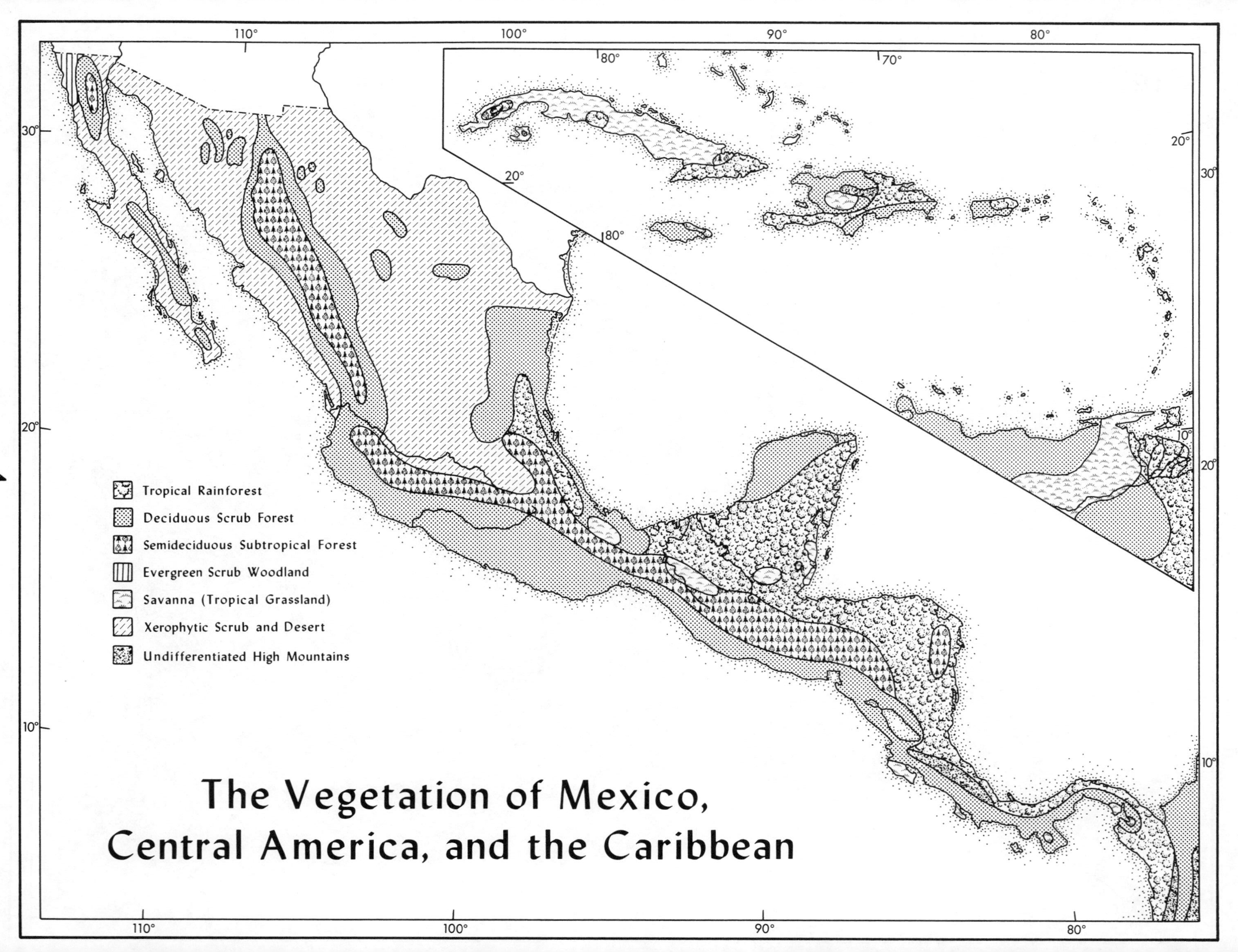

The Vegetation of Mexico, Central America, and the Caribbean

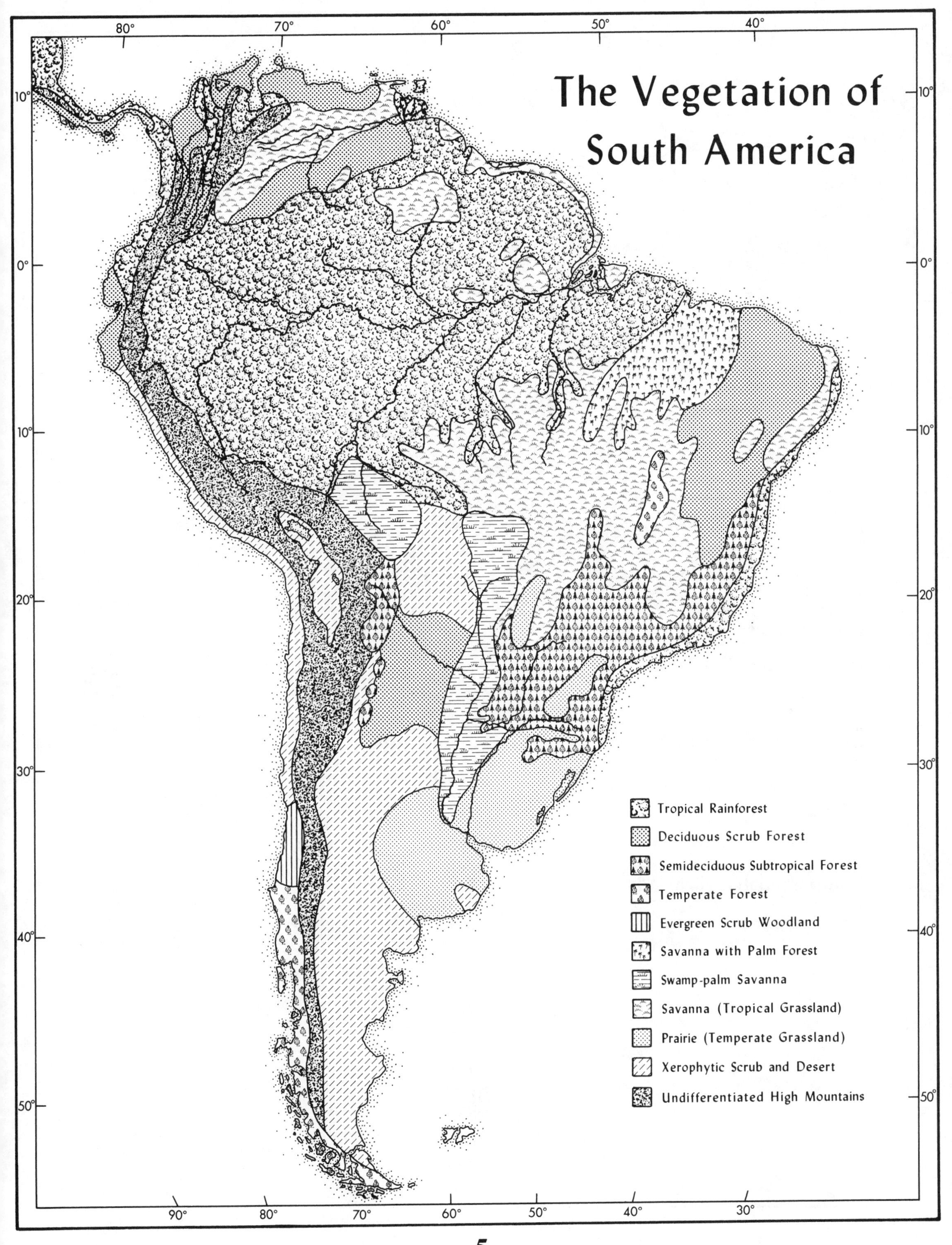
The Vegetation of South America
Tropical Rainforest
Deciduous Scrub Forest
Semideciduous Subtropical Forest
Temperate Forest
Evergreen Scrub Woodland
Savanna with Palm Forest
Swamp-palm Savanna
Savanna (Tropical Grassland)
Prairie (Temperate Grassland)
Xerophytic Scrub and Desert
Undifferentiated High Mountains
80°
70°
60°
50°
40°
10°
0°
10°
20°
30°
40°
50°
90°
80°
70°
60°
50°
40°
30°

The Climate of Latin America
Tropical Rainy Climates
Tropical Rainforest
Tropical Savanna
Dry Climates
Steppe
Desert
Humid Mesothermal Climates
Mediterranean Subtropical (Dry Summer)
Humid Subtropical (Warm Summer)
Marine West Coast (Cool Summer)
Undifferentiated Highlands
After Trewartha, 1957.
110°
100°
90°
80°
70°
60°
50°
40°
30°
20°
10°
0°
120°

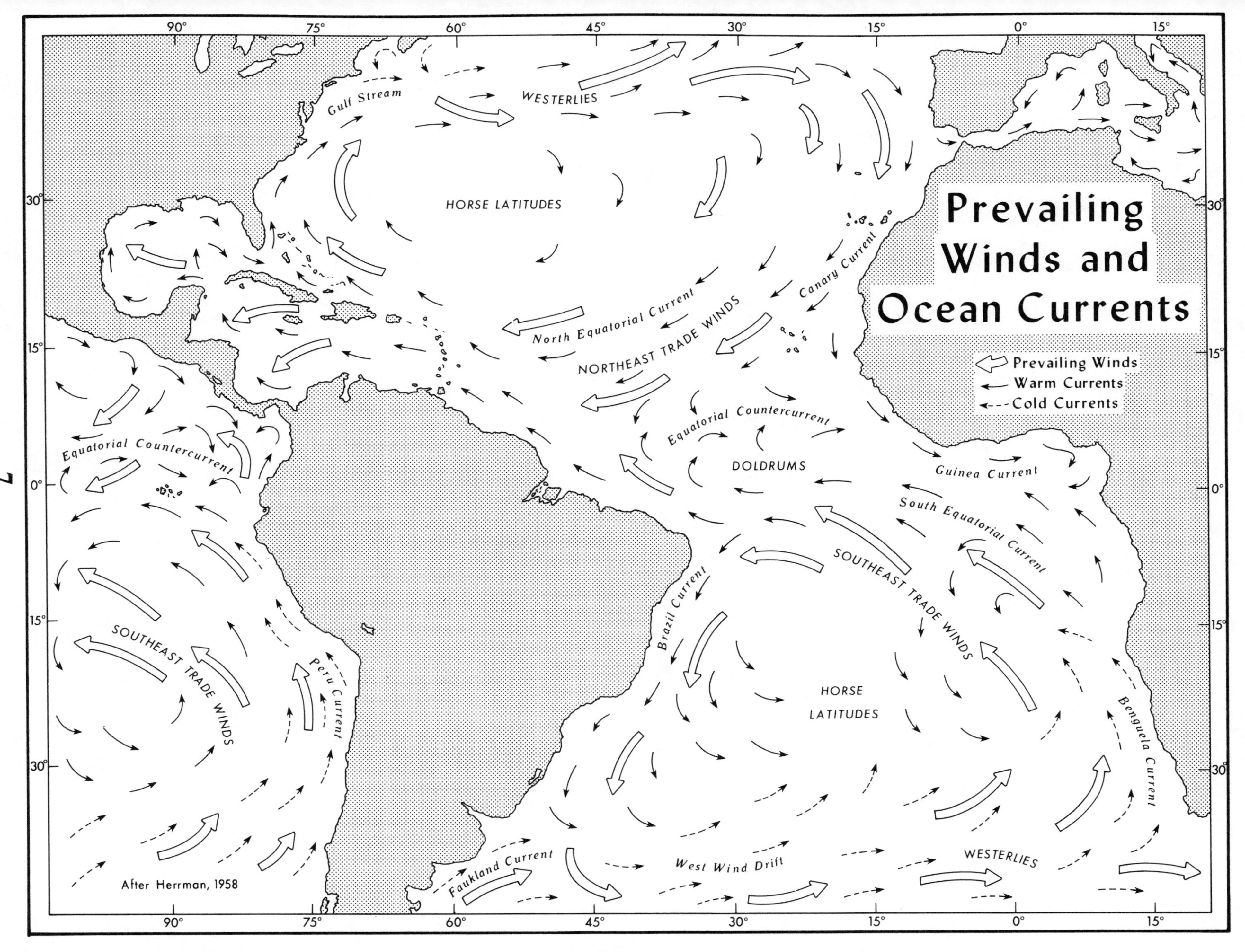
Prevailing Winds and Ocean Currents
Prevailing Winds
Warm Currents
Cold Currents
Gulf Stream
WESTERLIES
HORSE LATITUDES
Canary Current
North Equatorial Current
NORTHEAST TRADE WINDS
Equatorial Countercurrent
DOLDRUMS
Guinea Current
South Equatorial Current
SOUTHEAST TRADE WINDS
Brazil Current
HORSE LATITUDES
Benguela Current
Faukland Current
West Wind Drift
WESTERLIES
Equatorial Countercurrent
SOUTHEAST TRADE WINDS
Peru Current
After Herrman, 1958

THE COLONIAL PERIOD

The Iberian Background

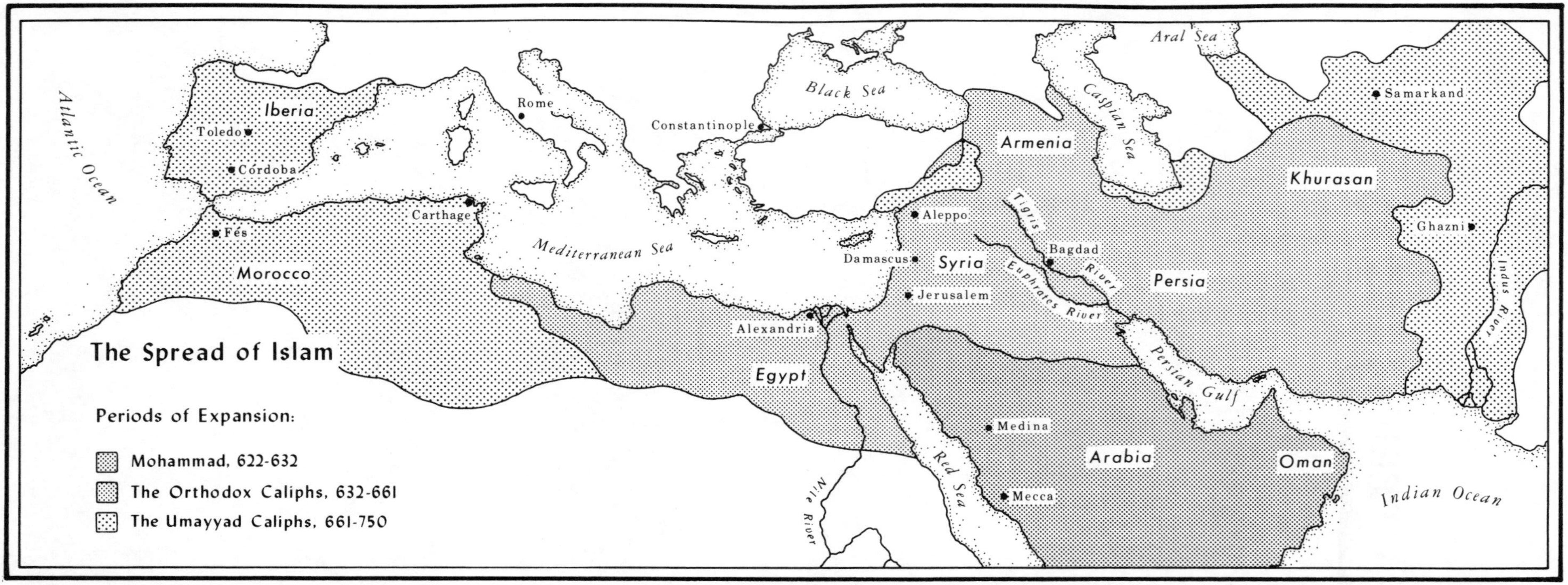

The Spread of Islam

Periods of Expansion:

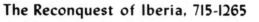

- Mohammad, 622-632
- The Orthodox Caliphs, 632-661
- The Umayyad Caliphs, 661-750

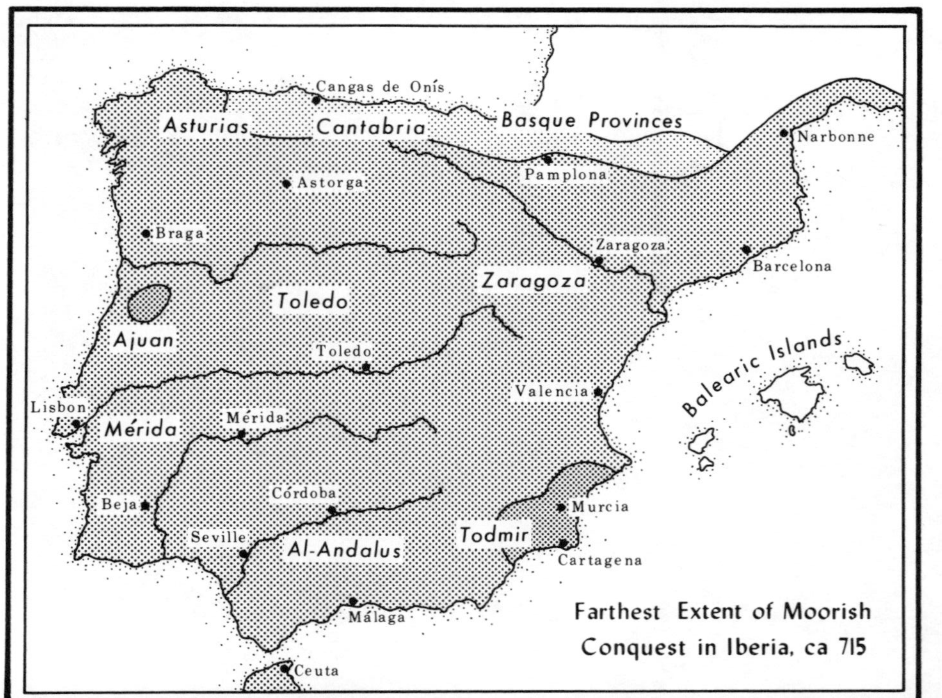

Farthest Extent of Moorish Conquest in Iberia, ca 715

The Reconquest of Iberia, 715-1265

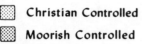

- Christian Controlled
- Moorish Controlled
- Independent States

The End of the Middle Ages, ca 1480

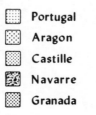

- Portugal
- Aragon
- Castille
- Navarre
- Granada

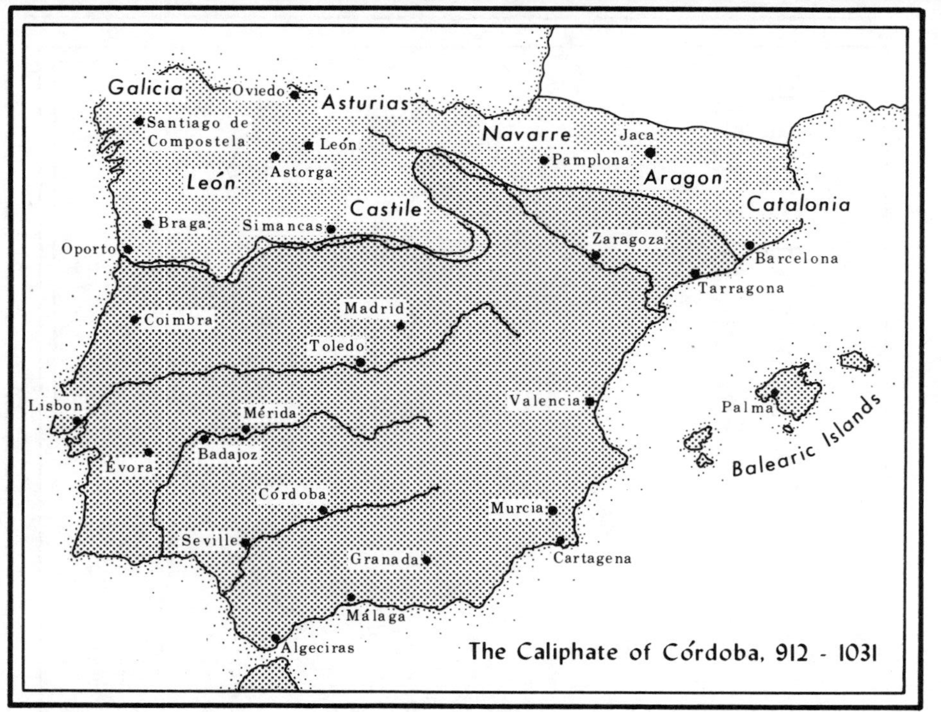

The Caliphate of Córdoba, 912 - 1031

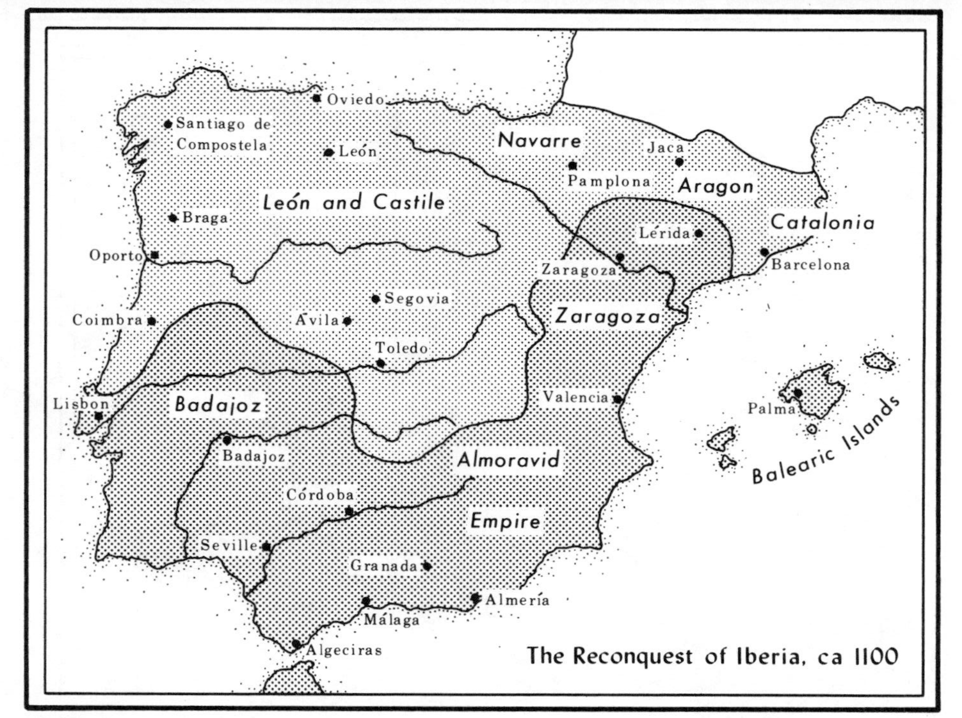

The Reconquest of Iberia, ca 1100

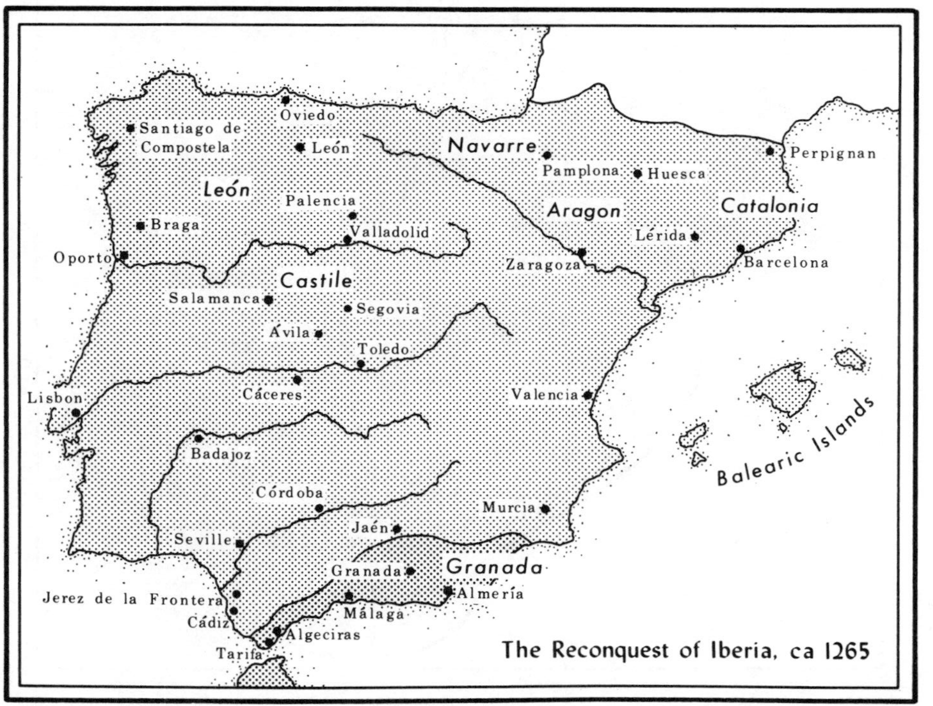

The Reconquest of Iberia, ca 1265

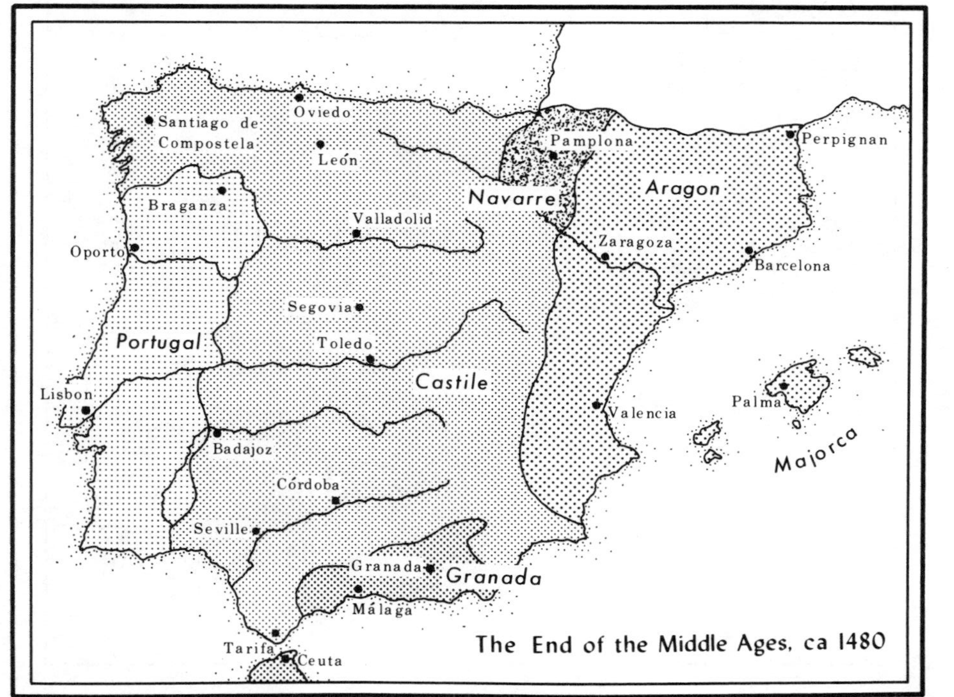

The End of the Middle Ages, ca 1480

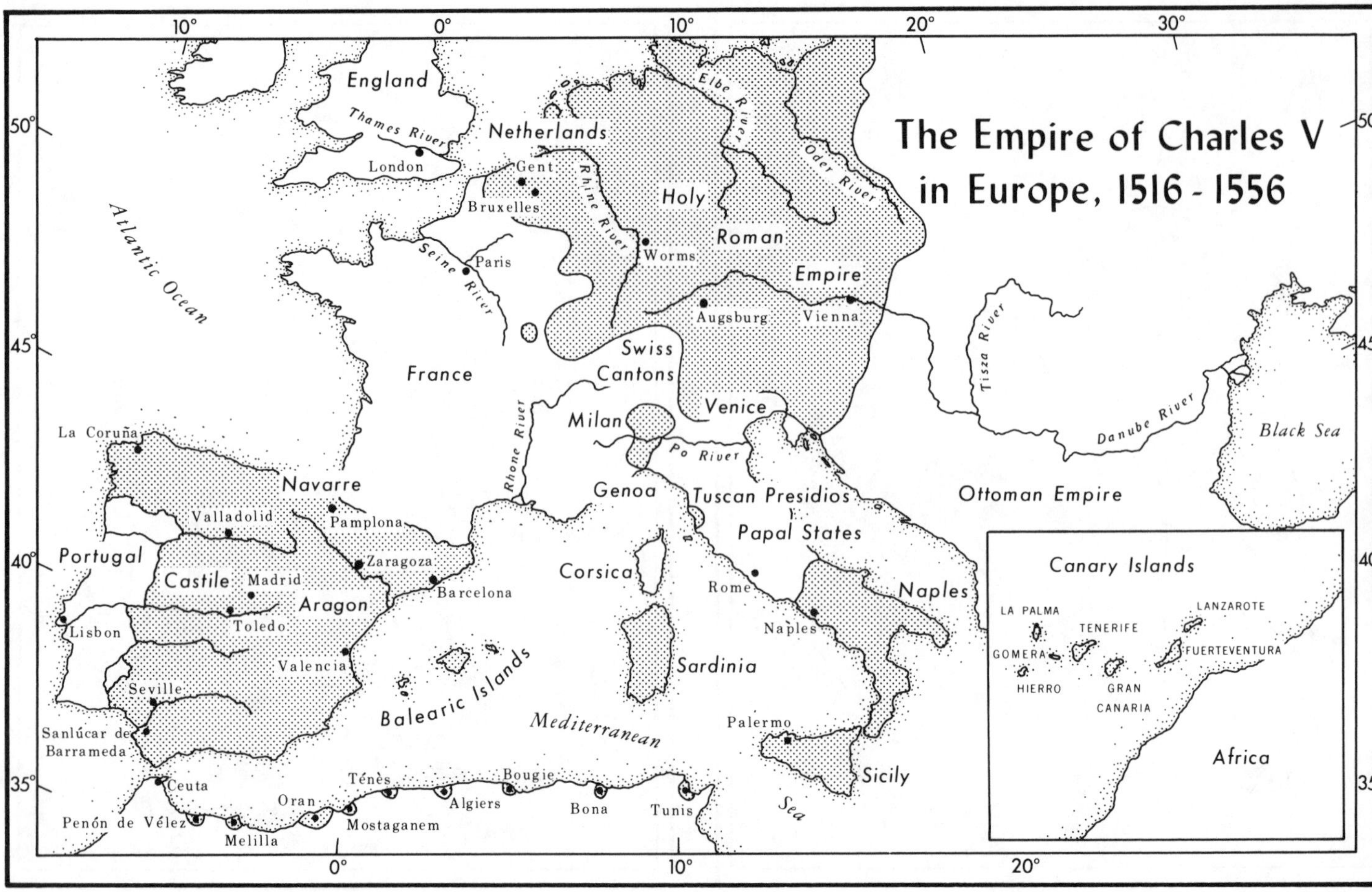

The Empire of Charles V in Europe, 1516 - 1556

England
Thames River
London
Netherlands
Gent
Bruxelles
Holy Roman Empire
Elbe River
Oder River
Rhine River
Worms
Augsburg
Vienna
Atlantic Ocean
Seine River
Paris
France
Swiss Cantons
Tisza River
Danube River
Black Sea
Venice
Milan
Po River
Rhone River
La Coruña
Navarre
Pamplona
Genoa
Tuscan Presidios
Papal States
Ottoman Empire
Valladolid
Portugal
Castile
Madrid
Zaragoza
Aragon
Barcelona
Toledo
Lisbon
Valencia
Corsica
Rome
Naples
Sardinia
Balearic Islands
Seville
Sanlúcar de Barrameda
Mediterranean Sea
Palermo
Sicily
Ceuta
Ténès
Bougie
Oran
Algiers
Bona
Tunis
Peñón de Vélez
Melilla
Mostaganem
Canary Islands
LA PALMA
TENERIFE
LANZAROTE
GOMERA
FUERTEVENTURA
HIERRO
GRAN CANARIA
Africa
10° 0° 10° 20° 30°
50° 45° 40° 35°

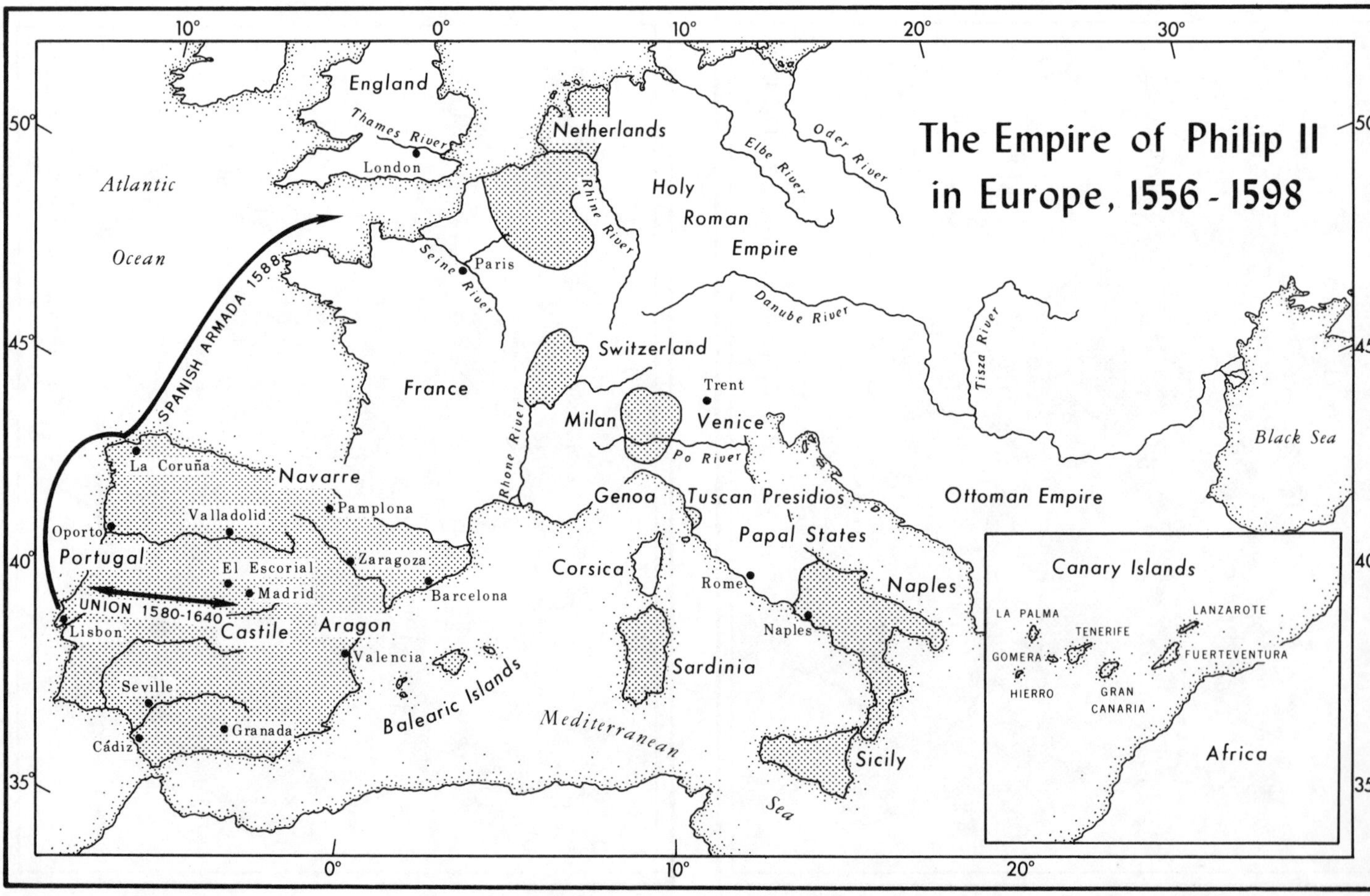

The Empire of Philip II in Europe, 1556 - 1598

England
Thames River
London
Netherlands
Holy Roman Empire
Elbe River
Oder River
Rhine River
Atlantic Ocean
SPANISH ARMADA 1588
Seine River
Paris
Danube River
Tisza River
Switzerland
France
Trent
Milan
Venice
Po River
Black Sea
Rhone River
La Coruña
Navarre
Genoa
Tuscan Presidios
Ottoman Empire
Valladolid
Pamplona
Oporto
Papal States
Portugal
El Escorial
Zaragoza
Madrid
Corsica
Rome
Naples
UNION 1580-1640
Barcelona
Lisbon
Castile
Aragon
Valencia
Sardinia
Balearic Islands
Seville
Granada
Cádiz
Mediterranean Sea
Sicily
Canary Islands
LA PALMA
LANZAROTE
TENERIFE
GOMERA
FUERTEVENTURA
HIERRO
GRAN CANARIA
Africa
10° 0° 10° 20° 30°
50° 45° 40° 35°

The Amerindian Background

Latin America:
Culture Levels
and
Tribal Groups
Prior to Contact with Europeans
1. High Civilization Empires
2. Theocratic and Militaristic Chiefdoms
3. Tropical Forest Farm Villages
4. Desert Farm Villages
5. Nomadic Hunting, Fishing, and Gathering Peoples
PAPAGO
PIMA
SERI
OPATA
CONCHO
GUAICURA
TARAHUMAR
YAQUI
PERICU
COAHUILTEC
TAMAULIPEC
ZACATEC
HUASTEC
SAYULTEC
OTOMI
TOTONAC
AZTEC
TARASCA
MIXTEC
ZOQUE
ZAPOTEC
MAYA
CHOL
CHORTI
LENCA
PAYA
PILPIL
MATAGALPA
MOSQUITO
ULVA
OROTIÑA
BORUCA
GUAYMI
CUNA
LUCAYO
CUBAN CIBONEY
SUBTAINO
AINO
HAITIAN CIBONEY
CIGUAYO
CARIB
GOAJIRO
MOTILON
CAQUETÍO
PALENQUE
CHAIMA
WARRAU
MAPOYE
YARURO
ARAWAK
CHIBCHA
CHOCÓ
ACHAGUA
CAYAPA
COLORADO
MACUSI
APARAI
WAICA
WITOTO
TUCANO
MACÚ
ARUA
TUPINAMBA
BORA
JIVARO
OMAGUA
MURA
ARARA
TEMBÉ
TREMEMBE
POTIGUARA
MUNDURUCÚ
CATUKINA
TIMBIRA
CHIMU
INCA
CAMPA
IPURINÁ
NORTHERN CAYAPÓ
AKWĒ-SHAVANTE
SHERENTE
JAICÓ
CAETÉ
CAWAHIB
CHINCHA
CHANCA
NAMBIKWÁRA
COLLA
ACRÓA
AYAMARA
CHIQUITO
BORORO
SOUTHERN CAYAPÓ
TUPINAMBÁ
BOTOCUDO
CHIRIGUANO
PAYAGUA
MBAYÁ
ATACAMA
CHOROTI
GUARANI
CAINGANG
DIAGUITA
ABIPON
MATARA
COMECHINGON
GUENOA
ARACHANE
HUARPE
QUERANDI
CHARRUA
MINUAN
ARAUCANIANS
CHIQUIYAMI
PUELCHE
PEHUENCHE
HET
MAPUCHE
POYA
NORTHERN TEHUELCHE
CHILOTE
CHONO
SOUTHERN TEHUELCHE
ALACALUF
TEUESH
ONA
YAHGAN
110°
100°
90°
80°
70°
60°
50°
40°
30°
20°
120°
10°
0°

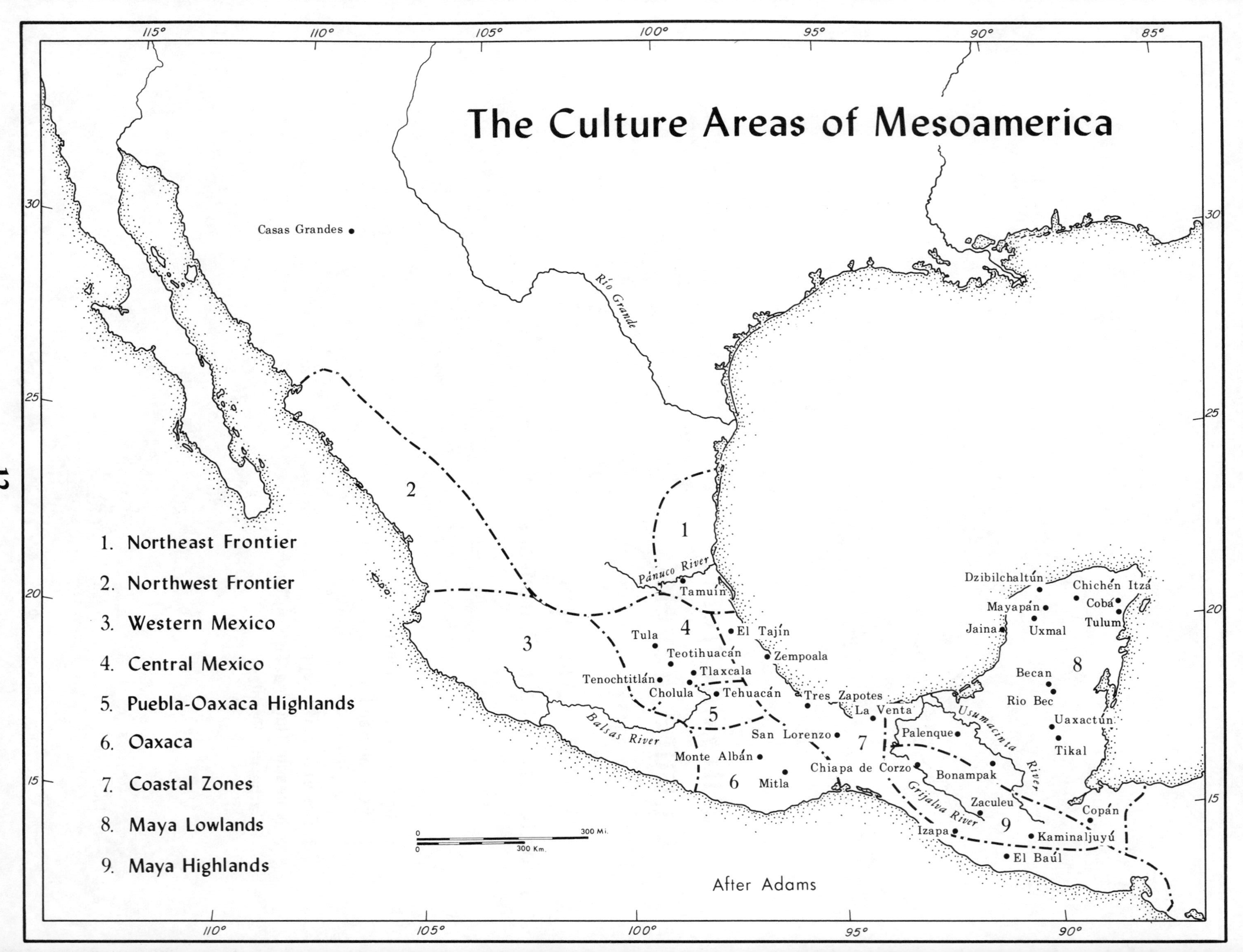
The Culture Areas of Mesoamerica
1. Northeast Frontier
2. Northwest Frontier
3. Western Mexico
4. Central Mexico
5. Puebla-Oaxaca Highlands
6. Oaxaca
7. Coastal Zones
8. Maya Lowlands
9. Maya Highlands
Casas Grandes
Río Grande
Pánuco River
Tamuín
Tula
El Tajín
Teotihuacán
Zempoala
Tlaxcala
Tenochtitlán
Cholula
Tehuacán
Tres Zapotes
Balsas River
La Venta
San Lorenzo
Monte Albán
Mitla
Chiapa de Corzo
Palenque
Usumacinta River
Bonampak
Grijalva River
Zaculeu
Izapa
Kaminaljuyú
El Baúl
Copán
Dzibilchaltún
Chichén Itzá
Mayapán
Cobá
Tulum
Jaina
Uxmal
Becan
Rio Bec
Uaxactún
Tikal
300 Mi.
300 Km.
After Adams

MESOAMERICA: ESTIMATED TIME LINE

PERIODS	DATES	CENTRAL VALLEY	HIGHLANDS OAXACA	GULF COAST	WEST COAST	MAYA
	B.C.					
EARLY	24,000	Tehuacán				
		Tlapacoya				
	20,000	Valsequillo				
	11,000			Diablo		
	10,000				Weicker Ranch	
	9,000	Tequixquiac				
		Tepexpan		Armadillo		
ARCHAIC	7,000	Iztapán		Cueva Humada		
		Coxcatlán				
	6,700		Santa Marta Rockshelter			
		Tehuacán				
					Puerto Marquez	
						Islona de Chantuto
	5,000	Yanhuitlán				
				Nogales		
	3,000			La Perra		
				Ocampo		
FORMATIVE	1,500	Tehuacan		San Lorenzo	Chiapa de Corzo	
	1,000	El Arbolillo				
	900	Zacatenco	Yagul	La Venta		Dizibilchaltún
		Copilco	Monte Albán	Potrero Nuevo	Chupícuaro	
			Monte Negro	Remojadas		
			Monte Flor	Tres Zapotes		
	800	Tlatilco		Cerro de las Mesas		
	600			El Tajín		
	500		Monte Albán II			Kaminaljuyú
	300	Cuiculico	Dainzú		La Victoria	
	100					Uaxactún
	B.C.-A.D.					
			Izapa		Tikal	
CLASSIC	300	Teotihuacán	Monte Albán III		Nayarit	Quiriquá
		Cholula	Zaachila		Jalisco	Jaina
			Puebla		Colima	Holmul
		Alta Vista de Chalchihuites	Tlaxcala			Palenque
	400	Schroeder	Yagul			Copán
		Atzcapotzalco	Mitla			Cobá
						Piedras Negras
						Yaxchilán
						Bonampak
					Becan	
					Palenque	
						Uxmal
	600	Xochicalco		Tamuín	La Quemada	
EARLY	900	Tula	Monte Albán IV			Rio Bec
POST						Puuc
CLASSIC						Chenes
(900-1200)						Pamplona
TOLTEC		Casas Grandes	Yagul			Tulum
						Izamal
						Chichén Itzá
POST	1,200	Tenayuca	Chinautla			Campeche
CLASSIC		Chapultepec				Mayapán
(1200-1500)						
AZTEC	1,300	Tenochtitlán		Zempoala		Xicalango
	1,400	Coxcatlán				
		Malinalco			Zaculeu	
		Cholula				
		Texcoco				

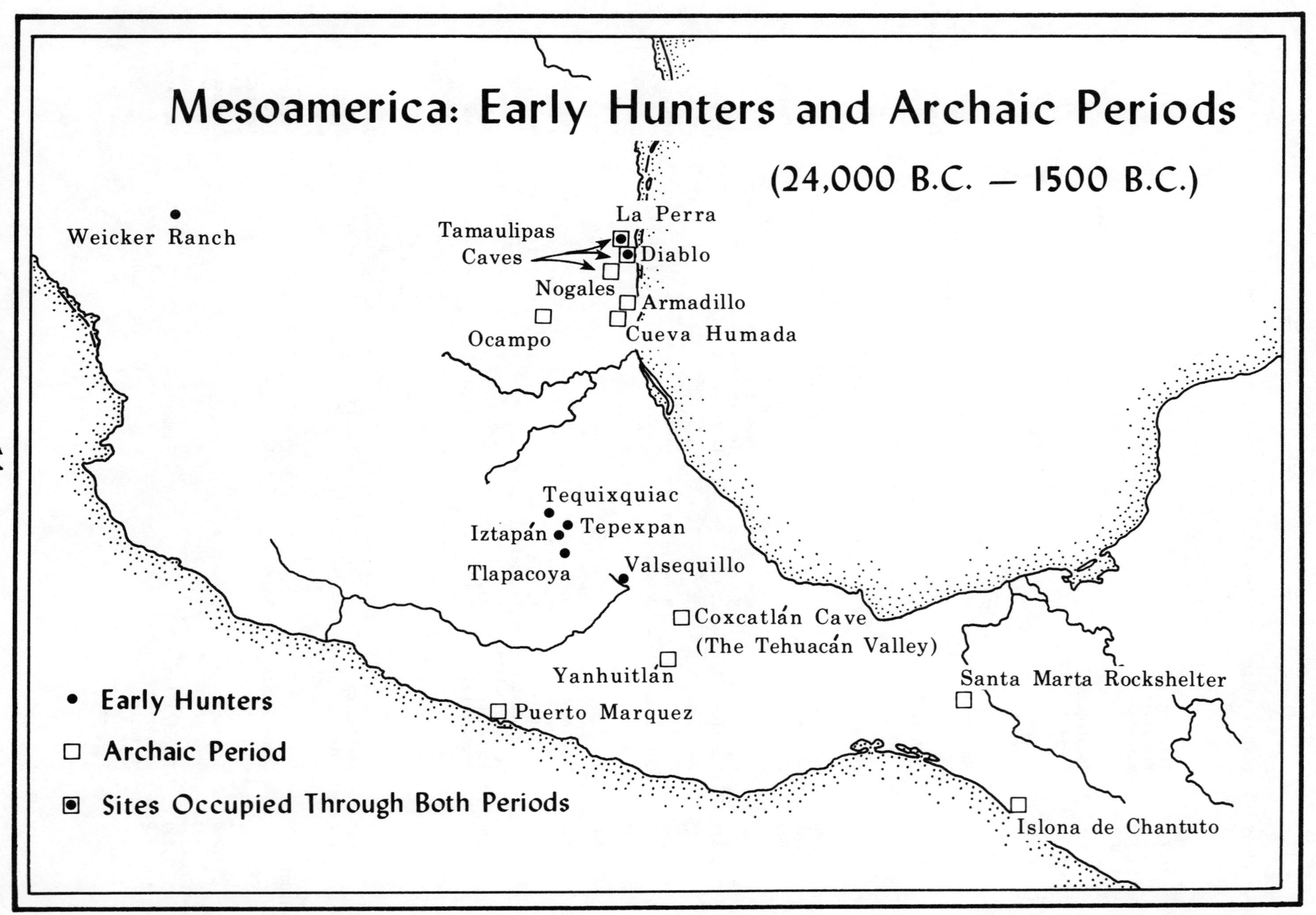

Mesoamerica: Early Hunters and Archaic Periods
(24,000 B.C. — 1500 B.C.)
Weicker Ranch
Tamaulipas Caves
La Perra
Diablo
Nogales
Armadillo
Ocampo
Cueva Humada
Tequixquiac
Iztapán
Tepexpan
Tlapacoya
Valsequillo
Coxcatlán Cave
(The Tehuacán Valley)
Yanhuitlán
Puerto Marquez
Santa Marta Rockshelter
Islona de Chantuto
Early Hunters
Archaic Period
Sites Occupied Through Both Periods

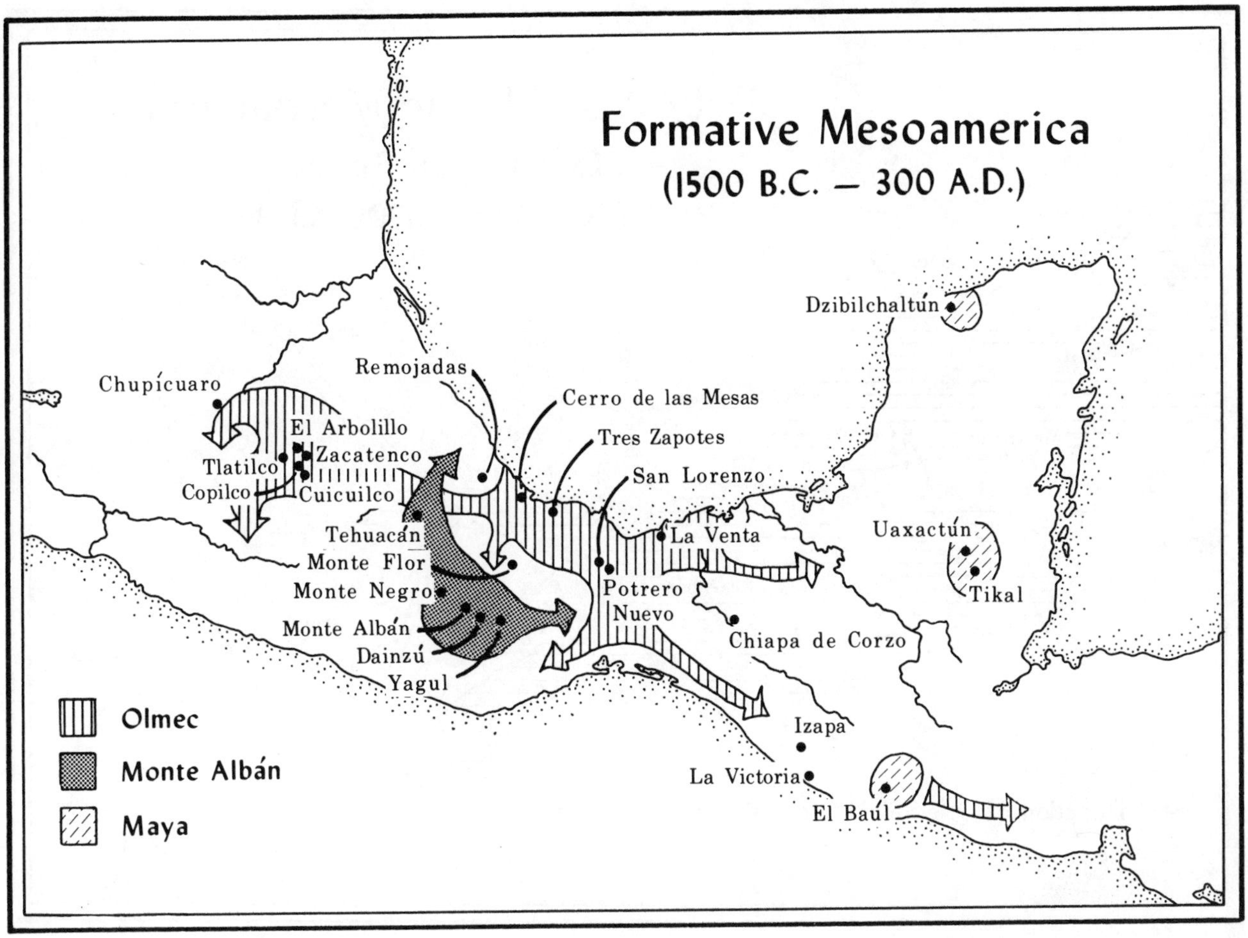

Formative Mesoamerica
(1500 B.C. – 300 A.D.)

Dzibilchaltún
Chupícuaro
Remojadas
Cerro de las Mesas
El Arbolillo
Zacatenco
Tres Zapotes
Tlatilco
San Lorenzo
Copilco
Cuicuilco
Tehuacán
La Venta
Uaxactún
Monte Flor
Monte Negro
Potrero Nuevo
Tikal
Monte Albán
Chiapa de Corzo
Dainzú
Yagul
Izapa
La Victoria
El Baúl

Olmec
Monte Albán
Maya

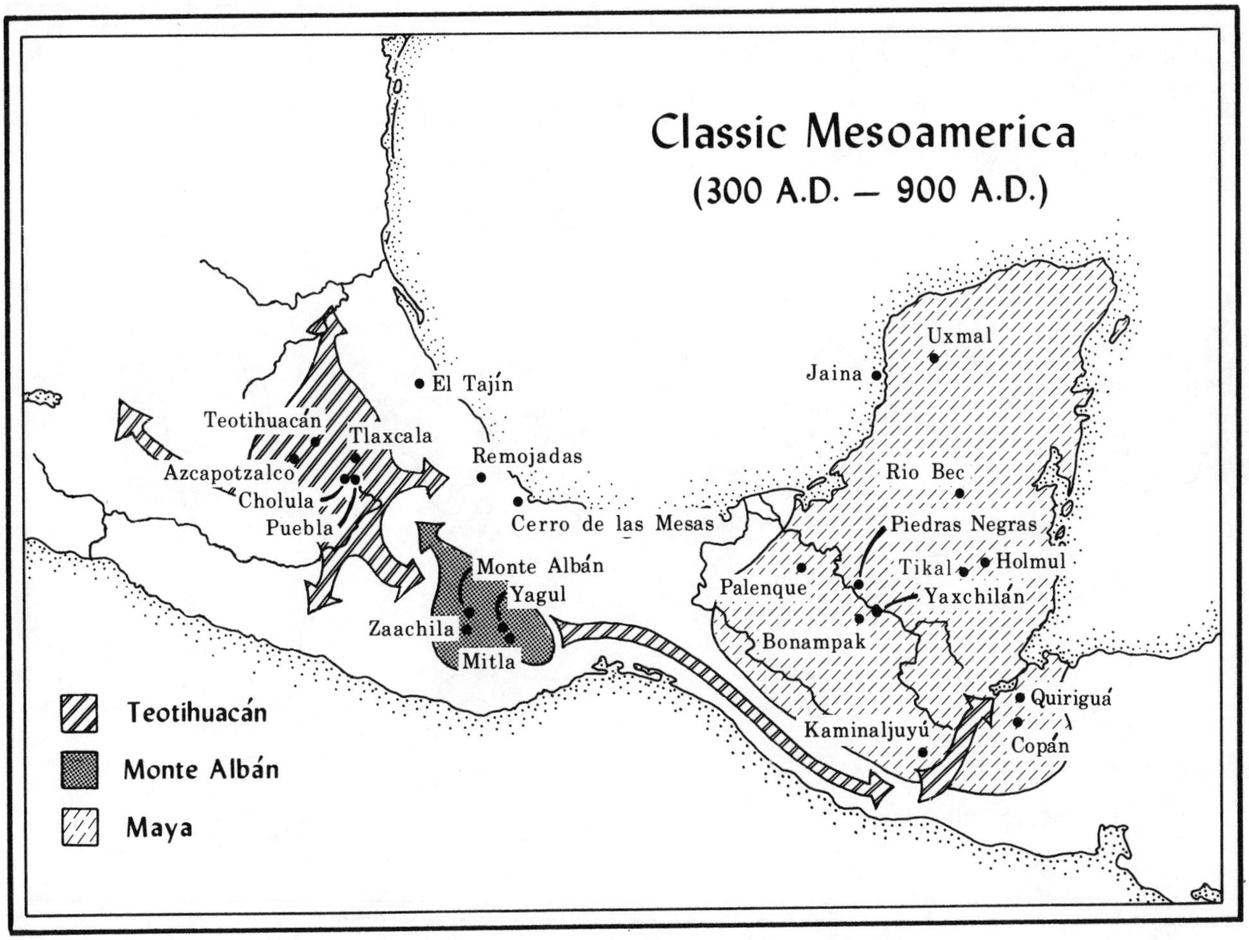

Classic Mesoamerica
(300 A.D. – 900 A.D.)

Uxmal
Jaina
El Tajín
Teotihuacán
Tlaxcala
Remojadas
Azcapotzalco
Rio Bec
Cholula
Puebla
Cerro de las Mesas
Piedras Negras
Monte Albán
Tikal
Holmul
Yagul
Palenque
Yaxchilán
Zaachila
Bonampak
Mitla
Quiriguá
Kaminaljuyú
Copán

Teotihuacán
Monte Albán
Maya

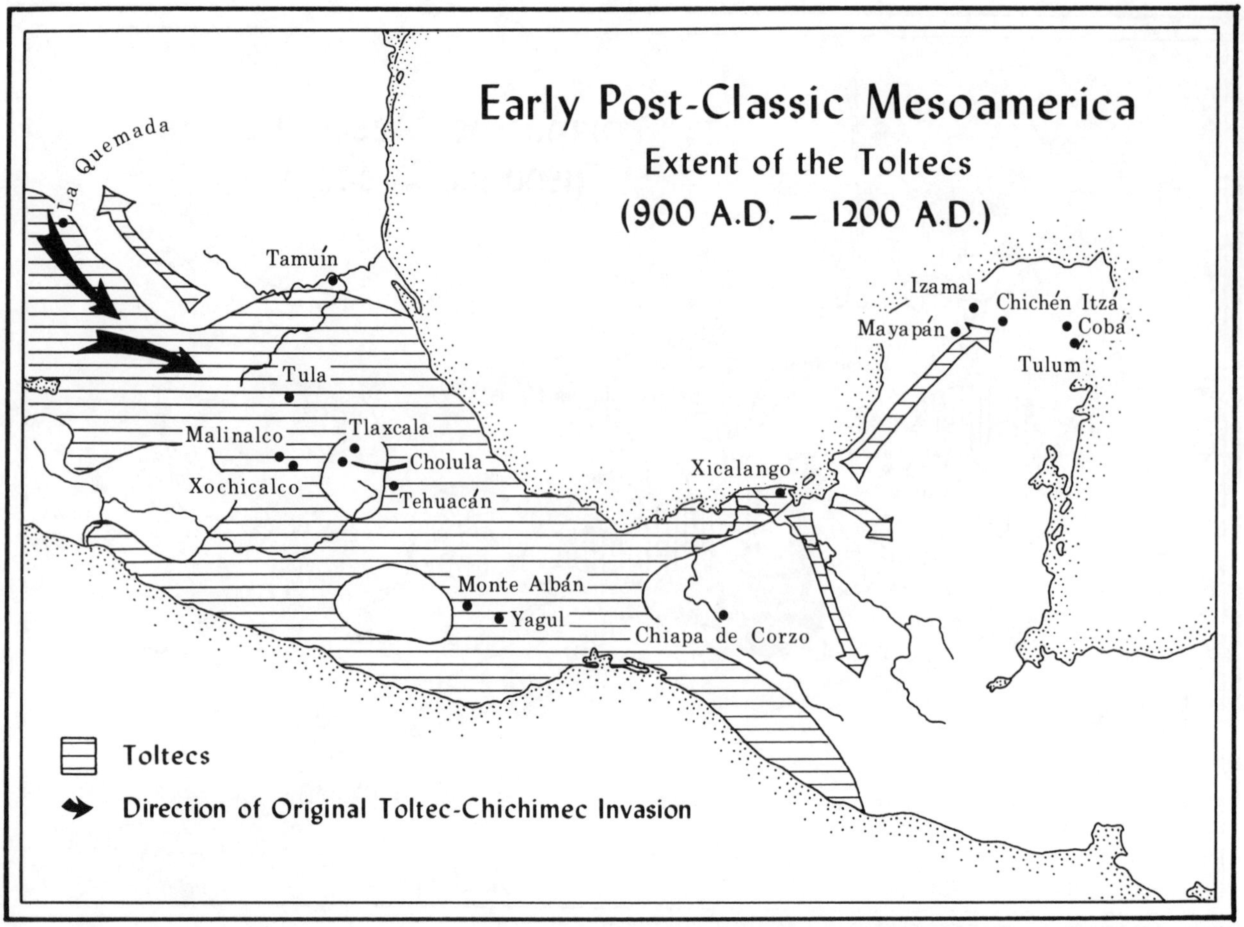

Early Post-Classic Mesoamerica

Extent of the Toltecs

(900 A.D. — 1200 A.D.)

La Quemada
Tamuín
Tula
Malinalco
Tlaxcala
Cholula
Xochicalco
Tehuacán
Monte Albán
Yagul
Chiapa de Corzo
Xicalango
Izamal
Chichén Itzá
Mayapán
Cobá
Tulum

Toltecs

Direction of Original Toltec-Chichimec Invasion

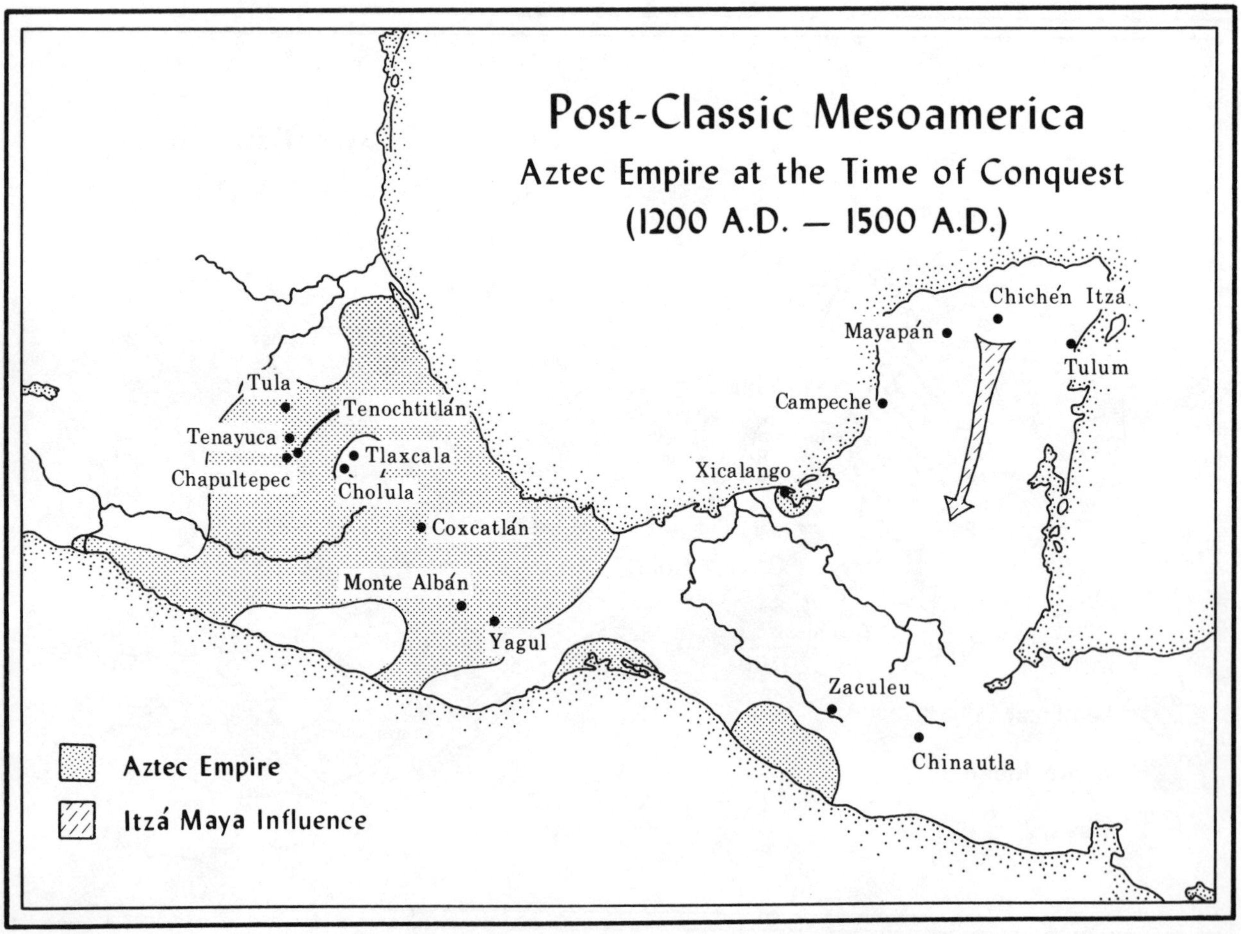

Post-Classic Mesoamerica

Aztec Empire at the Time of Conquest

(1200 A.D. — 1500 A.D.)

Tula
Tenochtitlán
Tenayuca
Chapultepec
Tlaxcala
Cholula
Coxcatlán
Monte Albán
Yagul
Chichén Itzá
Mayapán
Tulum
Campeche
Xicalango
Zaculeu
Chinautla

Aztec Empire

Itzá Maya Influence

South America:
Early Sites
(22,000 B.C. – 3000 B.C.)
• Sites of Pre-projectile Point Technology
▪ Sites of Projectile Point Technology
Muaco
Las Lagunas
Taima-taima
El Jobo
Orinoco River
Magdalena River
Cauca River
El Abra
El Inga
Punín
Las Vegas
Negro River
Amazon River
Marañón River
Ucayali R.
Madeira River
Tapajós River
Xingu River
Tocantins River
São Raimundo Nonato
São Francisco River
Quishqui Puncu
Lauricocha I
Lauricocha II and III
Cerro Chivateros
Ancón
Paccaicasa
Casavilca
Viscachani
Lagoa Santa Caves
Alice Boër
Paraguay River
Loma Negra
Tulan
Tres Morros
Ampajango
Totoral
Paraná River
Uruguay River
Ongamira
Quereo
Ayampitín
Gruta de Cadonga
Isla de Arriba
Intihuasi Cave
Laguna de Tagua Tagua
Arroyo Seco
Monte Verde
Las Buitreras Cave
Eberhardt Cave
Palli Aike Cave
Englefield Island
Fell's Cave

THE ANDEAN REGION: ESTIMATED TIME LINE

(after Rowe and Lanning)

```
PRECERAMIC     INITIAL        EARLY HORIZON  EARLY          MIDDLE         LATE          INCAS
                                             INTERMEDIATE   INTERMEDIATE   INTERMEDIATE
+--------------+--------------+--------------+--------------+--------------+-------------+--------------------+
8000  B.C.    1600  B.C.    900  B.C.     200  B.C.     600  A.D.      1000  A.D.    1476  A.D.            1534

Ancón------------------------------+
Paracas---------------------------------------------+
Huaca Negra-------------+
Las Haldas--------------+
Culebras----------------+
Chuquitanta----------------------------------+
Asia           Ica--------------------------------------------------------------------------------------------+
Rio Seco       Chiripa------------------------------+
Huaca Prieta   Kotosh------------------------+
Casavilca
Chanapata-----------------------------------------------------------------------------------------------------+
Huancarani                    Supe--------------------------------+
                              Chavín de Huántar----------------+
                              Cupisnique     Gallinazo------------+
                              Ocucaje        Tiahuanaco-----------+
                              Qaluyu         Huari----------------+
                              Paracas        Salinar        Recuay--------------------------------------------+
                                             Huaraz         Cajamarca-----------------------------------------+
                                             Pucará         Pachacamác----------------------------------------+
                                             Maranga        Huamachuco----------------------------------------+
                                             Cahuáchi       Nasca          Chancay----------------------------+
                                             Cerro de       Cajamarquilla  Cuzco------------------------------+
                                               Trinidad     Piura          Carabayllo-------------------------+
                                                            Pacheco        Chan Chan--------------------------+
                                                                           Purgatorio    Quito----------------+
                                                                           Pacatuamu     Huanuco--------------+
                                                                           Farfan        Huancayo-------------+
                                                                           Apurlé        Machu Picchu---------+

PRECERAMIC     INITIAL        EARLY HORIZON  EARLY          MIDDLE         LATE          INCAS
                                             INTERMEDIATE   INTERMEDIATE   INTERMEDIATE
+--------------+--------------+--------------+--------------+--------------+-------------+--------------------+
8000  B.C.    1600  B.C.    900  B.C.     200  B.C.     600  A.D.      1000  A.D.    1476  A.D.            1534
```

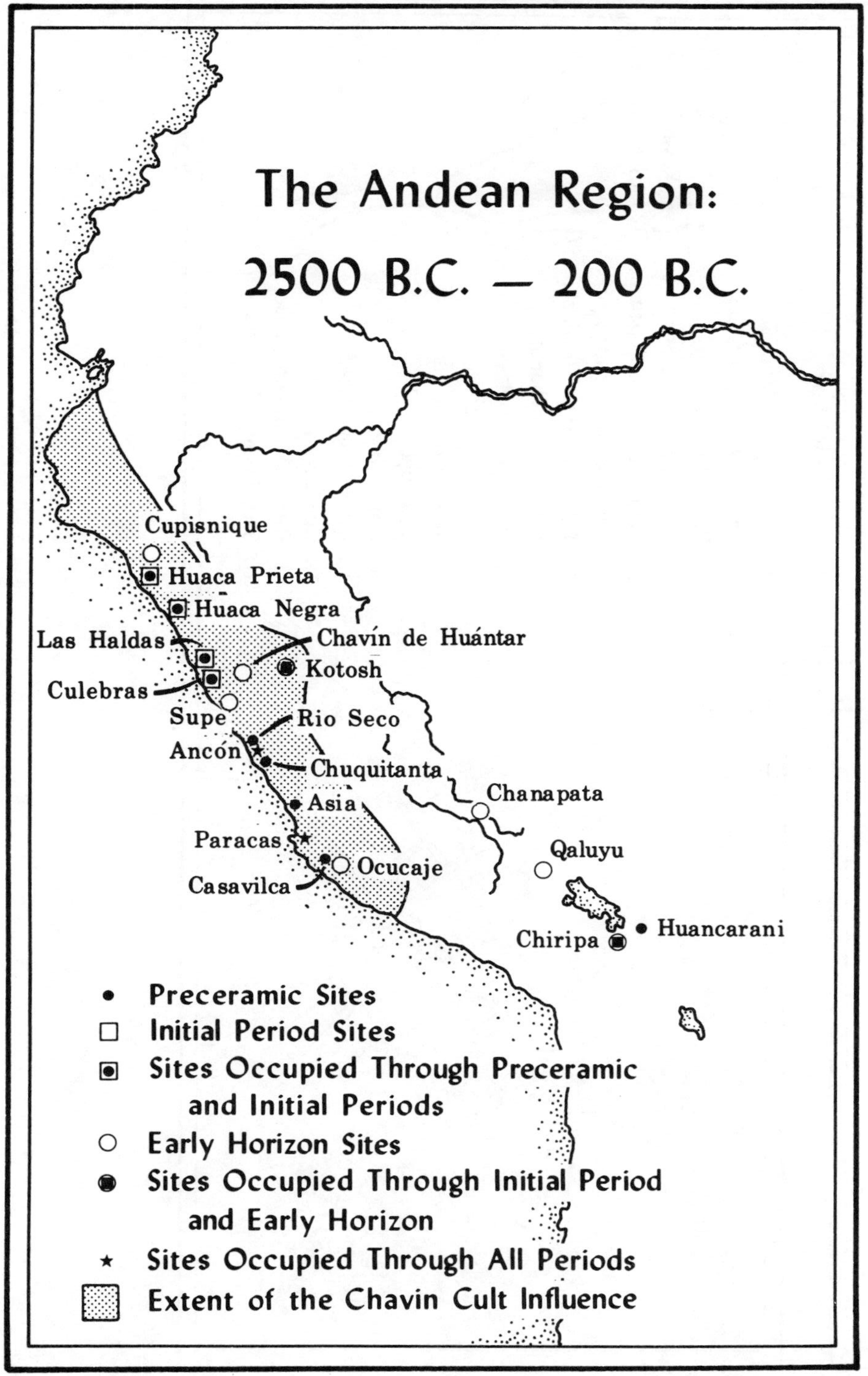

The Andean Region: 2500 B.C. — 200 B.C.

Cupisnique
Huaca Prieta
Huaca Negra
Las Haldas
Chavín de Huántar
Kotosh
Culebras
Supe
Rio Seco
Ancón
Chuquitanta
Chanapata
Asia
Paracas
Qaluyu
Ocucaje
Casavilca
Chiripa
Huancarani

- • Preceramic Sites
- □ Initial Period Sites
- ▣ Sites Occupied Through Preceramic and Initial Periods
- ○ Early Horizon Sites
- ◉ Sites Occupied Through Initial Period and Early Horizon
- ★ Sites Occupied Through All Periods
- Extent of the Chavin Cult Influence

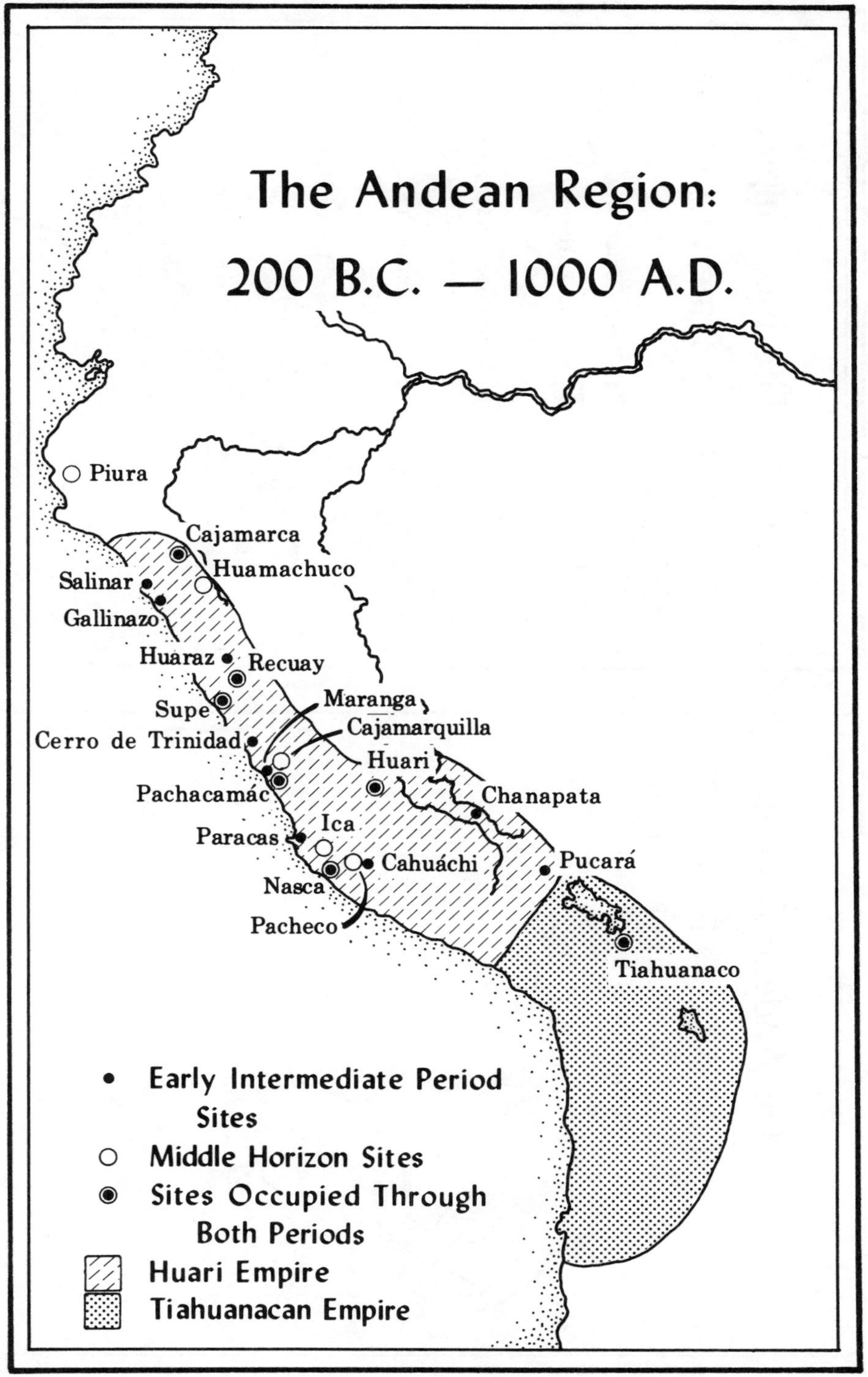

The Andean Region: 200 B.C. — 1000 A.D.

Piura
Cajamarca
Salinar
Huamachuco
Gallinazo
Huaraz
Recuay
Supe
Maranga
Cajamarquilla
Cerro de Trinidad
Huari
Pachacamác
Chanapata
Ica
Paracas
Cahuáchi
Pucará
Nasca
Pacheco
Tiahuanaco

- • Early Intermediate Period Sites
- ○ Middle Horizon Sites
- ◉ Sites Occupied Through Both Periods
- Huari Empire
- Tiahuanacan Empire

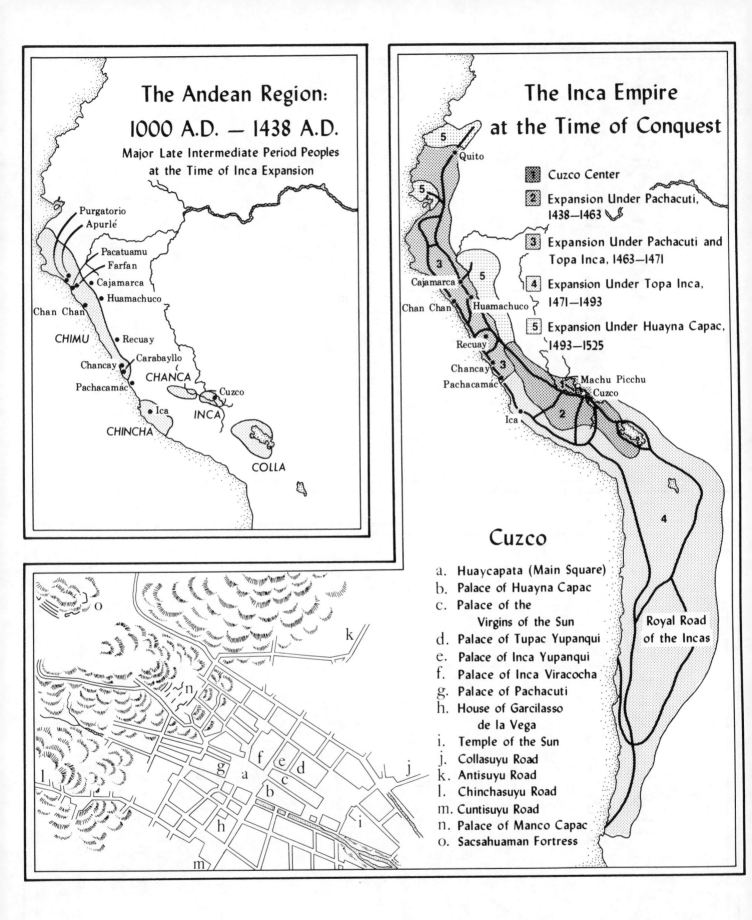

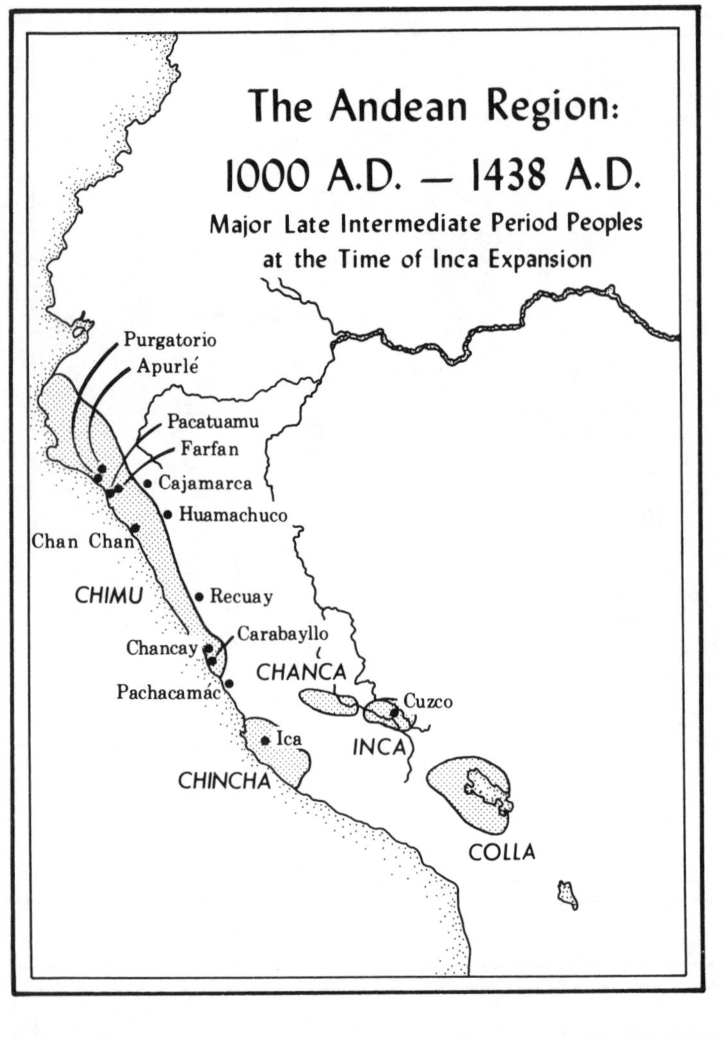

The Inca Empire at the Time of Conquest

1 Cuzco Center

2 Expansion Under Pachacuti, 1438—1463

3 Expansion Under Pachacuti and Topa Inca, 1463—1471

4 Expansion Under Topa Inca, 1471—1493

5 Expansion Under Huayna Capac, 1493—1525

Quito

Cajamarca

Chan Chan

Huamachuco

Recuay

Chancay

Pachacamác

Machu Picchu

Cuzco

Ica

Royal Road of the Incas

Cuzco

a. Huaycapata (Main Square)
b. Palace of Huayna Capac
c. Palace of the Virgins of the Sun
d. Palace of Tupac Yupanqui
e. Palace of Inca Yupanqui
f. Palace of Inca Viracocha
g. Palace of Pachacuti
h. House of Garcilasso de la Vega
i. Temple of the Sun
j. Collasuyu Road
k. Antisuyu Road
l. Chinchasuyu Road
m. Cuntisuyu Road
n. Palace of Manco Capac
o. Sacsahuaman Fortress

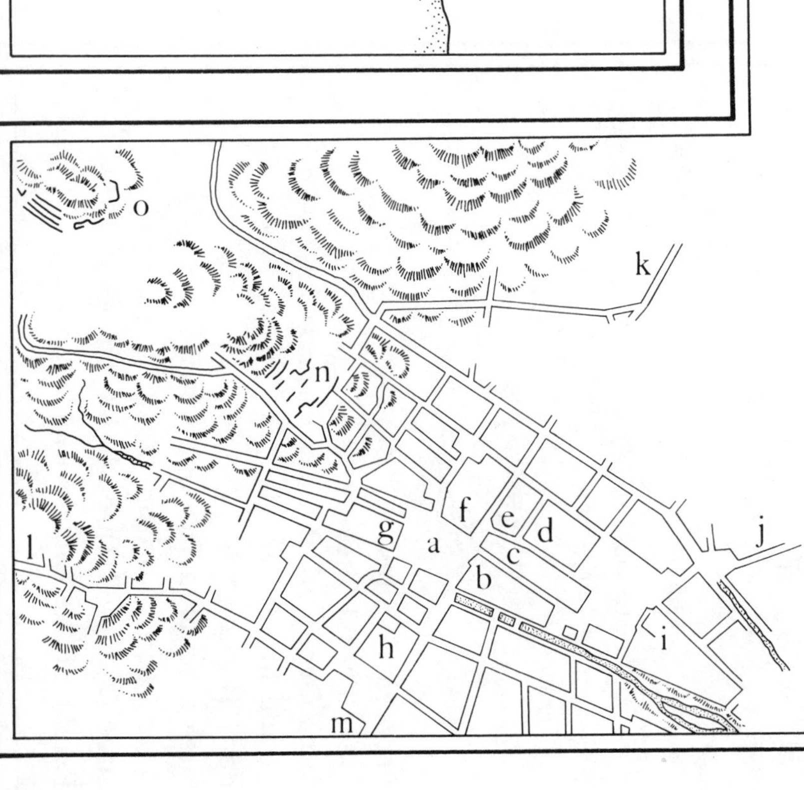

Discovery and Conquest

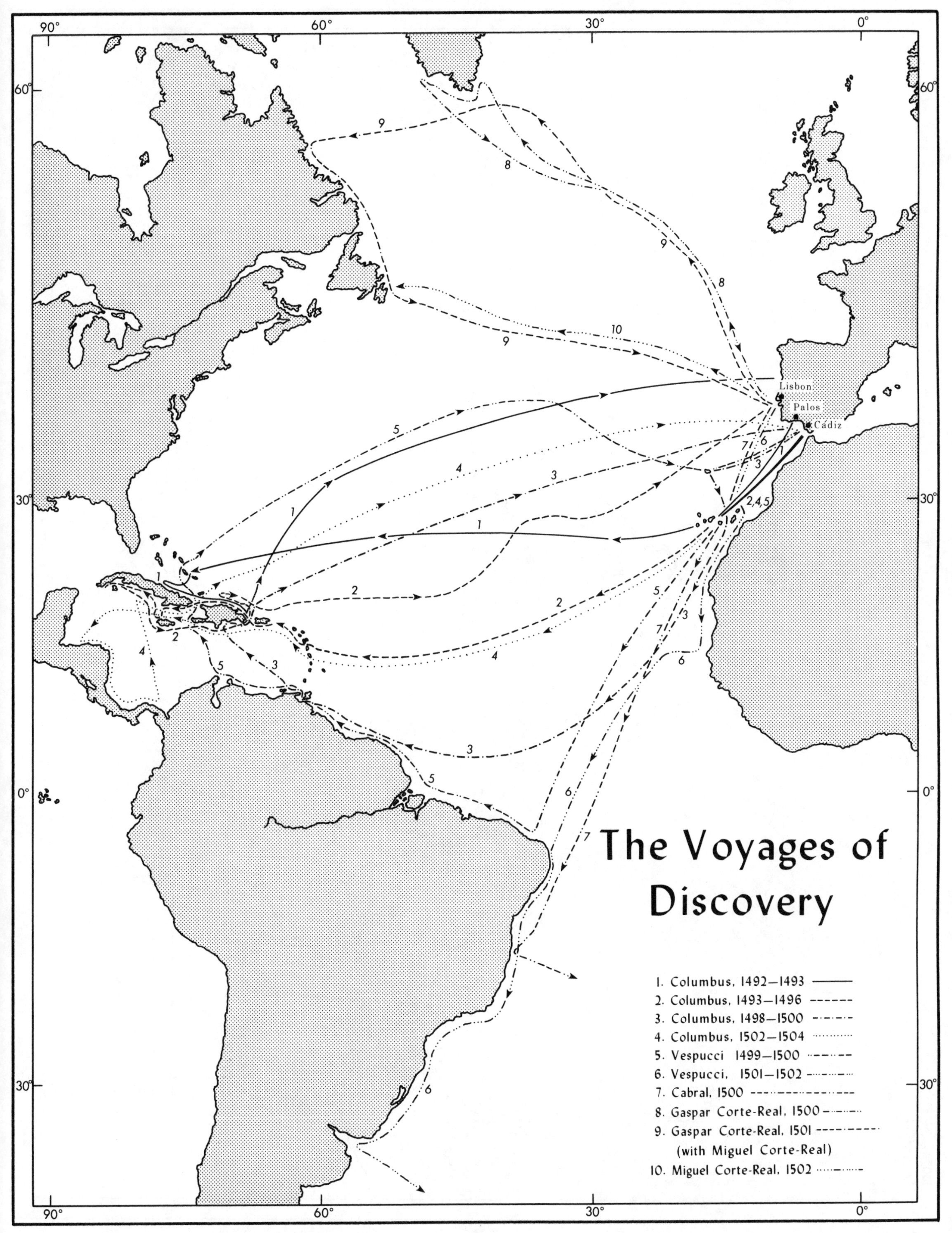
The Voyages of Discovery
1. Columbus, 1492–1493
2. Columbus, 1493–1496
3. Columbus, 1498–1500
4. Columbus, 1502–1504
5. Vespucci 1499–1500
6. Vespucci, 1501–1502
7. Cabral, 1500
8. Gaspar Corte-Real, 1500
9. Gaspar Corte-Real, 1501 (with Miguel Corte-Real)
10. Miguel Corte-Real, 1502
Lisbon
Palos
Cádiz
90°
60°
30°
0°

The Caribbean Explorations

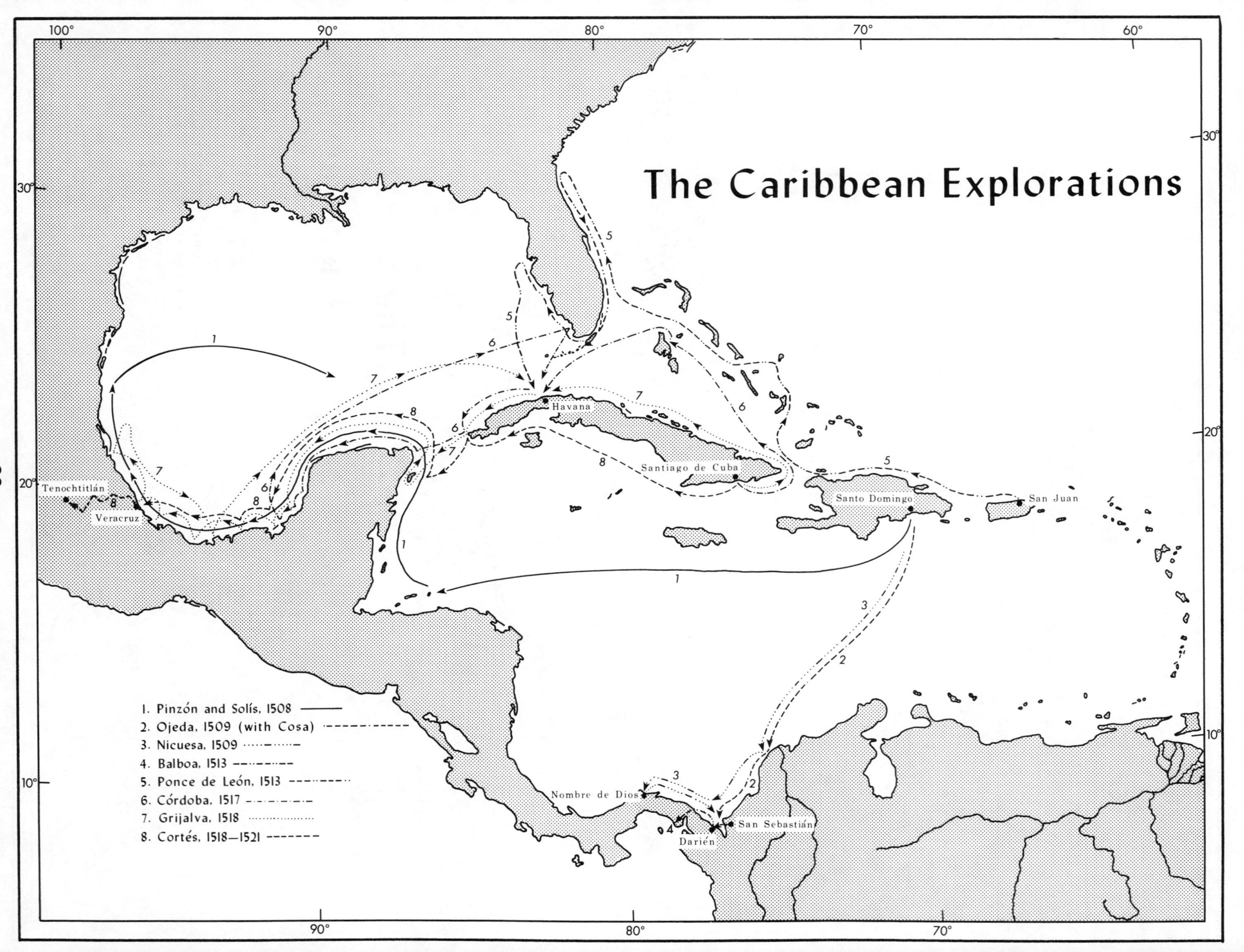

The Caribbean Explorations
1. Pinzón and Solís, 1508
2. Ojeda, 1509 (with Cosa)
3. Nicuesa, 1509
4. Balboa, 1513
5. Ponce de León, 1513
6. Córdoba, 1517
7. Grijalva, 1518
8. Cortés, 1518–1521
Tenochtitlán
Veracruz
Havana
Santiago de Cuba
Santo Domingo
San Juan
Nombre de Dios
San Sebastián
Darién
100°
90°
80°
70°
60°
30°
20°
10°

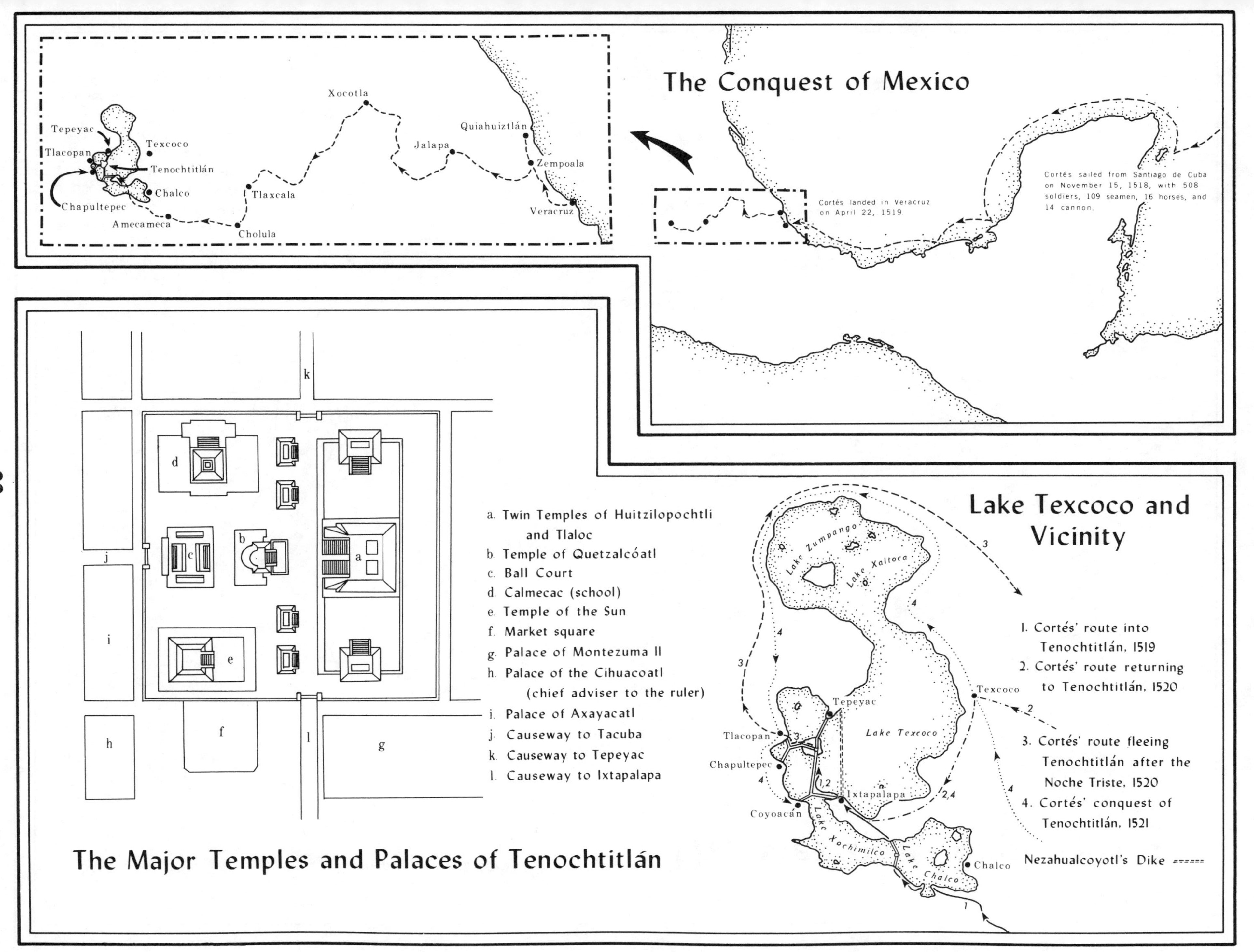

The Conquest of Mexico
Cortés sailed from Santiago de Cuba on November 15, 1518, with 508 soldiers, 109 seamen, 16 horses, and 14 cannon.
Cortés landed in Veracruz on April 22, 1519.
Tepeyac
Tlacopan
Texcoco
Tenochtitlán
Chalco
Chapultepec
Amecameca
Cholula
Tlaxcala
Xocotla
Jalapa
Quiahuiztlán
Zempoala
Veracruz
The Major Temples and Palaces of Tenochtitlán
a. Twin Temples of Huitzilopochtli and Tlaloc
b. Temple of Quetzalcóatl
c. Ball Court
d. Calmecac (school)
e. Temple of the Sun
f. Market square
g. Palace of Montezuma II
h. Palace of the Cihuacoatl (chief adviser to the ruler)
i. Palace of Axayacatl
j. Causeway to Tacuba
k. Causeway to Tepeyac
l. Causeway to Ixtapalapa
Lake Texcoco and Vicinity
Lake Zumpango
Lake Xaltoca
Lake Texcoco
Lake Xochimilco
Lake Chalco
Tepeyac
Tlacopan
Chapultepec
Coyoacán
Ixtapalapa
Texcoco
Chalco
1. Cortés' route into Tenochtitlán, 1519
2. Cortés' route returning to Tenochtitlán, 1520
3. Cortés' route fleeing Tenochtitlán after the Noche Triste, 1520
4. Cortés' conquest of Tenochtitlán, 1521
Nezahualcoyotl's Dike

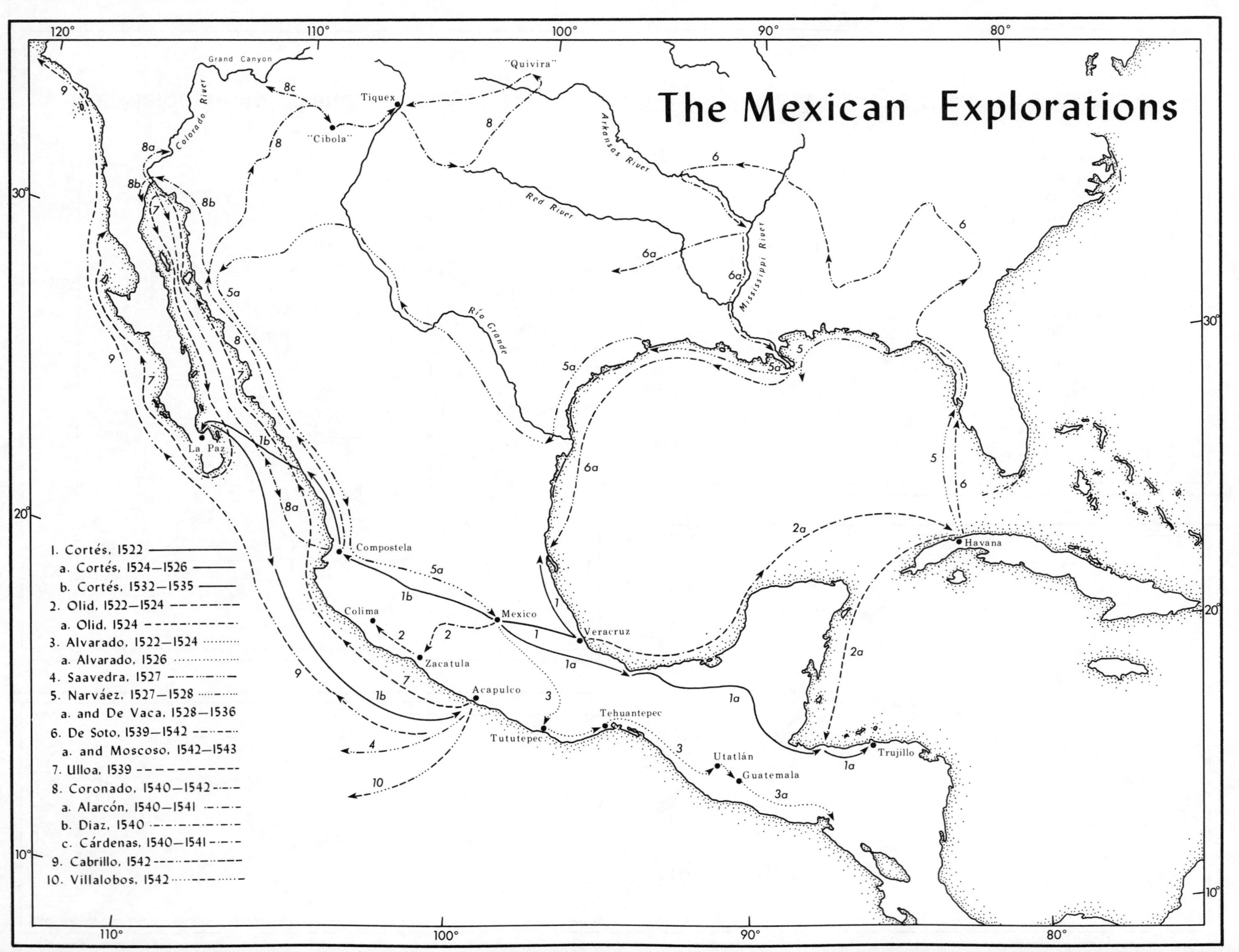
The Mexican Explorations
1. Cortés, 1522
a. Cortés, 1524–1526
b. Cortés, 1532–1535
2. Olid, 1522–1524
a. Olid, 1524
3. Alvarado, 1522–1524
a. Alvarado, 1526
4. Saavedra, 1527
5. Narváez, 1527–1528
a. and De Vaca, 1528–1536
6. De Soto, 1539–1542
a. and Moscoso, 1542–1543
7. Ulloa, 1539
8. Coronado, 1540–1542
a. Alarcón, 1540–1541
b. Diaz, 1540
c. Cárdenas, 1540–1541
9. Cabrillo, 1542
10. Villalobos, 1542
Grand Canyon
Colorado River
"Quivira"
Tiquex
"Cibola"
Arkansas River
Red River
Mississippi River
Río Grande
La Paz
Compostela
Colima
Zacatula
Acapulco
Mexico
Veracruz
Tututepec
Tehuantepec
Utatlán
Guatemala
Trujillo
Havana
120°
110°
100°
90°
80°
30°
20°
10°

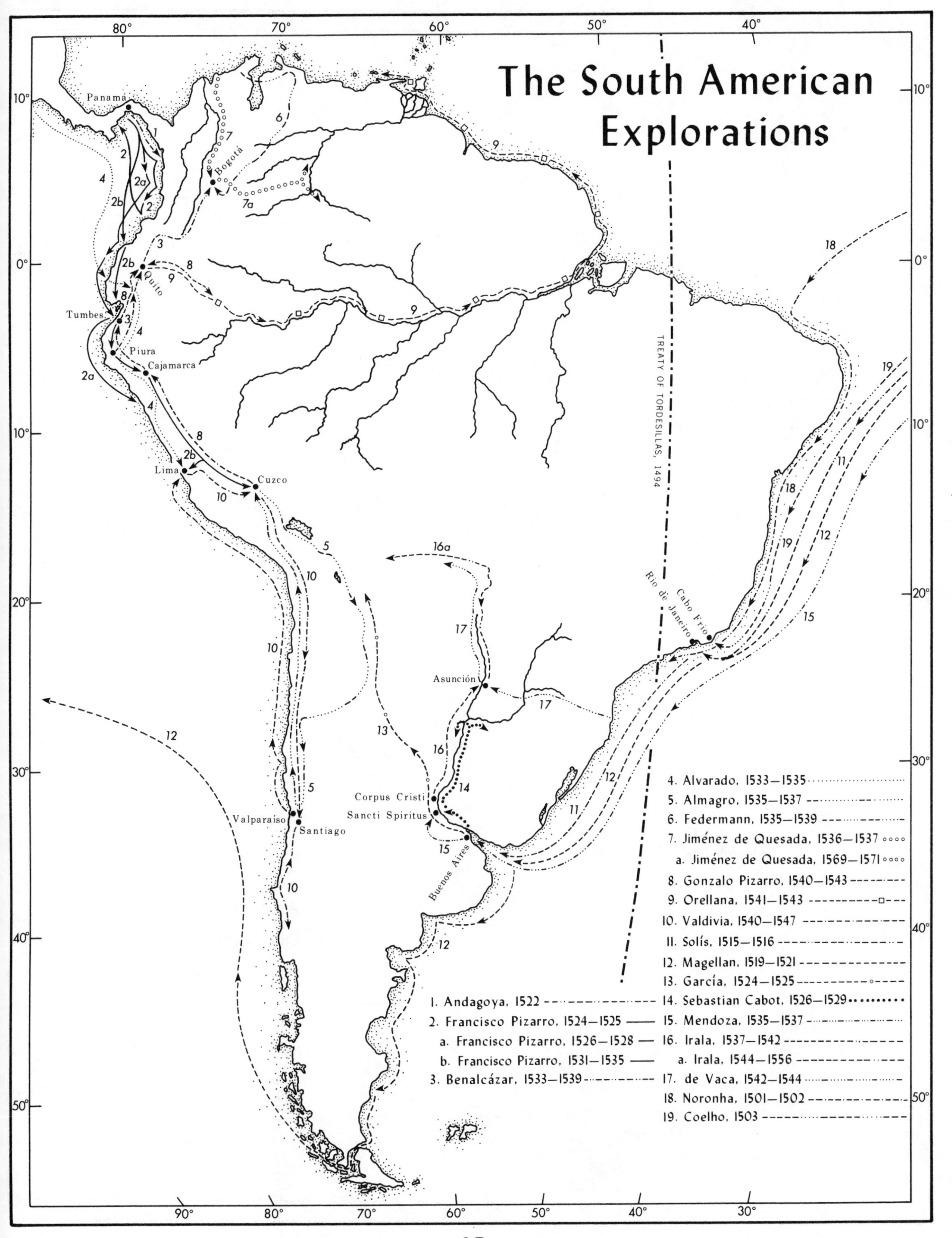
The South American Explorations
Panamá
Bogotá
Quito
Tumbes
Piura
Cajamarca
Lima
Cuzco
Asunción
Corpus Cristi
Sancti Spiritus
Valparaíso
Santiago
Buenos Aires
Río de Janeiro
Cabo Frío
TREATY OF TORDESILLAS, 1494
1. Andagoya, 1522
2. Francisco Pizarro, 1524–1525
a. Francisco Pizarro, 1526–1528
b. Francisco Pizarro, 1531–1535
3. Benalcázar, 1533–1539
4. Alvarado, 1533–1535
5. Almagro, 1535–1537
6. Federmann, 1535–1539
7. Jiménez de Quesada, 1536–1537
a. Jiménez de Quesada, 1569–1571
8. Gonzalo Pizarro, 1540–1543
9. Orellana, 1541–1543
10. Valdivia, 1540–1547
11. Solís, 1515–1516
12. Magellan, 1519–1521
13. García, 1524–1525
14. Sebastian Cabot, 1526–1529
15. Mendoza, 1535–1537
16. Irala, 1537–1542
a. Irala, 1544–1556
17. de Vaca, 1542–1544
18. Noronha, 1501–1502
19. Coelho, 1503

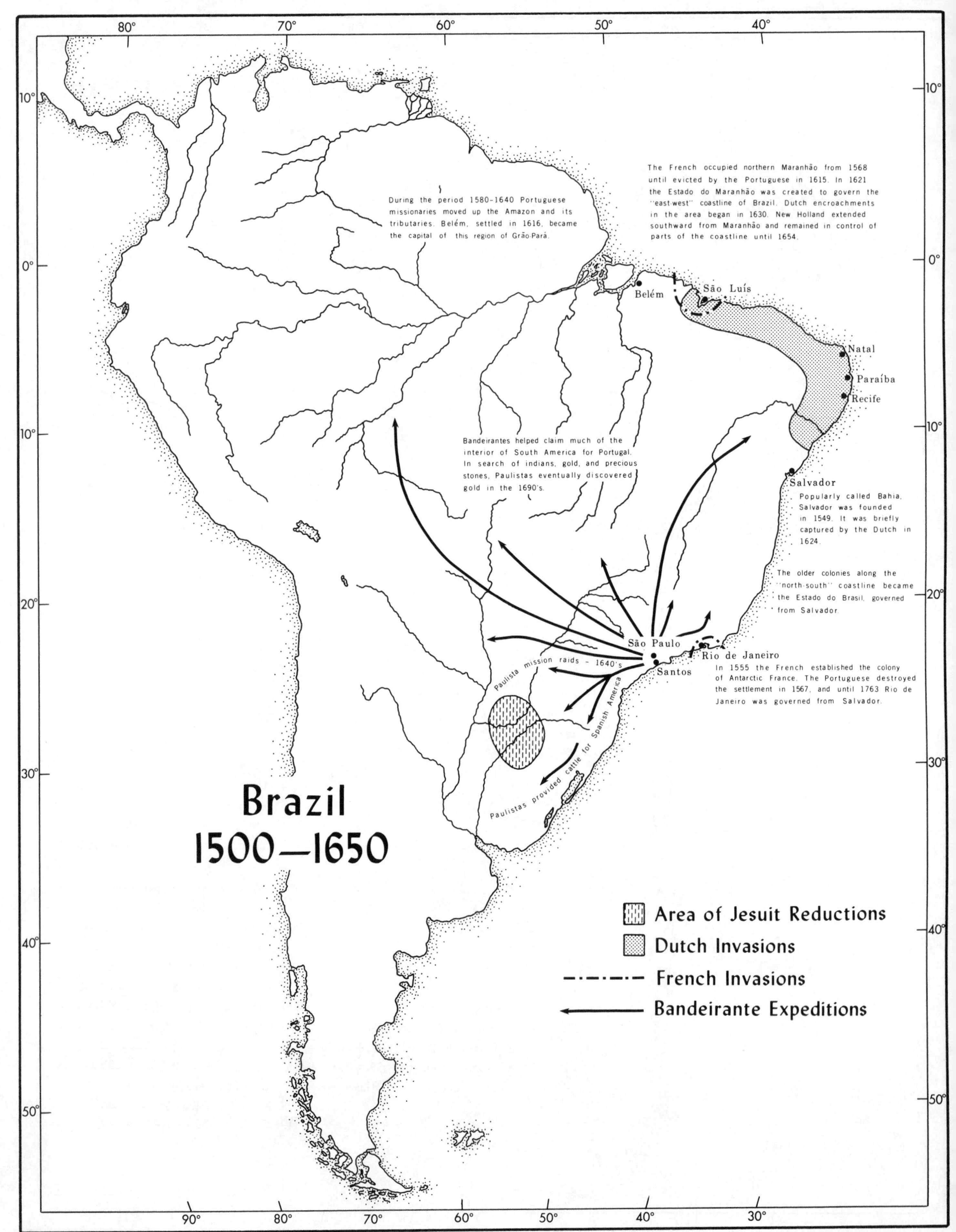

Brazil
1500—1650
During the period 1580-1640 Portuguese missionaries moved up the Amazon and its tributaries. Belém, settled in 1616, became the capital of this region of Grão-Pará.
The French occupied northern Maranhão from 1568 until evicted by the Portuguese in 1615. In 1621 the Estado do Maranhão was created to govern the "east-west" coastline of Brazil. Dutch encroachments in the area began in 1630. New Holland extended southward from Maranhão and remained in control of parts of the coastline until 1654.
Belém
São Luís
Natal
Paraíba
Recife
Salvador
Popularly called Bahia, Salvador was founded in 1549. It was briefly captured by the Dutch in 1624.
Bandeirantes helped claim much of the interior of South America for Portugal. In search of indians, gold, and precious stones, Paulistas eventually discovered gold in the 1690's.
The older colonies along the "north-south" coastline became the Estado do Brasil, governed from Salvador.
São Paulo
Santos
Rio de Janeiro
In 1555 the French established the colony of Antarctic France. The Portuguese destroyed the settlement in 1567, and until 1763 Rio de Janeiro was governed from Salvador.
Paulista mission raids - 1640's
Paulistas provided cattle for Spanish America
Area of Jesuit Reductions
Dutch Invasions
French Invasions
Bandeirante Expeditions

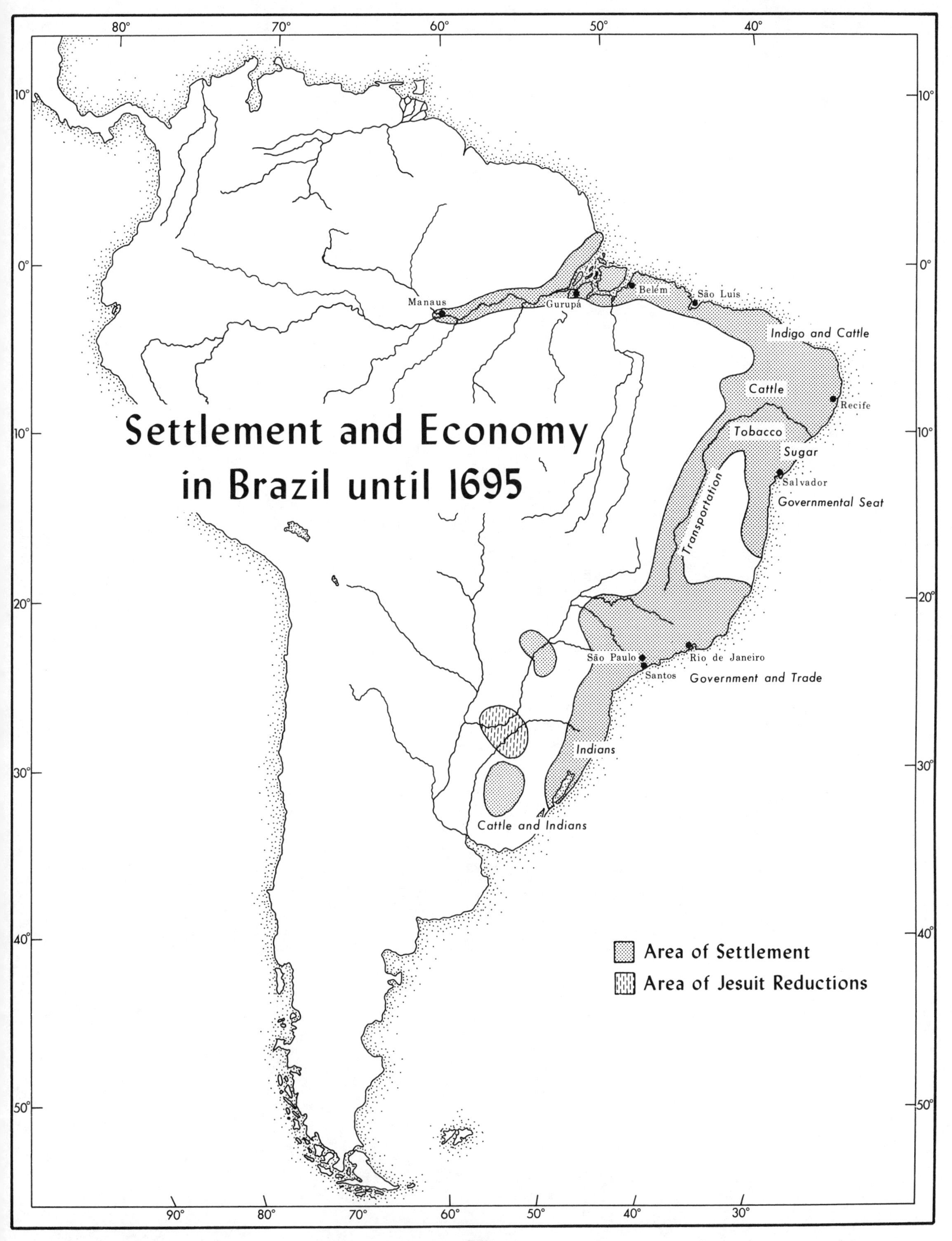
Settlement and Economy
in Brazil until 1695
80°
70°
60°
50°
40°
30°
90°
10°
0°
20°
Manaus
Gurupá
Belém
São Luís
Indigo and Cattle
Cattle
Recife
Tobacco
Sugar
Salvador
Governmental Seat
Transportation
São Paulo
Rio de Janeiro
Santos
Government and Trade
Indians
Cattle and Indians
Area of Settlement
Area of Jesuit Reductions

The Colonial Governments

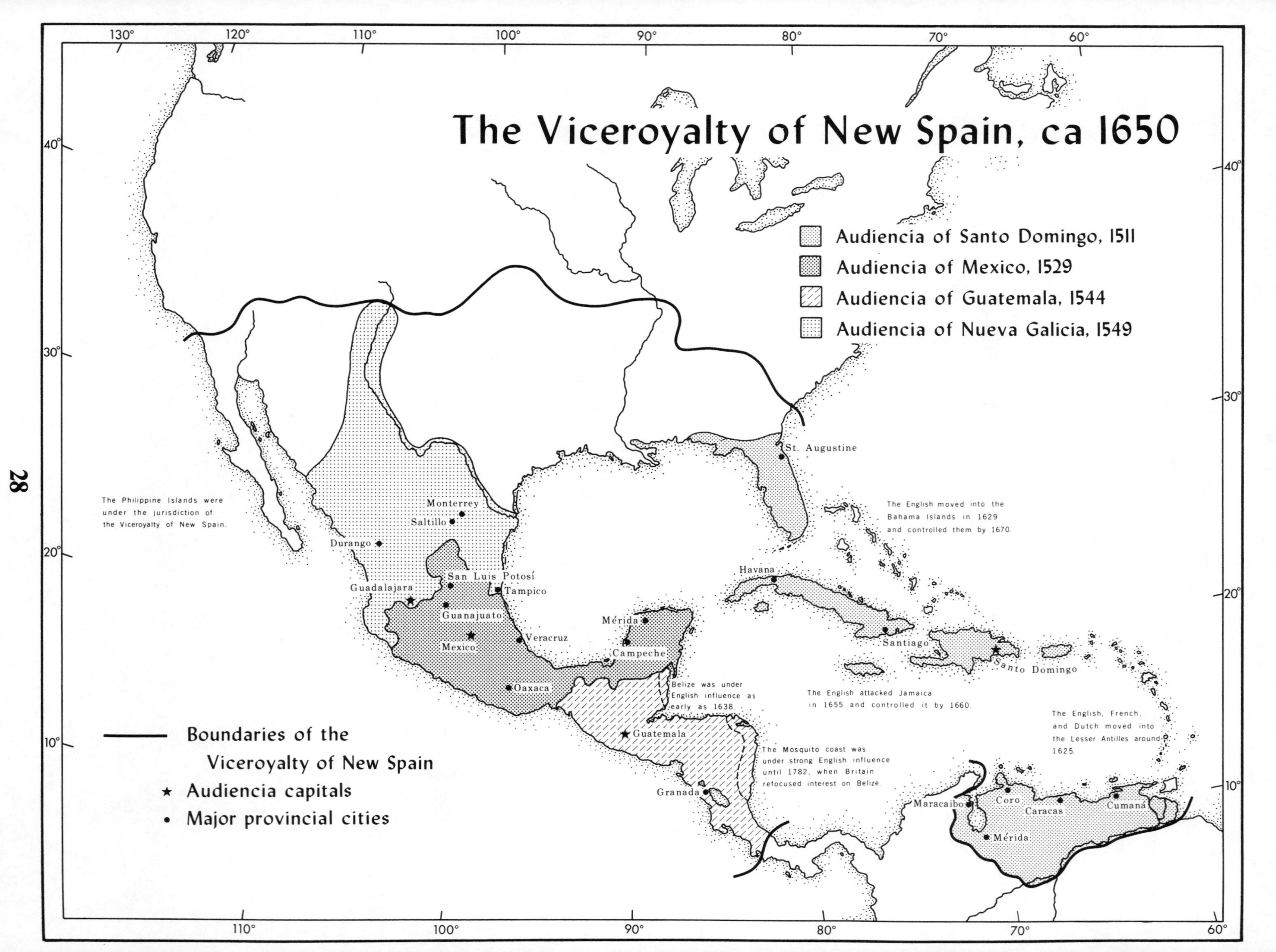
The Viceroyalty of New Spain, ca 1650
Audiencia of Santo Domingo, 1511
Audiencia of Mexico, 1529
Audiencia of Guatemala, 1544
Audiencia of Nueva Galicia, 1549
Boundaries of the Viceroyalty of New Spain
Audiencia capitals
Major provincial cities
The Philippine Islands were under the jurisdiction of the Viceroyalty of New Spain.
The English moved into the Bahama Islands in 1629 and controlled them by 1670.
The English attacked Jamaica in 1655 and controlled it by 1660.
Belize was under English influence as early as 1638.
The Mosquito coast was under strong English influence until 1782, when Britain refocused interest on Belize.
The English, French, and Dutch moved into the Lesser Antilles around 1625.
St. Augustine
Monterrey
Saltillo
Durango
San Luis Potosí
Tampico
Guadalajara
Guanajuato
Mexico
Veracruz
Oaxaca
Mérida
Campeche
Guatemala
Granada
Havana
Santiago
Santo Domingo
Maracaibo
Coro
Caracas
Cumaná
Mérida
130°
120°
110°
100°
90°
80°
70°
60°
40°
30°
20°
10°

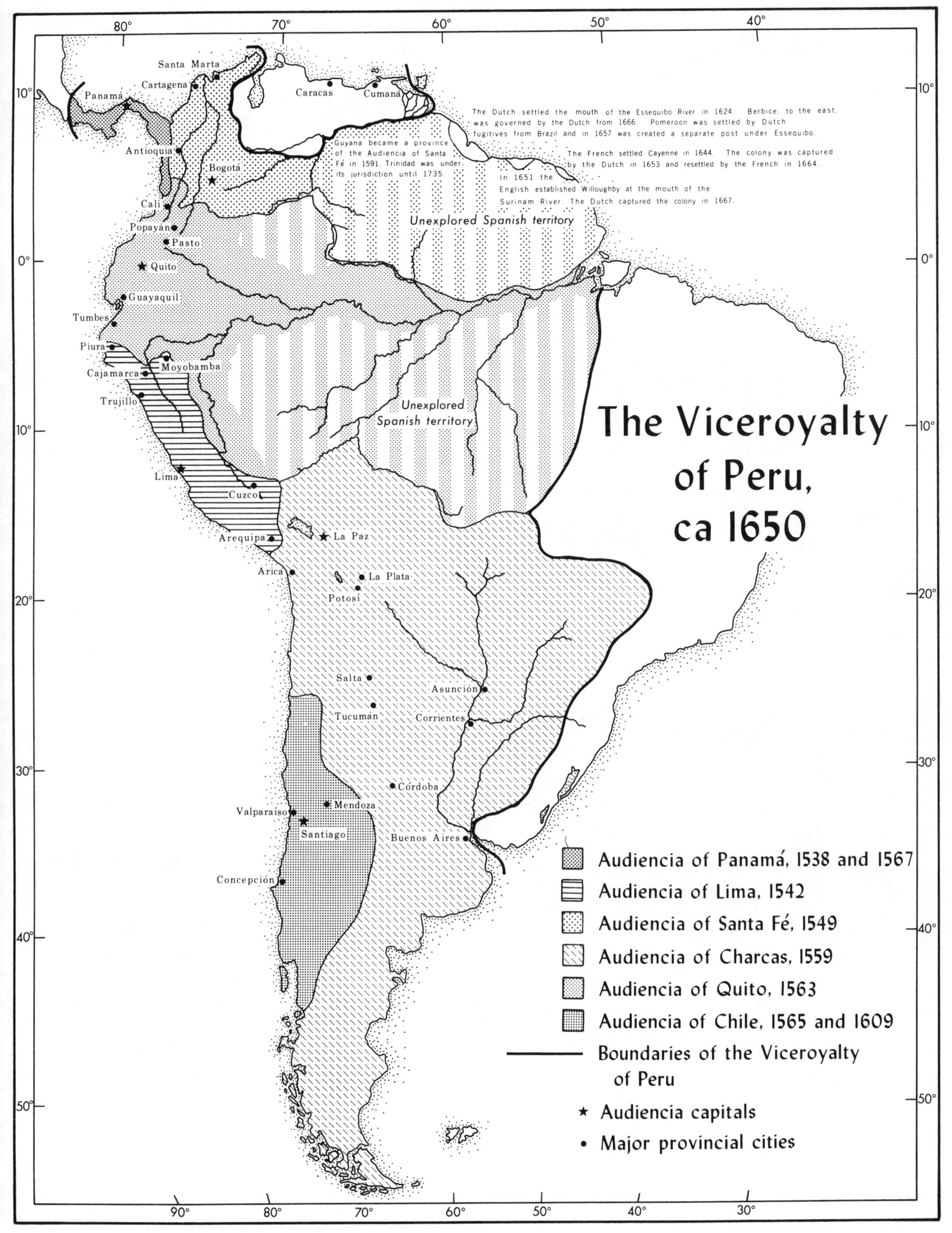

The Viceroyalty of Peru, ca 1650
80°
70°
60°
50°
40°
10°
0°
10°
20°
30°
40°
50°
90°
80°
70°
60°
50°
40°
30°
Santa Marta
Cartagena
Panamá
Caracas
Cumaná
Antioquia
Bogotá
Cali
Popayán
Pasto
Quito
Guayaquil
Tumbes
Piura
Moyobamba
Cajamarca
Trujillo
Lima
Cuzco
Arequipa
La Paz
Arica
La Plata
Potosí
Salta
Asunción
Tucumán
Corrientes
Córdoba
Mendoza
Valparaíso
Santiago
Buenos Aires
Concepción
The Dutch settled the mouth of the Essequibo River in 1624. Berbice, to the east, was governed by the Dutch from 1666. Pomeroon was settled by Dutch fugitives from Brazil and in 1657 was created a separate post under Essequibo.
Guyana became a province of the Audiencia of Santa Fé in 1591. Trinidad was under its jurisdiction until 1735.
The French settled Cayenne in 1644. The colony was captured by the Dutch in 1653 and resettled by the French in 1664.
In 1651 the English established Willoughby at the mouth of the Surinam River. The Dutch captured the colony in 1667.
Unexplored Spanish territory
Unexplored Spanish territory
Audiencia of Panamá, 1538 and 1567
Audiencia of Lima, 1542
Audiencia of Santa Fé, 1549
Audiencia of Charcas, 1559
Audiencia of Quito, 1563
Audiencia of Chile, 1565 and 1609
Boundaries of the Viceroyalty of Peru
Audiencia capitals
Major provincial cities

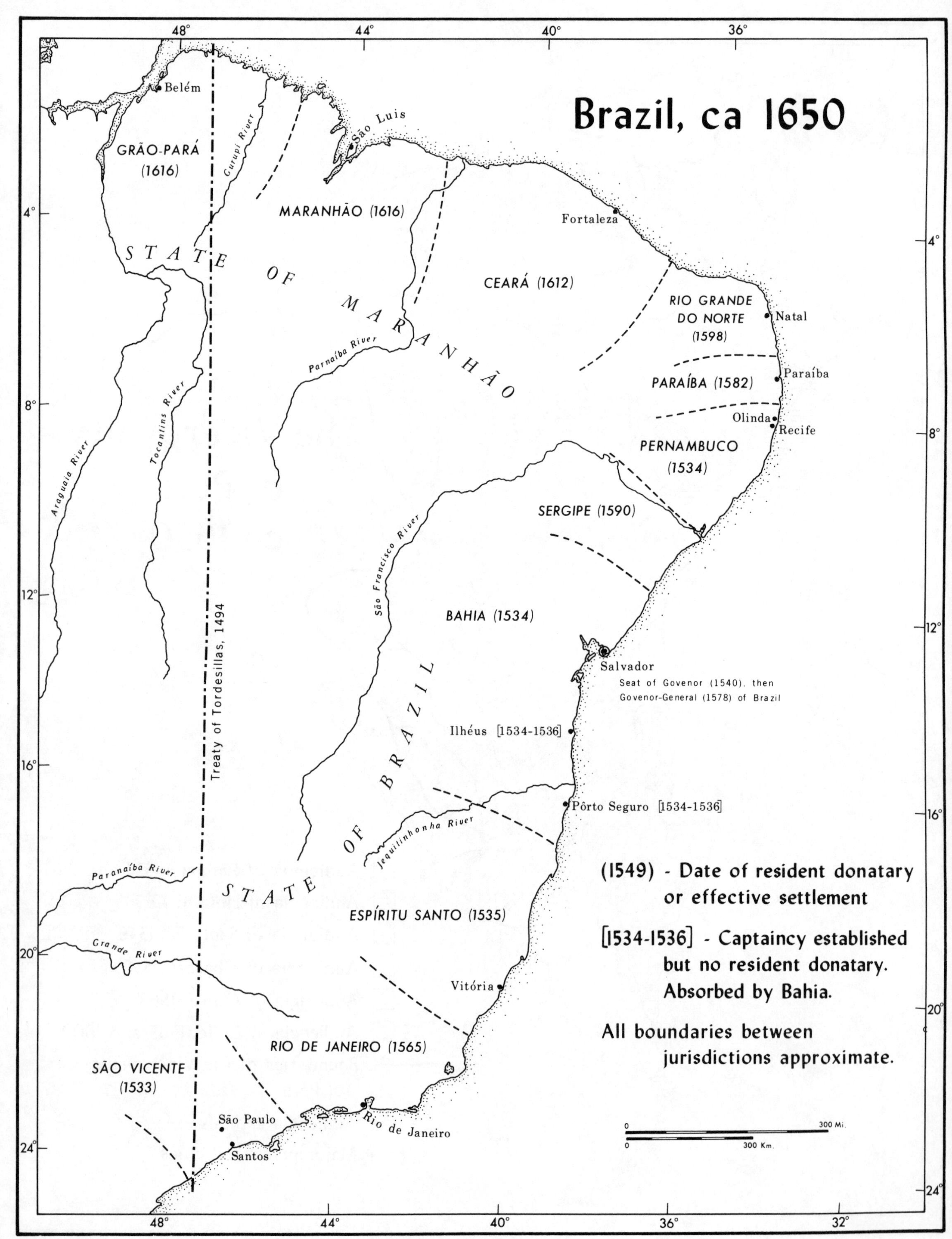

Brazil, ca 1650
48°
44°
40°
36°
32°
4°
8°
12°
16°
20°
24°
Belém
GRÃO-PARÁ
(1616)
Gurupi River
São Luis
MARANHÃO (1616)
Fortaleza
STATE OF MARANHÃO
CEARÁ (1612)
RIO GRANDE
DO NORTE
(1598)
Natal
Parnaíba River
PARAÍBA (1582)
Paraíba
Olinda
Recife
PERNAMBUCO
(1534)
Araguaia River
Tocantins River
SERGIPE (1590)
São Francisco River
BAHIA (1534)
Treaty of Tordesillas, 1494
Salvador
Seat of Govenor (1540), then
Govenor-General (1578) of Brazil
Ilhéus [1534-1536]
Pôrto Seguro [1534-1536]
Jequitinhonha River
STATE OF BRAZIL
Paranaíba River
(1549) - Date of resident donatary
or effective settlement
ESPÍRITU SANTO (1535)
[1534-1536] - Captaincy established
but no resident donatary.
Absorbed by Bahia.
Grande River
Vitória
All boundaries between
jurisdictions approximate.
RIO DE JANEIRO (1565)
SÃO VICENTE
(1533)
São Paulo
Rio de Janeiro
Santos
0
300 Mi.
0
300 Km.

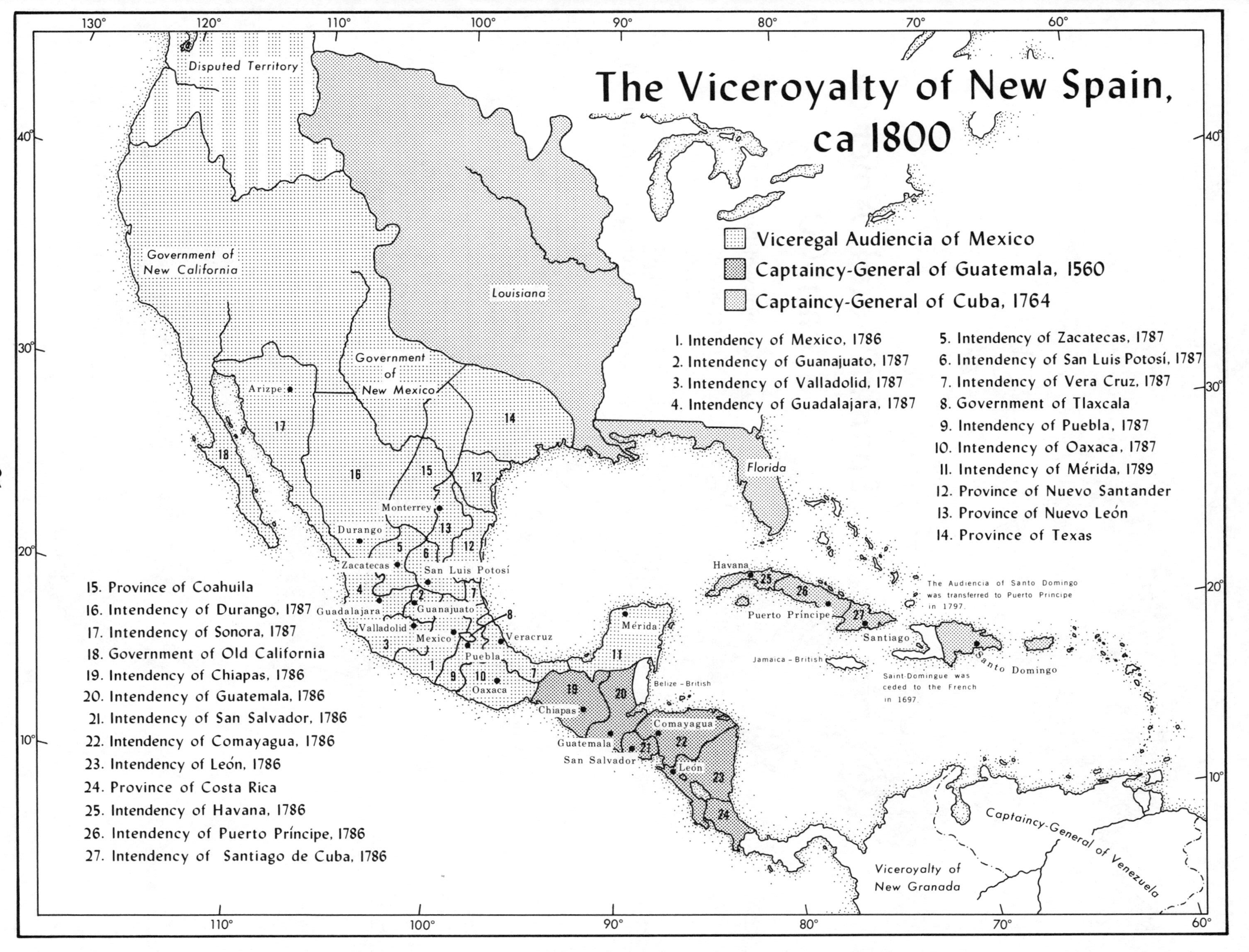
The Viceroyalty of New Spain, ca 1800
Viceregal Audiencia of Mexico
Captaincy-General of Guatemala, 1560
Captaincy-General of Cuba, 1764
1. Intendency of Mexico, 1786
2. Intendency of Guanajuato, 1787
3. Intendency of Valladolid, 1787
4. Intendency of Guadalajara, 1787
5. Intendency of Zacatecas, 1787
6. Intendency of San Luis Potosí, 1787
7. Intendency of Vera Cruz, 1787
8. Government of Tlaxcala
9. Intendency of Puebla, 1787
10. Intendency of Oaxaca, 1787
11. Intendency of Mérida, 1789
12. Province of Nuevo Santander
13. Province of Nuevo León
14. Province of Texas
15. Province of Coahuila
16. Intendency of Durango, 1787
17. Intendency of Sonora, 1787
18. Government of Old California
19. Intendency of Chiapas, 1786
20. Intendency of Guatemala, 1786
21. Intendency of San Salvador, 1786
22. Intendency of Comayagua, 1786
23. Intendency of León, 1786
24. Province of Costa Rica
25. Intendency of Havana, 1786
26. Intendency of Puerto Príncipe, 1786
27. Intendency of Santiago de Cuba, 1786
Disputed Territory
Government of New California
Louisiana
Government of New Mexico
Florida
Arizpe
Monterrey
Durango
Zacatecas
San Luis Potosí
Guadalajara
Guanajuato
Valladolid
Mexico
Veracruz
Puebla
Oaxaca
Mérida
Chiapas
Guatemala
San Salvador
Comayagua
León
Belize - British
Havana
Puerto Principe
Santiago
Jamaica - British
Santo Domingo
The Audiencia of Santo Domingo was transferred to Puerto Principe in 1797.
Saint-Domingue was ceded to the French in 1697.
Captaincy-General of Venezuela
Viceroyalty of New Granada

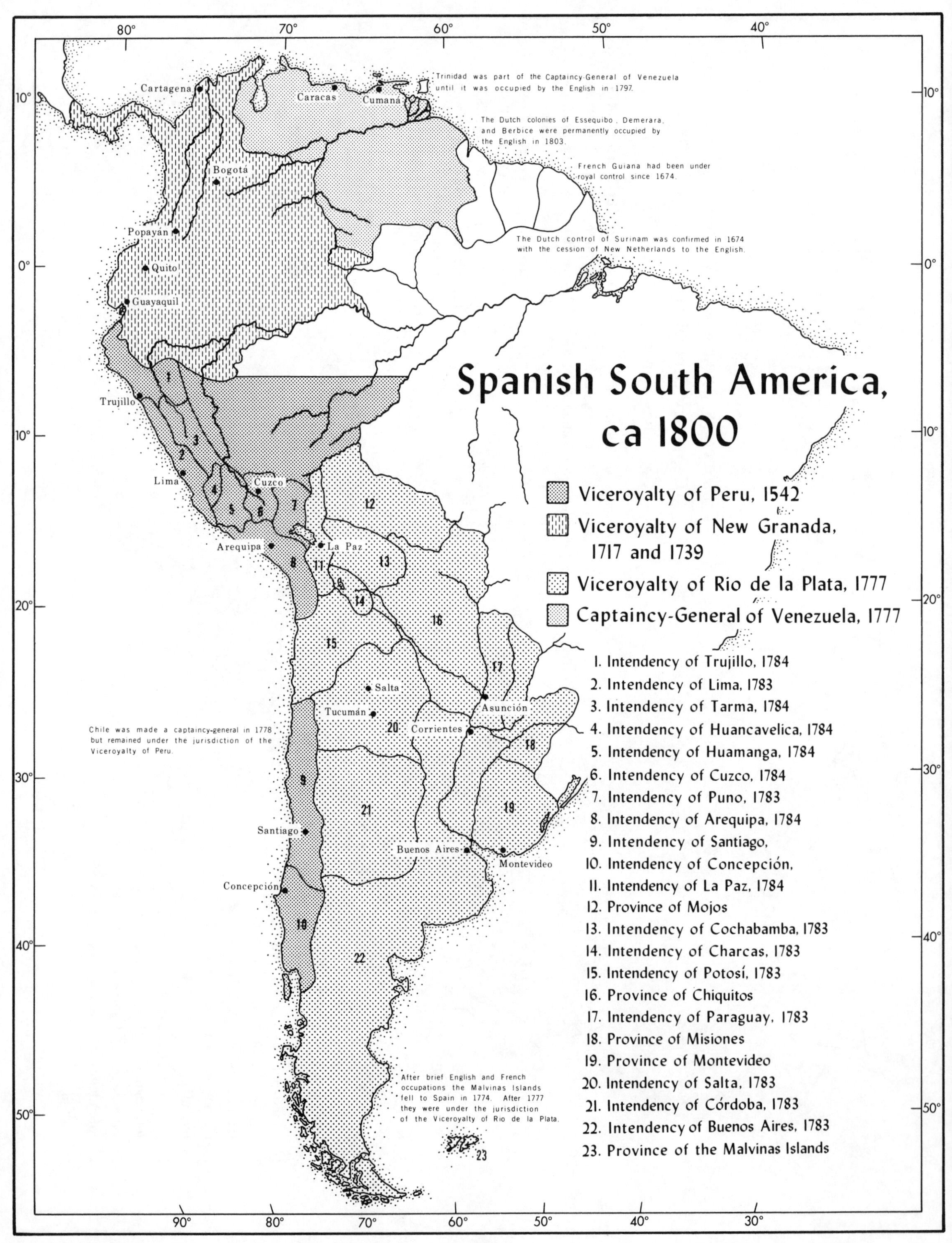

Spanish South America, ca 1800
Viceroyalty of Peru, 1542
Viceroyalty of New Granada, 1717 and 1739
Viceroyalty of Rio de la Plata, 1777
Captaincy-General of Venezuela, 1777
1. Intendency of Trujillo, 1784
2. Intendency of Lima, 1783
3. Intendency of Tarma, 1784
4. Intendency of Huancavelica, 1784
5. Intendency of Huamanga, 1784
6. Intendency of Cuzco, 1784
7. Intendency of Puno, 1783
8. Intendency of Arequipa, 1784
9. Intendency of Santiago,
10. Intendency of Concepción,
11. Intendency of La Paz, 1784
12. Province of Mojos
13. Intendency of Cochabamba, 1783
14. Intendency of Charcas, 1783
15. Intendency of Potosí, 1783
16. Province of Chiquitos
17. Intendency of Paraguay, 1783
18. Province of Misiones
19. Province of Montevideo
20. Intendency of Salta, 1783
21. Intendency of Córdoba, 1783
22. Intendency of Buenos Aires, 1783
23. Province of the Malvinas Islands
Trinidad was part of the Captaincy-General of Venezuela until it was occupied by the English in 1797.
The Dutch colonies of Essequibo, Demerara, and Berbice were permanently occupied by the English in 1803.
French Guiana had been under royal control since 1674.
The Dutch control of Surinam was confirmed in 1674 with the cession of New Netherlands to the English.
Chile was made a captaincy-general in 1778 but remained under the jurisdiction of the Viceroyalty of Peru.
After brief English and French occupations the Malvinas Islands fell to Spain in 1774. After 1777 they were under the jurisdiction of the Viceroyalty of Rio de la Plata.
Cartagena
Caracas
Cumaná
Bogotá
Popayán
Quito
Guayaquil
Trujillo
Lima
Cuzco
Arequipa
La Paz
Salta
Tucumán
Asunción
Corrientes
Santiago
Buenos Aires
Montevideo
Concepción
80°
70°
60°
50°
40°
30°
90°
10°
0°
20°

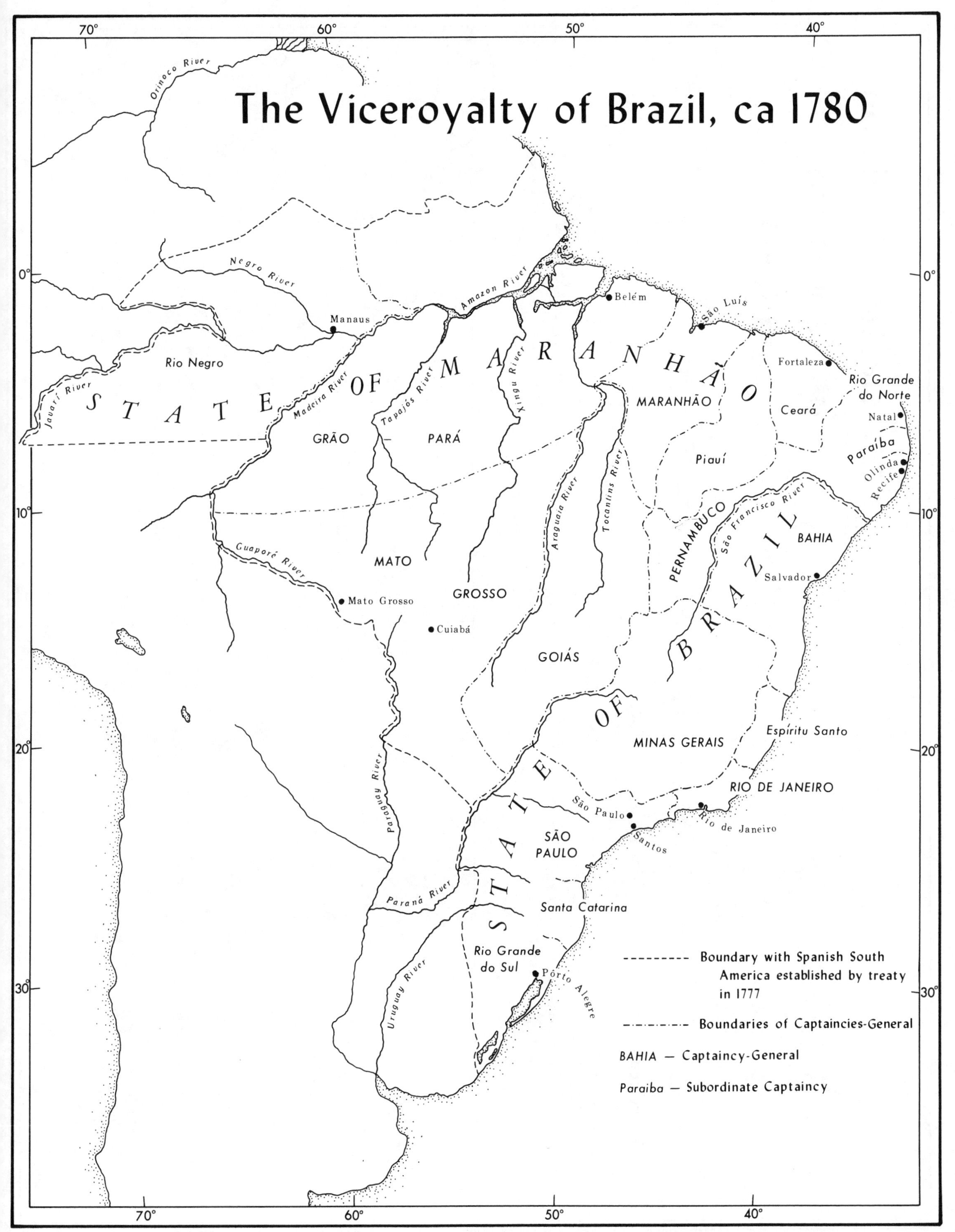

The Viceroyalty of Brazil, ca 1780
70°
60°
50°
40°
0°
10°
20°
30°
Orinoco River
Negro River
Amazon River
Manaus
Belém
São Luís
Fortaleza
Rio Grande do Norte
Natal
Ceará
Paraíba
Olinda
Recife
Rio Negro
Javarí River
Madeira River
Tapajós River
Xingu River
STATE OF MARANHÃO
MARANHÃO
Piauí
GRÃO
PARÁ
PERNAMBUCO
São Francisco River
BAHIA
Salvador
Araguaia River
Tocantins River
MATO
GROSSO
Guaporé River
Mato Grosso
Cuiabá
GOIÁS
STATE OF BRAZIL
MINAS GERAIS
Espíritu Santo
RIO DE JANEIRO
Rio de Janeiro
São Paulo
Santos
SÃO PAULO
Paraguay River
Paraná River
Santa Catarina
Rio Grande do Sul
Pôrto Alegre
Uruguay River
Boundary with Spanish South America established by treaty in 1777
Boundaries of Captaincies-General
BAHIA — Captaincy-General
Paraiba — Subordinate Captaincy

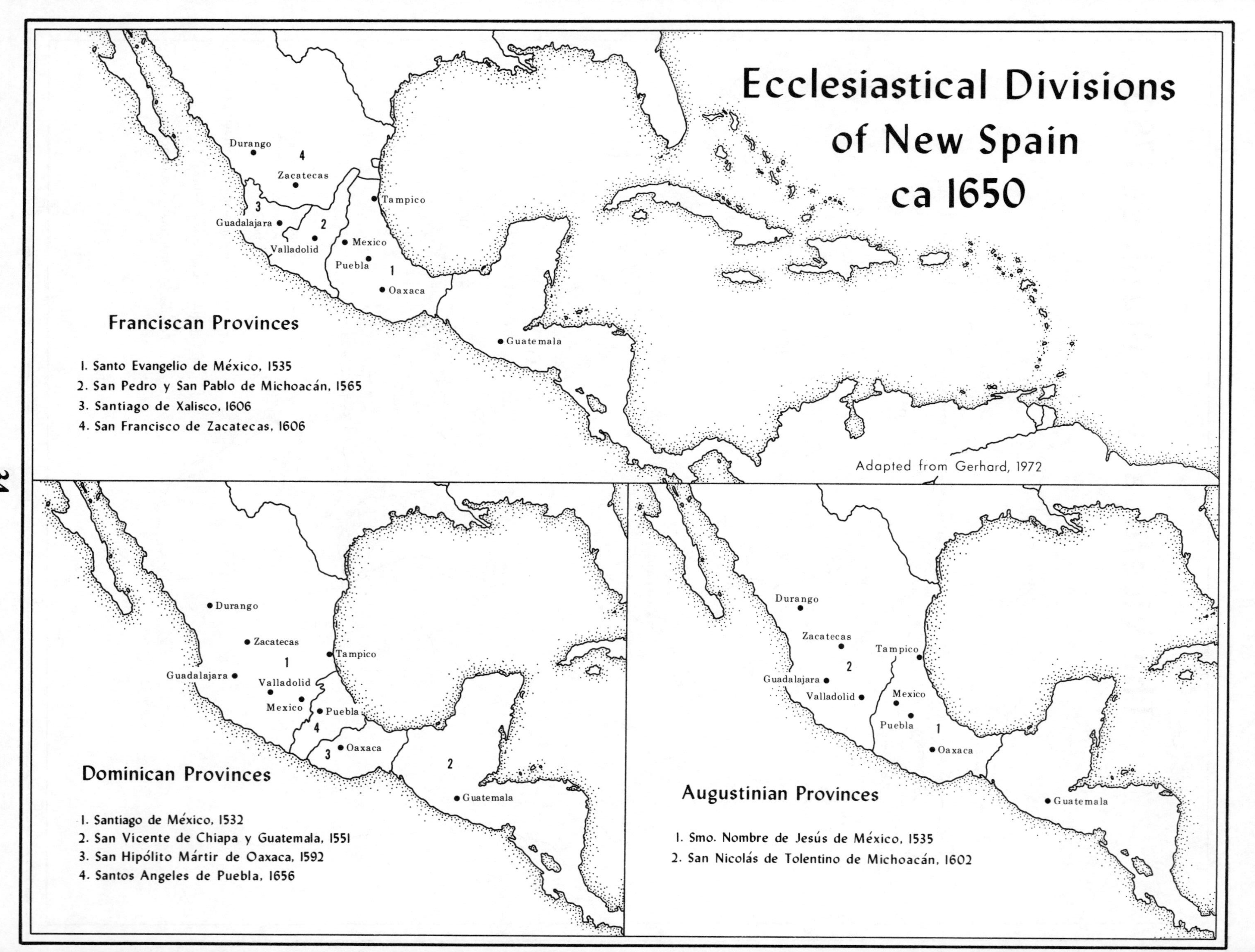
Ecclesiastical Divisions
of New Spain
ca 1650
Durango
4
Zacatecas
3
Tampico
Guadalajara
2
Valladolid
Mexico
Puebla
1
Oaxaca
Franciscan Provinces
Guatemala
1. Santo Evangelio de México, 1535
2. San Pedro y San Pablo de Michoacán, 1565
3. Santiago de Xalisco, 1606
4. San Francisco de Zacatecas, 1606
Adapted from Gerhard, 1972
Durango
Zacatecas
Tampico
1
Guadalajara
Valladolid
Mexico
Puebla
4
3
Oaxaca
2
Dominican Provinces
Guatemala
1. Santiago de México, 1532
2. San Vicente de Chiapa y Guatemala, 1551
3. San Hipólito Mártir de Oaxaca, 1592
4. Santos Angeles de Puebla, 1656
Durango
Zacatecas
Tampico
2
Guadalajara
Valladolid
Mexico
Puebla
1
Oaxaca
Augustinian Provinces
Guatemala
1. Smo. Nombre de Jesús de México, 1535
2. San Nicolás de Tolentino de Michoacán, 1602

Trade, Resources, and Competition

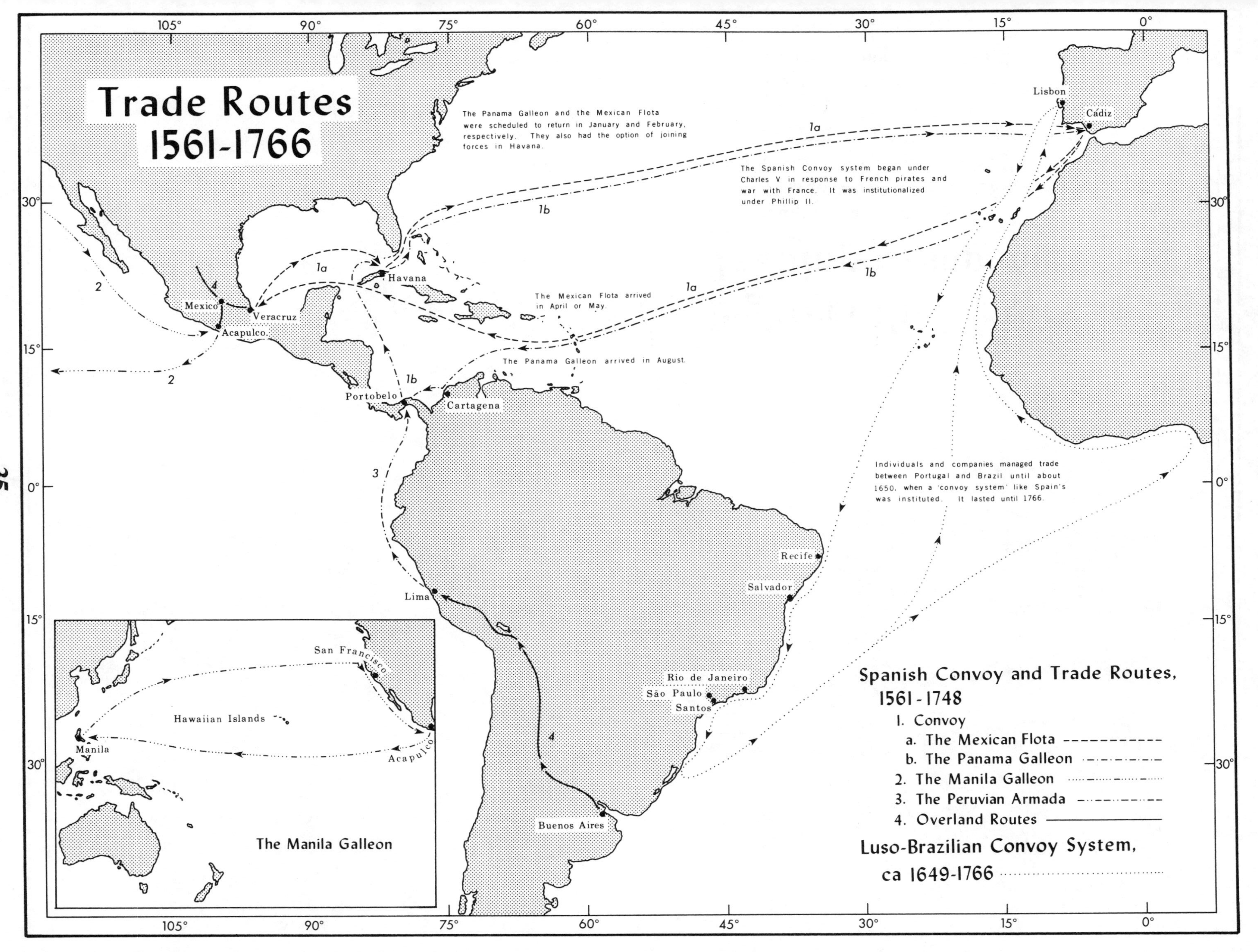

Trade Routes
1561-1766
The Panama Galleon and the Mexican Flota were scheduled to return in January and February, respectively. They also had the option of joining forces in Havana.
The Spanish Convoy system began under Charles V in response to French pirates and war with France. It was institutionalized under Phillip II.
The Mexican Flota arrived in April or May.
The Panama Galleon arrived in August.
Individuals and companies managed trade between Portugal and Brazil until about 1650, when a 'convoy system' like Spain's was instituted. It lasted until 1766.
Lisbon
Cádiz
Havana
Mexico
Veracruz
Acapulco
Portobelo
Cartagena
Lima
Recife
Salvador
Rio de Janeiro
São Paulo
Santos
Buenos Aires
1a
1b
2
3
4
The Manila Galleon
San Francisco
Hawaiian Islands
Manila
Acapulco
Spanish Convoy and Trade Routes, 1561-1748
1. Convoy
a. The Mexican Flota
b. The Panama Galleon
2. The Manila Galleon
3. The Peruvian Armada
4. Overland Routes
Luso-Brazilian Convoy System, ca 1649-1766
105°
90°
75°
60°
45°
30°
15°
0°

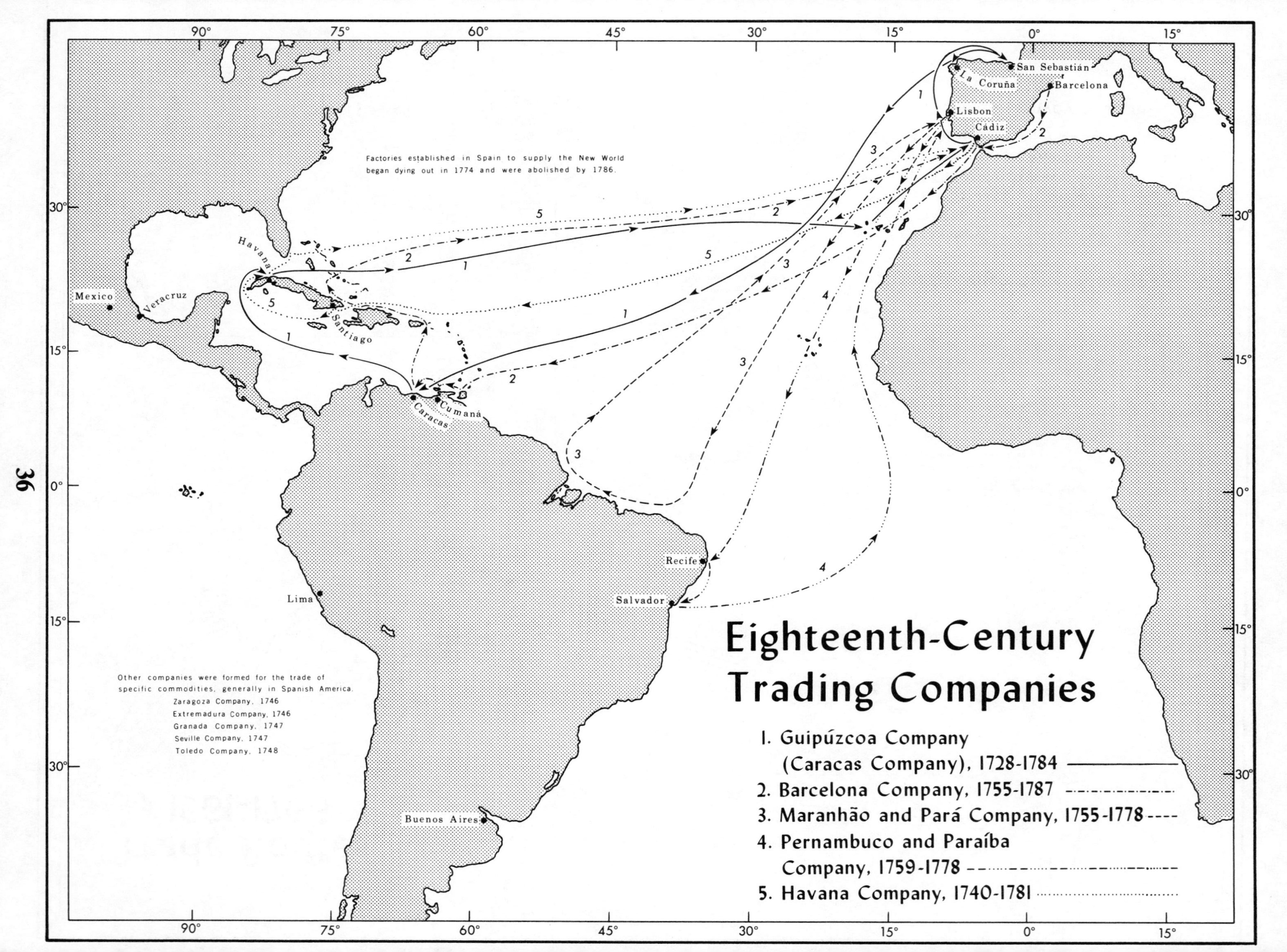
Eighteenth-Century Trading Companies
1. Guipúzcoa Company (Caracas Company), 1728-1784
2. Barcelona Company, 1755-1787
3. Maranhão and Pará Company, 1755-1778
4. Pernambuco and Paraíba Company, 1759-1778
5. Havana Company, 1740-1781
Factories established in Spain to supply the New World began dying out in 1774 and were abolished by 1786.
Other companies were formed for the trade of specific commodities, generally in Spanish America.
Zaragoza Company, 1746
Extremadura Company, 1746
Granada Company, 1747
Seville Company, 1747
Toledo Company, 1748
San Sebastián
La Coruña
Barcelona
Lisbon
Cádiz
Havana
Mexico
Veracruz
Santiago
Caracas
Cumaná
Recife
Salvador
Lima
Buenos Aires

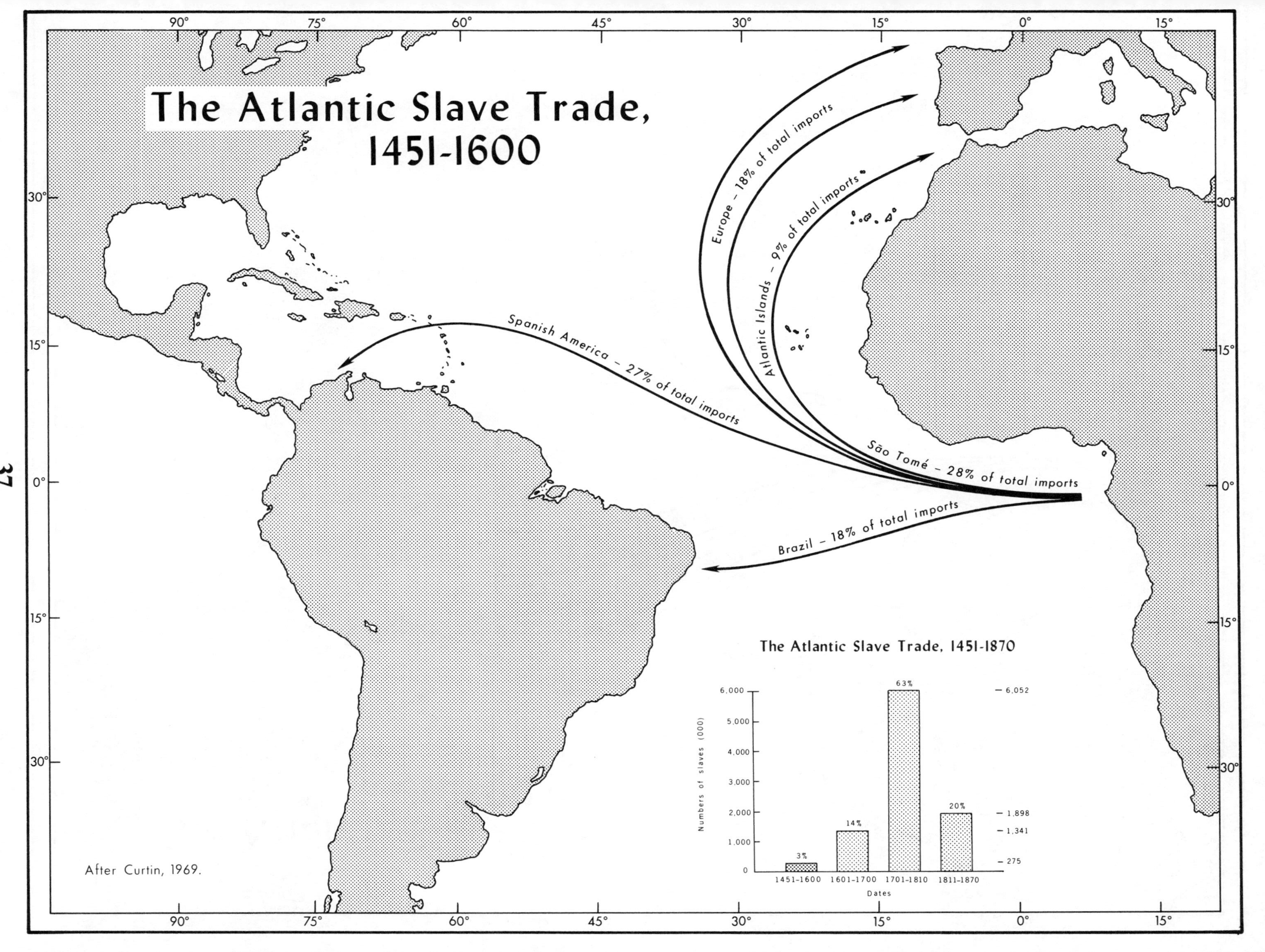
The Atlantic Slave Trade,
1451-1600
Europe – 18% of total imports
Atlantic Islands – 9% of total imports
Spanish America – 27% of total imports
São Tomé – 28% of total imports
Brazil – 18% of total imports
The Atlantic Slave Trade, 1451-1870
Numbers of slaves (000)
6,000
5,000
4,000
3,000
2,000
1,000
0
3%
14%
63%
20%
– 6,052
– 1,898
– 1,341
– 275
1451-1600
1601-1700
1701-1810
1811-1870
Dates
90°
75°
60°
45°
30°
15°
0°
After Curtin, 1969.

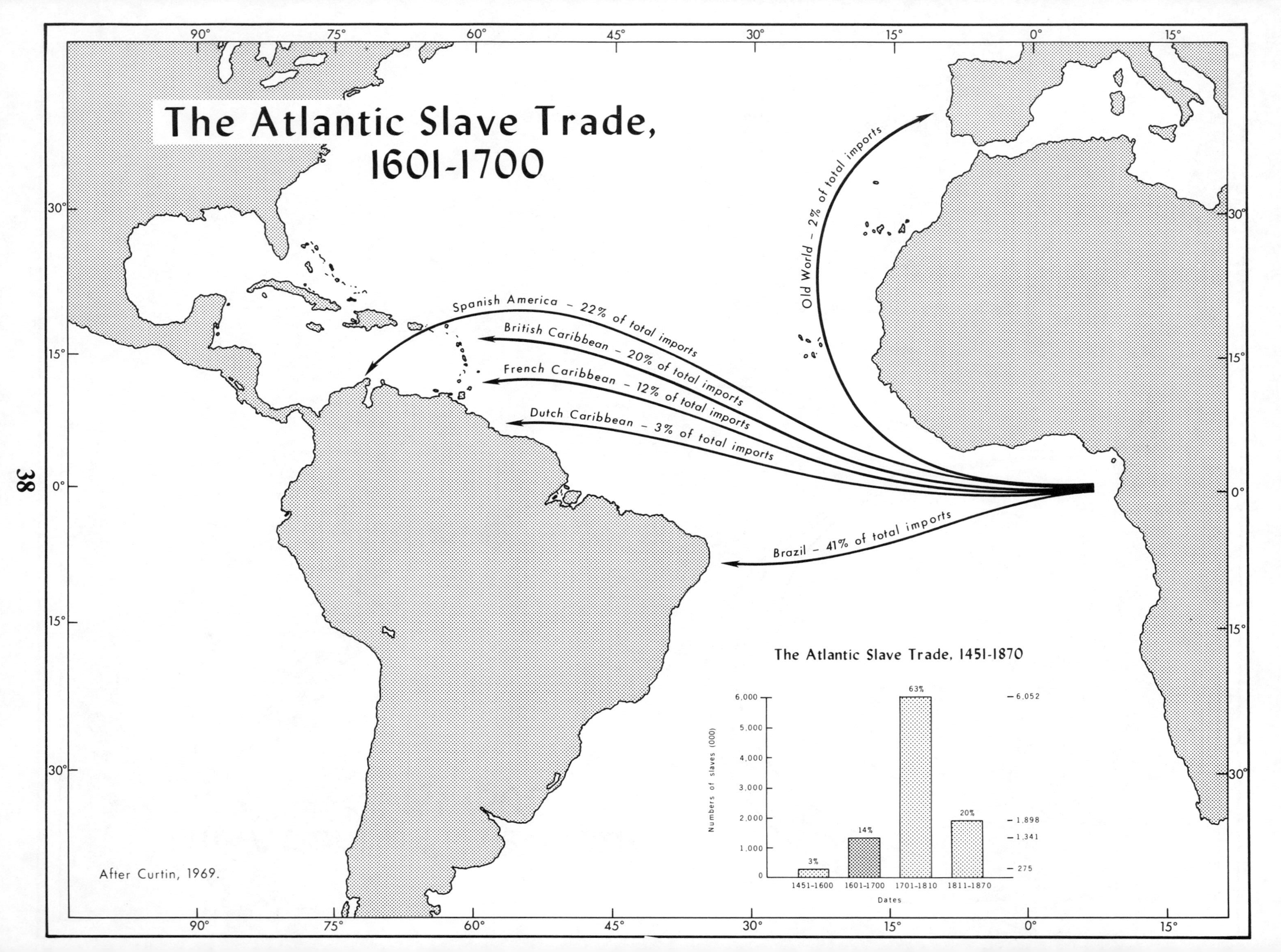
The Atlantic Slave Trade, 1601-1700
Old World – 2% of total imports
Spanish America – 22% of total imports
British Caribbean – 20% of total imports
French Caribbean – 12% of total imports
Dutch Caribbean – 3% of total imports
Brazil – 41% of total imports
The Atlantic Slave Trade, 1451-1870
Numbers of slaves (000)
6,000
5,000
4,000
3,000
2,000
1,000
0
3%
14%
63%
20%
– 6,052
– 1,898
– 1,341
– 275
1451-1600
1601-1700
1701-1810
1811-1870
Dates
After Curtin, 1969.
90°
75°
60°
45°
30°
15°
0°

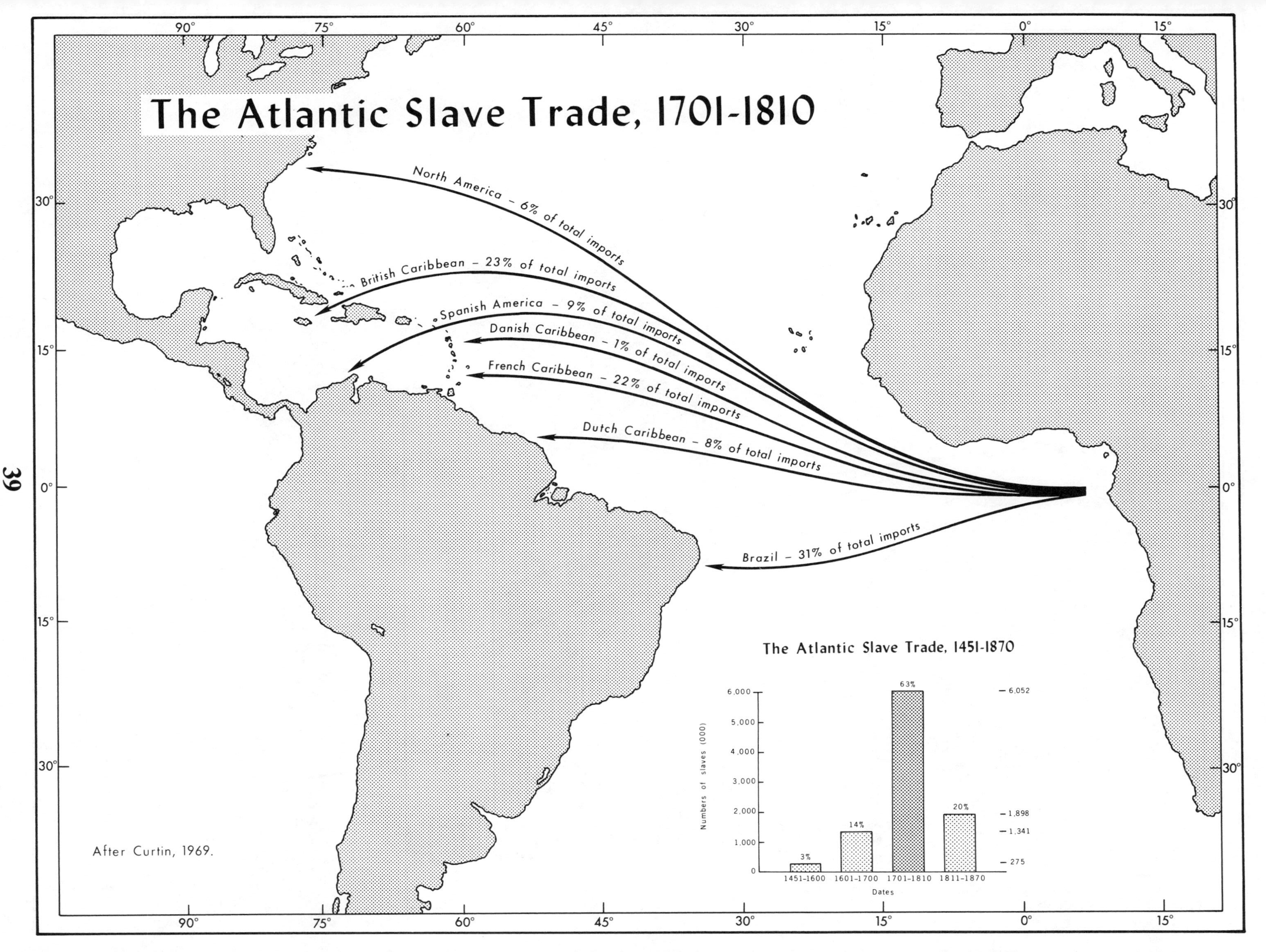
The Atlantic Slave Trade, 1701-1810
North America – 6% of total imports
British Caribbean – 23% of total imports
Spanish America – 9% of total imports
Danish Caribbean – 1% of total imports
French Caribbean – 22% of total imports
Dutch Caribbean – 8% of total imports
Brazil – 31% of total imports
The Atlantic Slave Trade, 1451-1870
Numbers of slaves (000)
6,000
5,000
4,000
3,000
2,000
1,000
0
3%
14%
63%
20%
1451-1600
1601-1700
1701-1810
1811-1870
Dates
– 6,052
– 1,898
– 1,341
– 275
After Curtin, 1969.

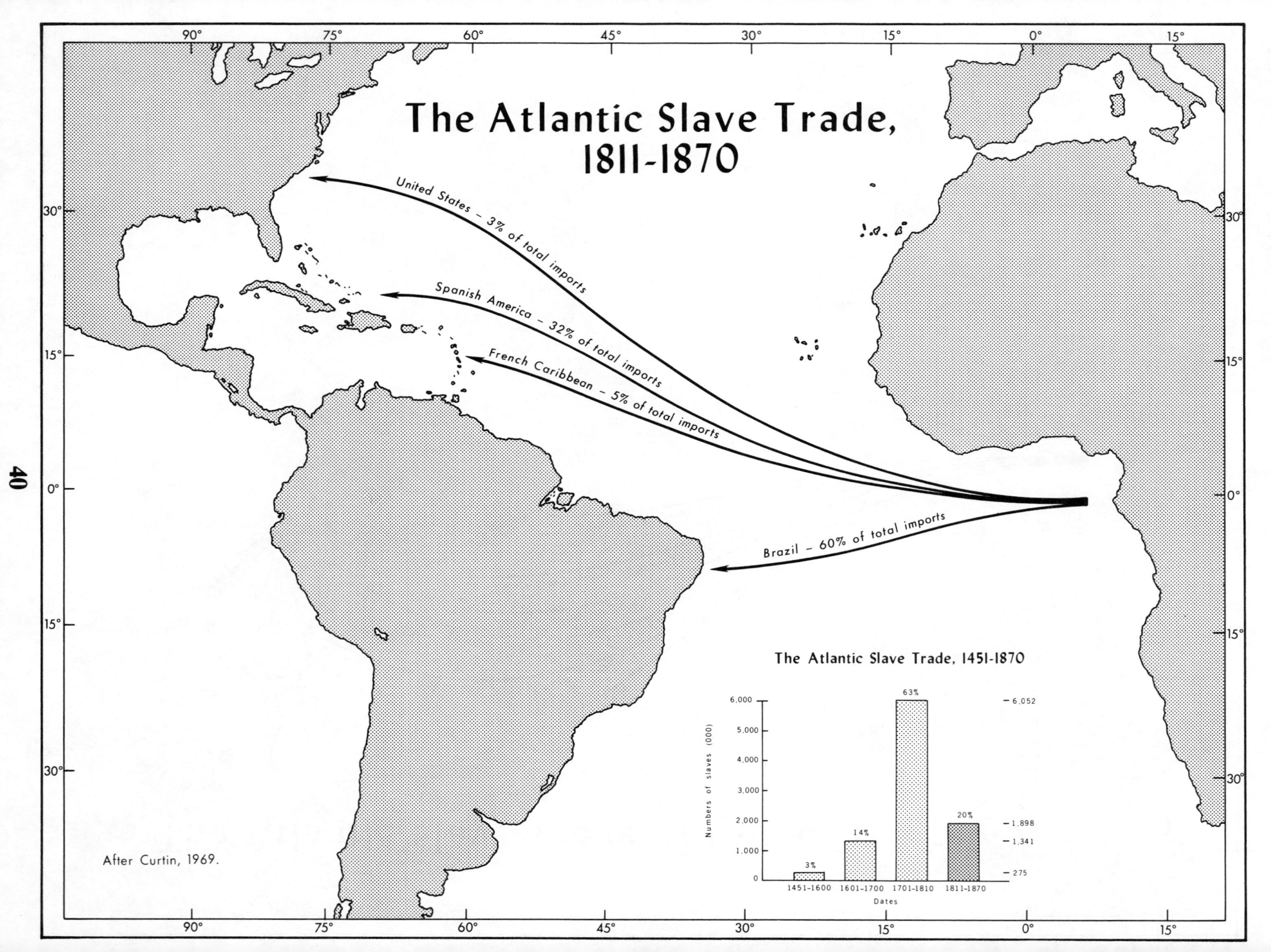

The Atlantic Slave Trade, 1811-1870
United States – 3% of total imports
Spanish America – 32% of total imports
French Caribbean – 5% of total imports
Brazil – 60% of total imports
The Atlantic Slave Trade, 1451-1870
Numbers of slaves (000)
6,000
5,000
4,000
3,000
2,000
1,000
0
3%
14%
63%
20%
– 6,052
– 1,898
– 1,341
– 275
1451-1600
1601-1700
1701-1810
1811-1870
Dates
90°
75°
60°
45°
30°
15°
0°
15°
30°
15°
0°
15°
30°
After Curtin, 1969.

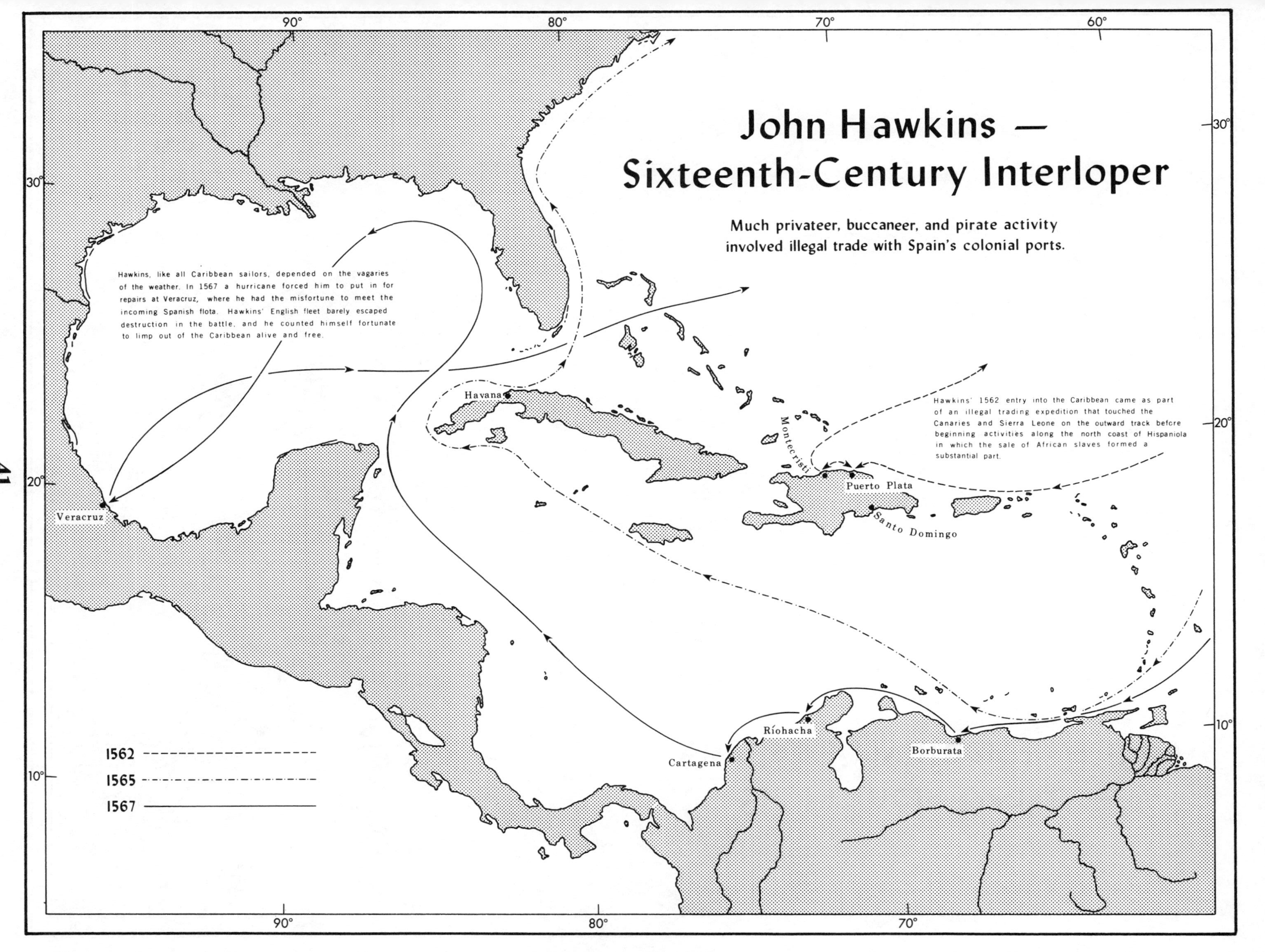

John Hawkins —
Sixteenth-Century Interloper
Much privateer, buccaneer, and pirate activity
involved illegal trade with Spain's colonial ports.
Hawkins, like all Caribbean sailors, depended on the vagaries of the weather. In 1567 a hurricane forced him to put in for repairs at Veracruz, where he had the misfortune to meet the incoming Spanish flota. Hawkins' English fleet barely escaped destruction in the battle, and he counted himself fortunate to limp out of the Caribbean alive and free.
Hawkins' 1562 entry into the Caribbean came as part of an illegal trading expedition that touched the Canaries and Sierra Leone on the outward track before beginning activities along the north coast of Hispaniola in which the sale of African slaves formed a substantial part.
Havana
Montecristi
Puerto Plata
Santo Domingo
Veracruz
Ríohacha
Cartagena
Borburata
1562
1565
1567
90°
80°
70°
60°
30°
20°
10°

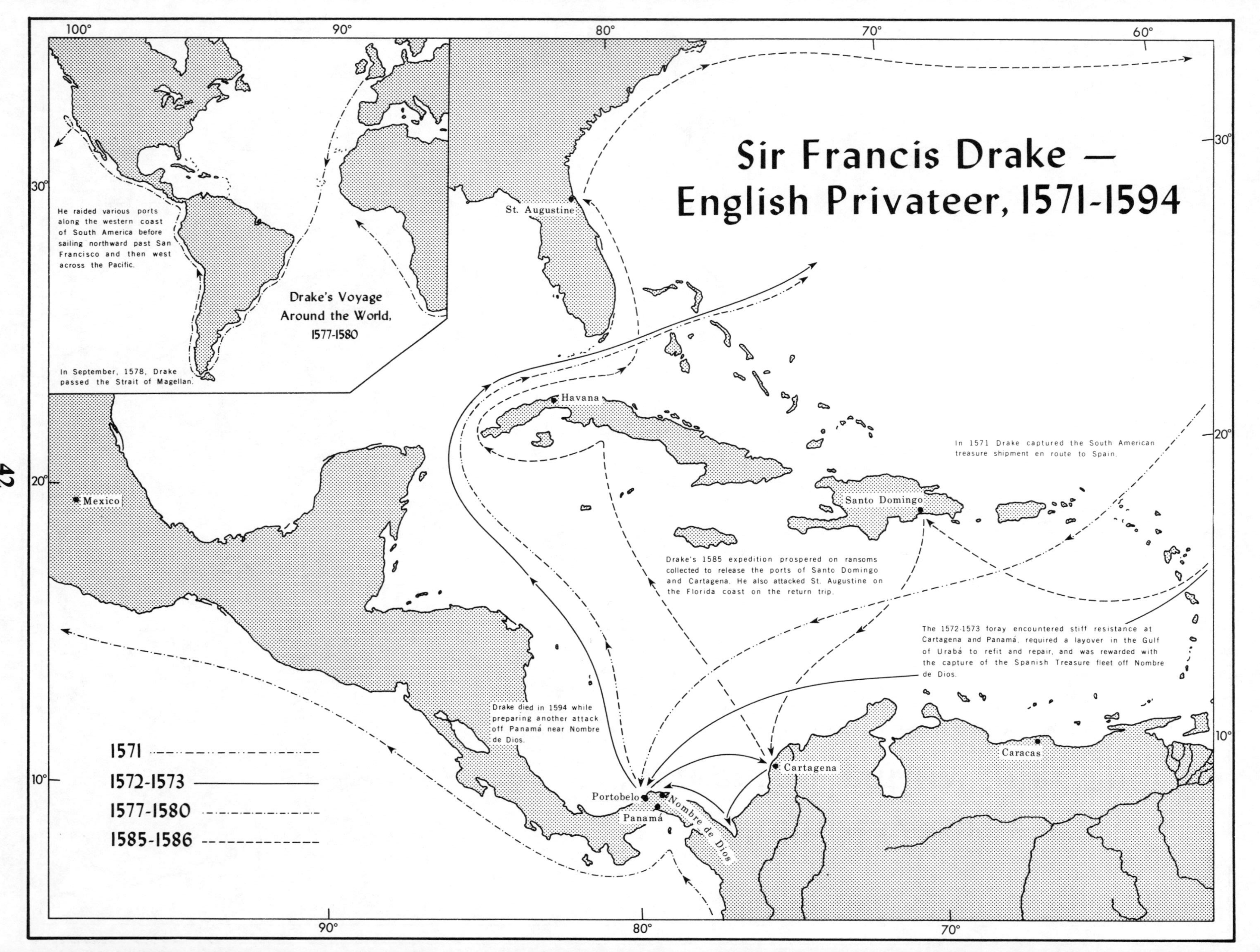

Sir Francis Drake —
English Privateer, 1571-1594
Drake's Voyage Around the World, 1577-1580
He raided various ports along the western coast of South America before sailing northward past San Francisco and then west across the Pacific.
In September, 1578, Drake passed the Strait of Magellan.
In 1571 Drake captured the South American treasure shipment en route to Spain.
Drake's 1585 expedition prospered on ransoms collected to release the ports of Santo Domingo and Cartagena. He also attacked St. Augustine on the Florida coast on the return trip.
The 1572-1573 foray encountered stiff resistance at Cartagena and Panamá, required a layover in the Gulf of Urabá to refit and repair, and was rewarded with the capture of the Spanish Treasure fleet off Nombre de Dios.
Drake died in 1594 while preparing another attack off Panamá near Nombre de Dios.
St. Augustine
Havana
Mexico
Santo Domingo
Caracas
Cartagena
Portobelo
Nombre de Dios
Panamá
1571
1572-1573
1577-1580
1585-1586
100°
90°
80°
70°
60°
30°
20°
10°

Piet Heyn — Dutch Privateer
Unlike other seventeenth-century interlopers, Piet Heyn was commissioned by the Dutch government to attack Spanish territory and shipping.
1623
1627
1628
In 1628 Piet Heyn captured the entire Mexican Flota in the Matanzas harbor, the richest bounty from a single flota in the history of Caribbean piracy.
In 1623, he captured and looted the city of Salvador returning to Holland a hero. This initiated Dutch control of much of north-eastern Brazil.
The Dutch under the command of Piet Heyn captured a Spanish fleet anchored in the Salvador harbor in 1627.
Matanzas
Havana
Mexico
Salvador
Santos
100°
80°
60°
40°
20°
120°
30°
20°
10°
0°
10°
20°
30°
40°
50°

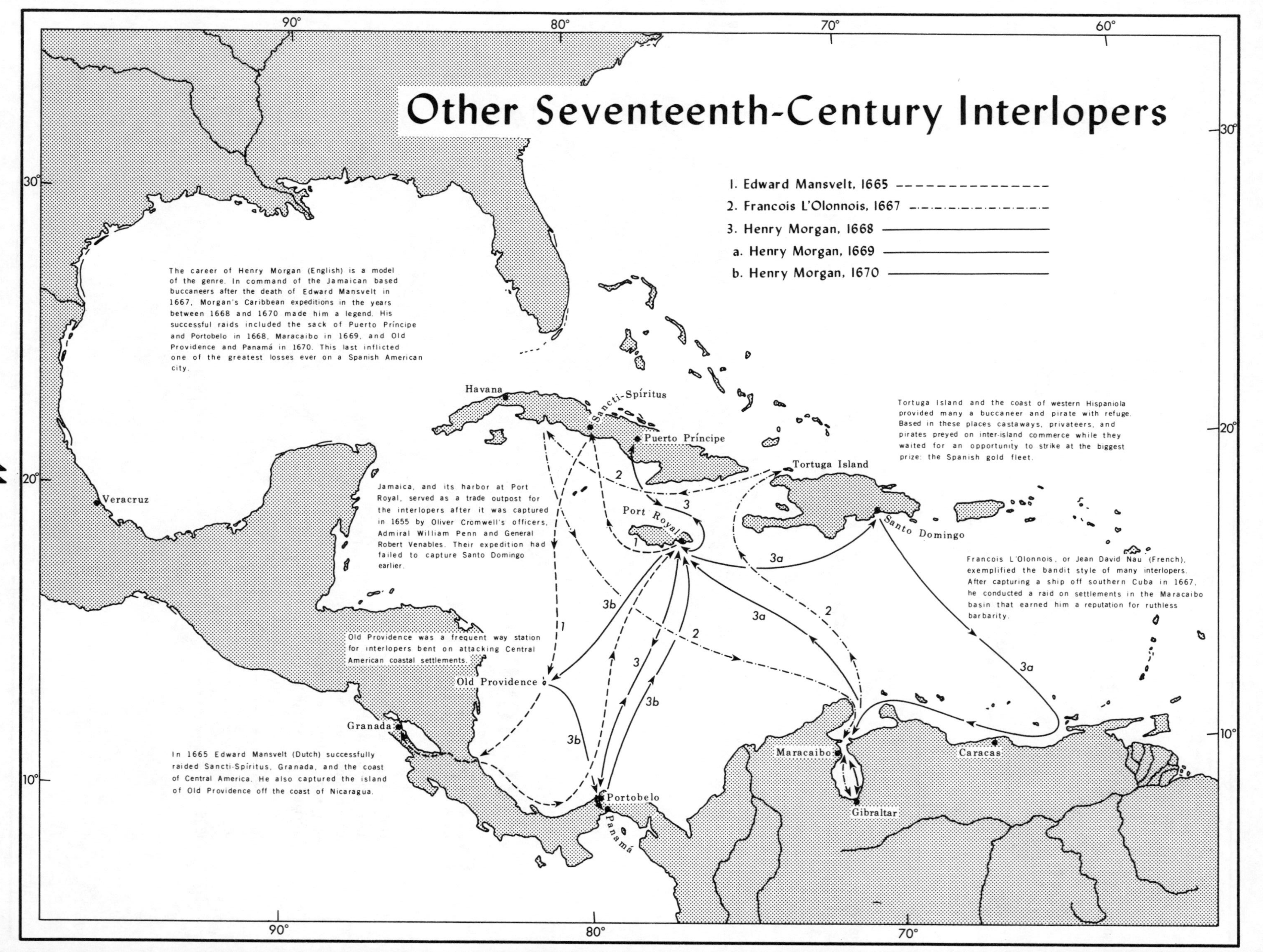
Other Seventeenth-Century Interlopers
1. Edward Mansvelt, 1665
2. Francois L'Olonnois, 1667
3. Henry Morgan, 1668
a. Henry Morgan, 1669
b. Henry Morgan, 1670
The career of Henry Morgan (English) is a model of the genre. In command of the Jamaican based buccaneers after the death of Edward Mansvelt in 1667, Morgan's Caribbean expeditions in the years between 1668 and 1670 made him a legend. His successful raids included the sack of Puerto Príncipe and Portobelo in 1668, Maracaibo in 1669, and Old Providence and Panamá in 1670. This last inflicted one of the greatest losses ever on a Spanish American city.
Tortuga Island and the coast of western Hispaniola provided many a buccaneer and pirate with refuge. Based in these places castaways, privateers, and pirates preyed on inter-island commerce while they waited for an opportunity to strike at the biggest prize: the Spanish gold fleet.
Jamaica, and its harbor at Port Royal, served as a trade outpost for the interlopers after it was captured in 1655 by Oliver Cromwell's officers, Admiral William Penn and General Robert Venables. Their expedition had failed to capture Santo Domingo earlier.
Francois L'Olonnois, or Jean David Nau (French), exemplified the bandit style of many interlopers. After capturing a ship off southern Cuba in 1667, he conducted a raid on settlements in the Maracaibo basin that earned him a reputation for ruthless barbarity.
Old Providence was a frequent way station for interlopers bent on attacking Central American coastal settlements.
In 1665 Edward Mansvelt (Dutch) successfully raided Sancti-Spíritus, Granada, and the coast of Central America. He also captured the island of Old Providence off the coast of Nicaragua.
Havana
Sancti-Spíritus
Puerto Príncipe
Tortuga Island
Port Royal
Santo Domingo
Veracruz
Old Providence
Granada
Portobelo
Panamá
Maracaibo
Gibraltar
Caracas
90°
80°
70°
60°
30°
20°
10°
1
2
3
3a
3b

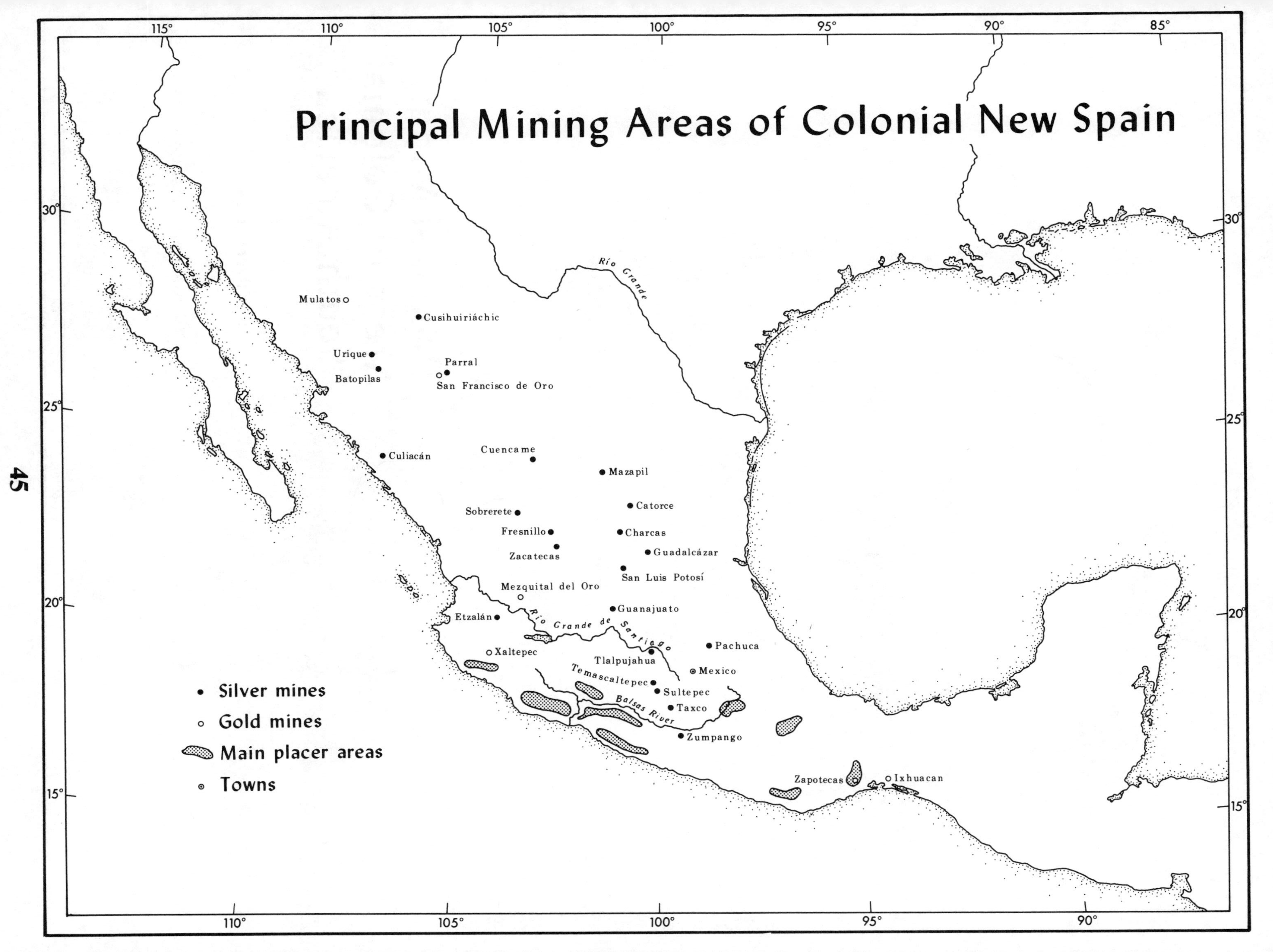
Principal Mining Areas of Colonial New Spain
Mulatos
Cusihuiriáchic
Urique
Batopilas
Parral
San Francisco de Oro
Culiacán
Cuencame
Mazapil
Catorce
Sobrerete
Fresnillo
Charcas
Zacatecas
Guadalcázar
San Luis Potosí
Mezquital del Oro
Guanajuato
Etzalán
Río Grande de Santiago
Río Grande
Xaltepec
Tlalpujahua
Pachuca
Mexico
Temascaltepec
Sultepec
Taxco
Balsas River
Zumpango
Zapotecas
Ixhuacan
Silver mines
Gold mines
Main placer areas
Towns
115°
110°
105°
100°
95°
90°
85°
30°
25°
20°
15°

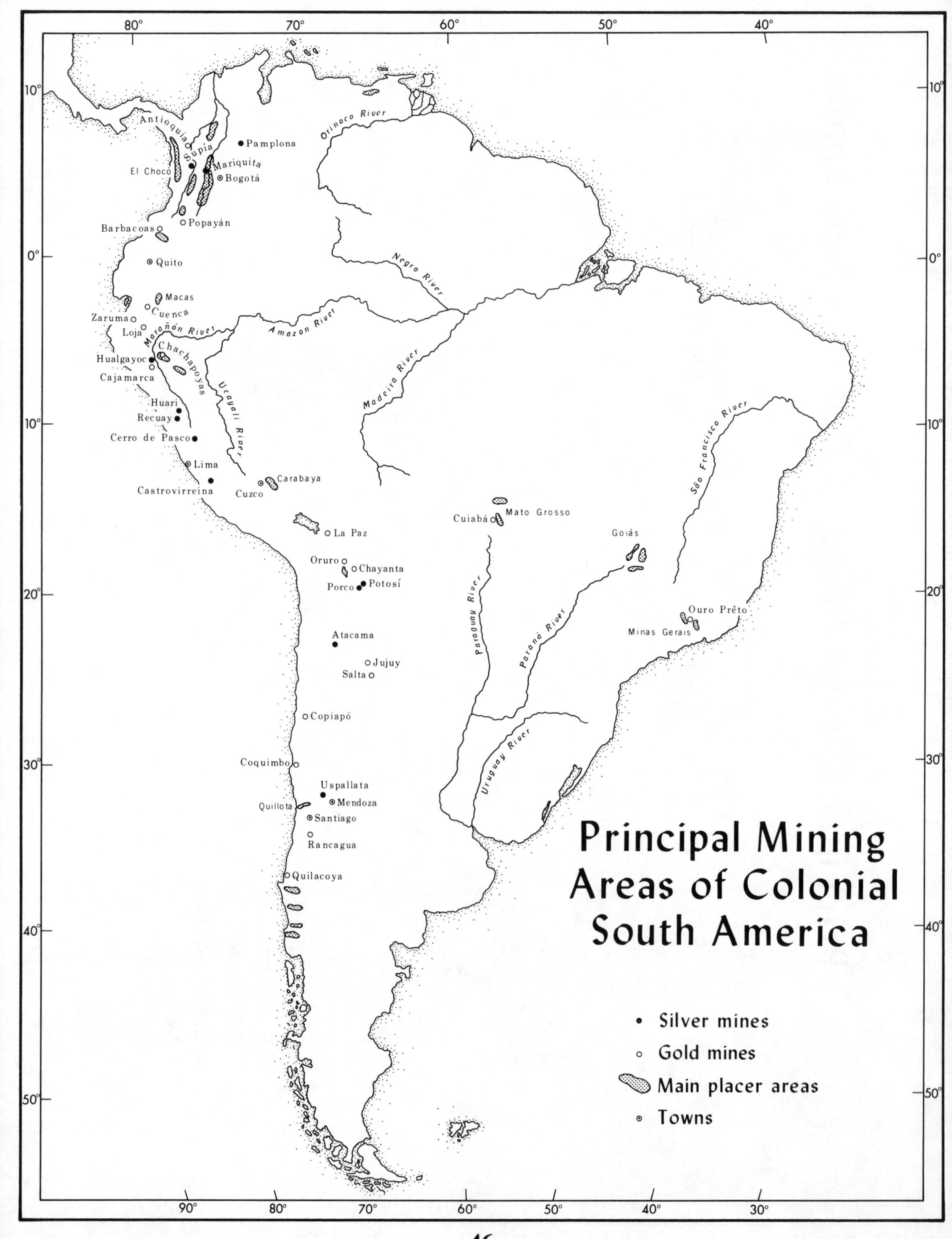
Principal Mining Areas of Colonial South America
Silver mines
Gold mines
Main placer areas
Towns
Antioquia
Supía
Pamplona
El Chocó
Mariquita
Bogotá
Popayán
Barbacoas
Quito
Macas
Cuenca
Zaruma
Loja
Marañón River
Chachapoyas
Hualgayoc
Cajamarca
Huari
Recuay
Cerro de Pasco
Lima
Castrovirreina
Cuzco
Carabaya
La Paz
Oruro
Chayanta
Porco
Potosí
Atacama
Jujuy
Salta
Copiapó
Coquimbo
Uspallata
Mendoza
Quillota
Santiago
Rancagua
Quilacoya
Orinoco River
Negro River
Amazon River
Ucayali River
Madeira River
Cuiabá
Mato Grosso
Goiás
São Francisco River
Ouro Prêto
Minas Gerais
Paraguay River
Paraná River
Uruguay River
80°
70°
60°
50°
40°
90°
30°
10°
0°
20°

The Independence of Spanish America

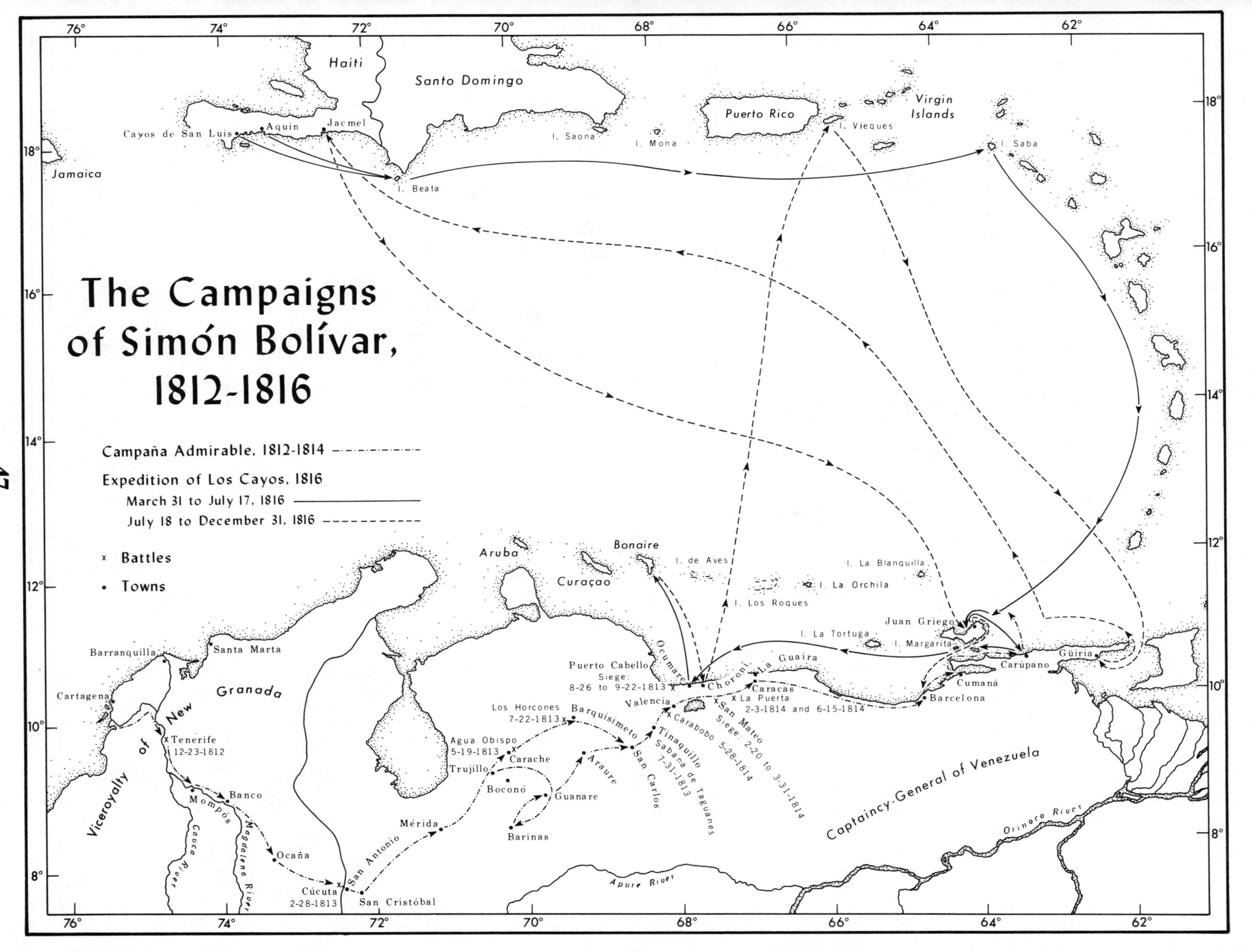
The Campaigns of Simón Bolívar, 1812-1816
Campaña Admirable, 1812-1814
Expedition of Los Cayos, 1816
March 31 to July 17, 1816
July 18 to December 31, 1816
Battles
Towns
Haiti
Santo Domingo
Puerto Rico
Virgin Islands
Jamaica
Cayos de San Luis
Aquin
Jacmel
I. Beata
I. Saona
I. Mona
I. Vieques
I. Saba
Aruba
Curaçao
Bonaire
I. de Aves
I. Los Roques
I. La Orchila
I. La Blanquilla
I. La Tortuga
I. Margarita
Juan Griego
Güiria
Carúpano
Cumaná
Barcelona
La Guaira
Caracas
Choroni
Ocumare
Puerto Cabello
Siege:
8-26 to 9-22-1813
La Puerta
2-3-1814 and 6-15-1814
San Mateo
Siege: 2-20 to 3-31-1814
Valencia
Carabobo 5-28-1814
Tinaquillo
Sabana de Taguanes
7-31-1813
San Carlos
Barquisimeto
Los Horcones
7-22-1813
Araure
Guanare
Barinas
Boconó
Agua Obispo
5-19-1813
Carache
Trujillo
Mérida
San Antonio
San Cristóbal
Cúcuta
2-28-1813
Ocaña
Banco
Mompós
Tenerife
12-23-1812
Cartagena
Barranquilla
Santa Marta
New Granada
Viceroyalty of New Granada
Cauca River
Magdalena River
Apure River
Orinoco River
Captaincy-General of Venezuela
76°
74°
72°
70°
68°
66°
64°
62°
18°
16°
14°
12°
10°
8°

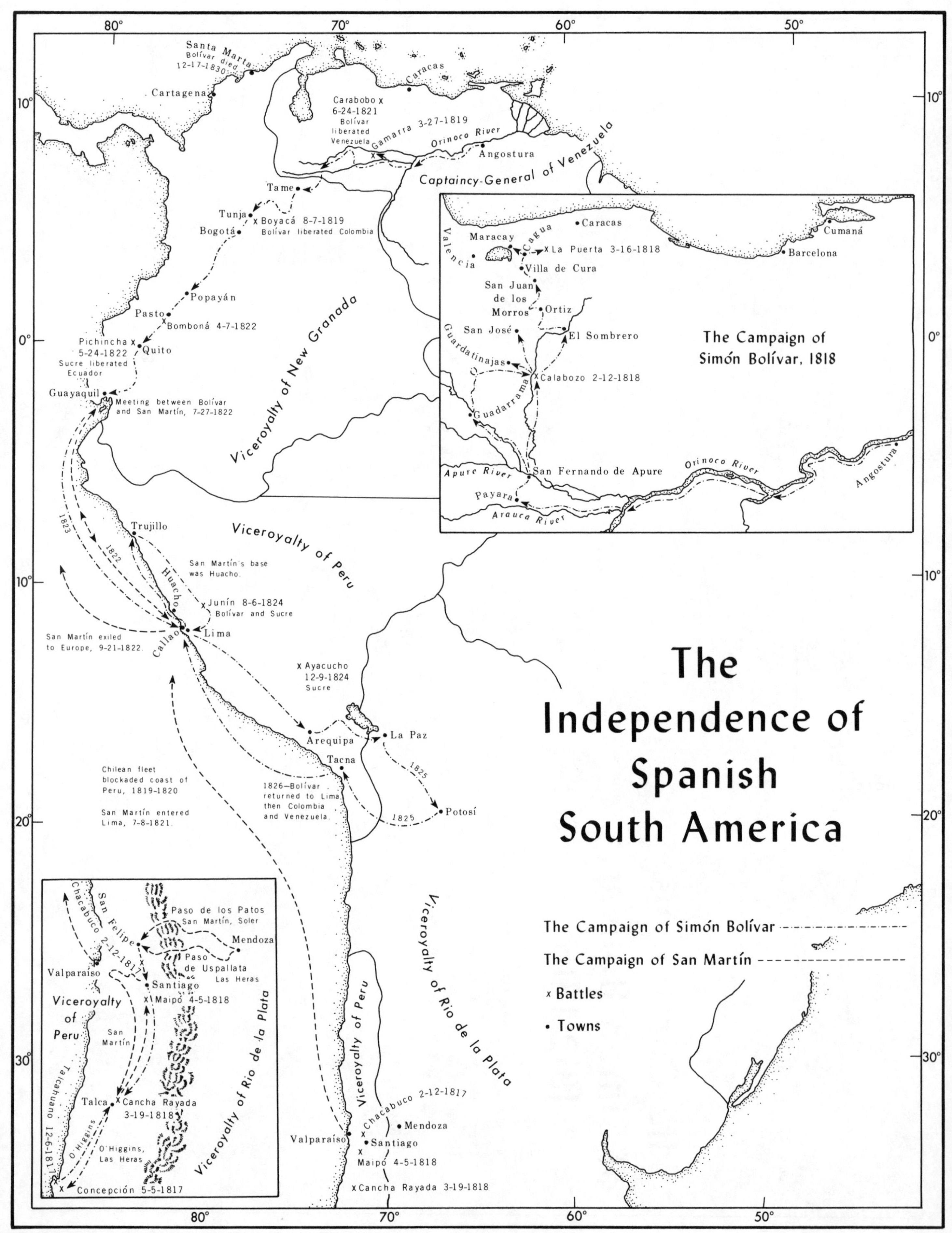
The Independence of Spanish South America
The Campaign of Simón Bolívar
The Campaign of San Martín
x Battles
• Towns
Santa Marta
Bolívar died 12-17-1830
Cartagena
Caracas
Carabobo 6-24-1821 Bolívar liberated Venezuela
Gamarra 3-27-1819
Orinoco River
Angostura
Captaincy-General of Venezuela
Tame
Tunja
Boyacá 8-7-1819 Bolívar liberated Colombia
Bogotá
Popayán
Pasto
Bomboná 4-7-1822
Pichincha 5-24-1822 Sucre liberated Ecuador
Quito
Guayaquil
Meeting between Bolívar and San Martín, 7-27-1822
Viceroyalty of New Granada
Viceroyalty of Peru
1823
1822
Trujillo
Huacho
San Martín's base was Huacho.
Junín 8-6-1824 Bolívar and Sucre
Callao
Lima
San Martín exiled to Europe, 9-21-1822.
Ayacucho 12-9-1824 Sucre
Arequipa
La Paz
Tacna
1825
Potosí
Chilean fleet blockaded coast of Peru, 1819-1820
San Martín entered Lima, 7-8-1821.
1826—Bolívar returned to Lima then Colombia and Venezuela.
Viceroyalty of Rio de la Plata
Chacabuco 2-12-1817
Mendoza
Valparaíso
Santiago
Maipó 4-5-1818
Cancha Rayada 3-19-1818
The Campaign of Simón Bolívar, 1818
Cumaná
Barcelona
Maracay
Cagua
La Puerta 3-16-1818
Valencia
Villa de Cura
San Juan de los Morros
Ortiz
San José
El Sombrero
Guardatinajas
Calabozo 2-12-1818
Guadarrama
Apure River
San Fernando de Apure
Payara
Arauca River
Paso de los Patos San Martín, Soler
San Felipe
Paso de Uspallata Las Heras
Viceroyalty of Peru
San Martín
Viceroyalty of Rio de la Plata
Talca
Cancha Rayada 3-19-1818
O'Higgins
O'Higgins, Las Heras
Talcahuano 12-6-1817
Concepción 5-5-1817
80°
70°
60°
50°
10°
0°
20°
30°

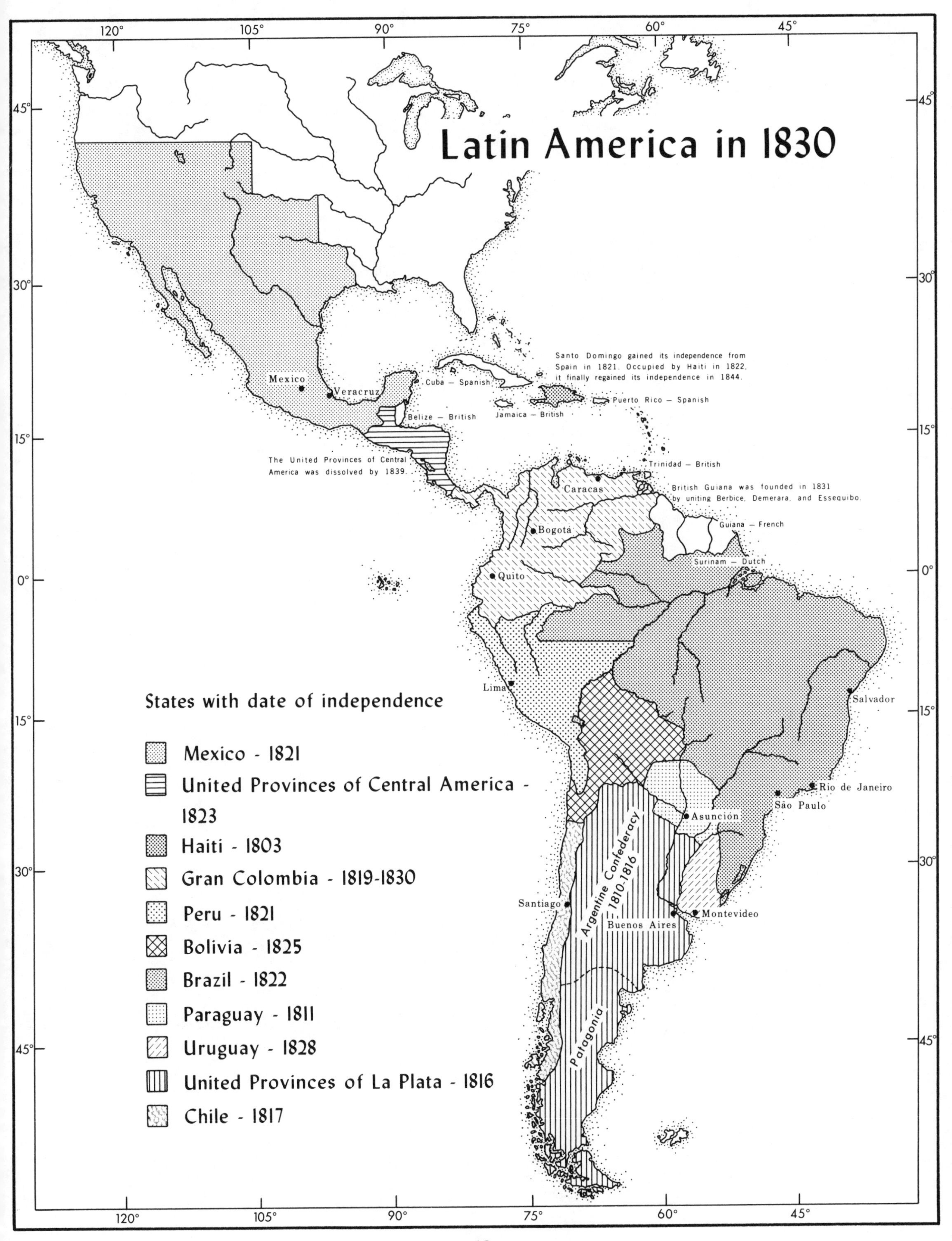

Latin America in 1830
States with date of independence
Mexico - 1821
United Provinces of Central America - 1823
Haiti - 1803
Gran Colombia - 1819-1830
Peru - 1821
Bolivia - 1825
Brazil - 1822
Paraguay - 1811
Uruguay - 1828
United Provinces of La Plata - 1816
Chile - 1817
Santo Domingo gained its independence from Spain in 1821. Occupied by Haiti in 1822, it finally regained its independence in 1844.
Cuba – Spanish
Puerto Rico – Spanish
Jamaica – British
Belize – British
Trinidad – British
British Guiana was founded in 1831 by uniting Berbice, Demerara, and Essequibo.
Guiana – French
Surinam – Dutch
The United Provinces of Central America was dissolved by 1839.
Mexico
Veracruz
Caracas
Bogotá
Quito
Lima
Salvador
Rio de Janeiro
São Paulo
Asunción
Santiago
Buenos Aires
Montevideo
Argentine Confederacy 1810-1816
Patagonia

THE MODERN PERIOD

Latin American Boundaries

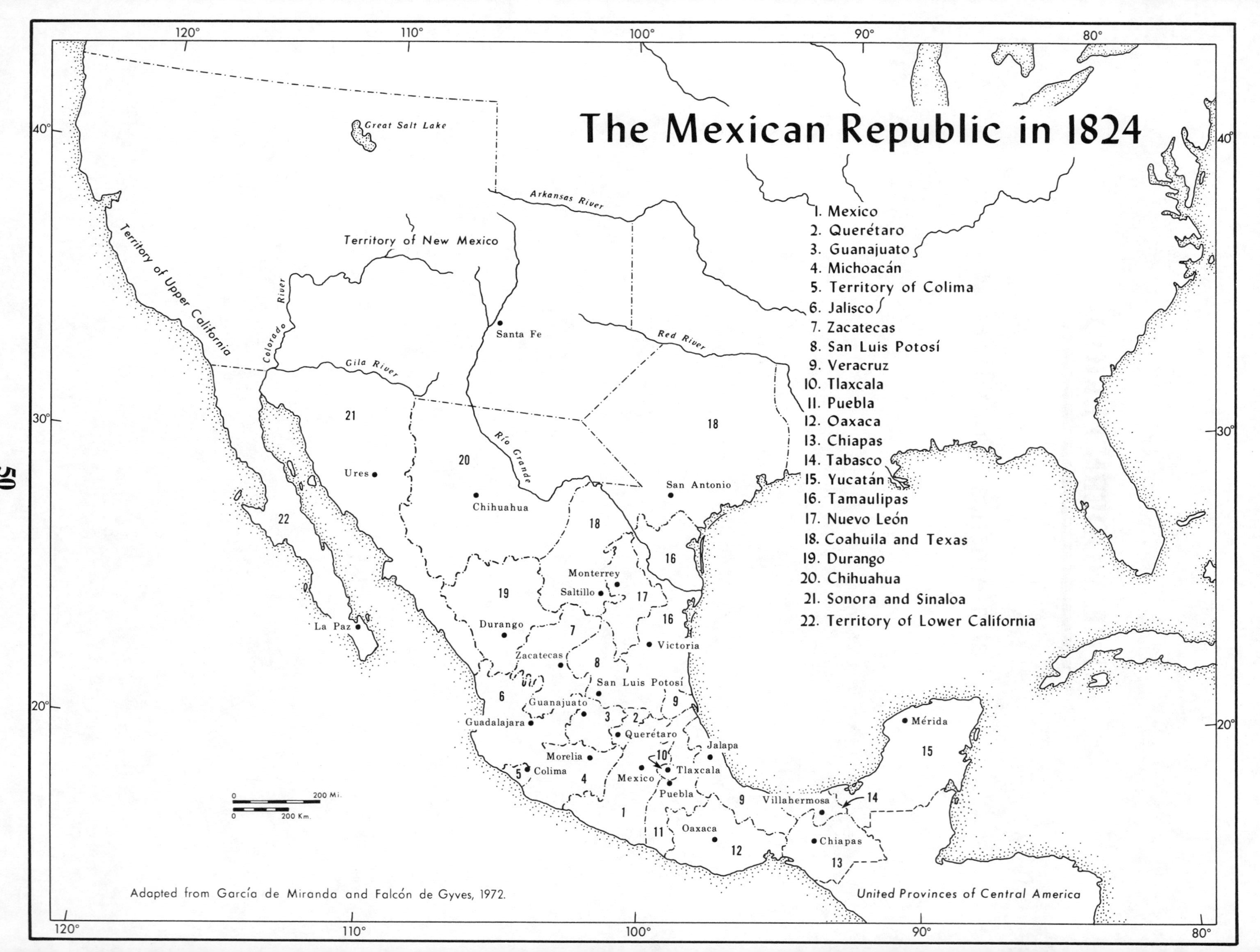
The Mexican Republic in 1824
1. Mexico
2. Querétaro
3. Guanajuato
4. Michoacán
5. Territory of Colima
6. Jalisco
7. Zacatecas
8. San Luis Potosí
9. Veracruz
10. Tlaxcala
11. Puebla
12. Oaxaca
13. Chiapas
14. Tabasco
15. Yucatán
16. Tamaulipas
17. Nuevo León
18. Coahuila and Texas
19. Durango
20. Chihuahua
21. Sonora and Sinaloa
22. Territory of Lower California
Great Salt Lake
Territory of Upper California
Territory of New Mexico
Arkansas River
Red River
Colorado River
Gila River
Río Grande
Santa Fe
San Antonio
Ures
Chihuahua
Monterrey
Saltillo
Durango
Victoria
Zacatecas
San Luis Potosí
Guanajuato
Querétaro
Guadalajara
Jalapa
Morelia
Colima
Mexico
Tlaxcala
Puebla
Villahermosa
Oaxaca
Chiapas
Mérida
La Paz
United Provinces of Central America
0 200 Mi.
0 200 Km.
120°
110°
100°
90°
80°
40°
30°
20°
Adapted from García de Miranda and Falcón de Gyves, 1972.

The Dissolution of Gran Colombia, 1830

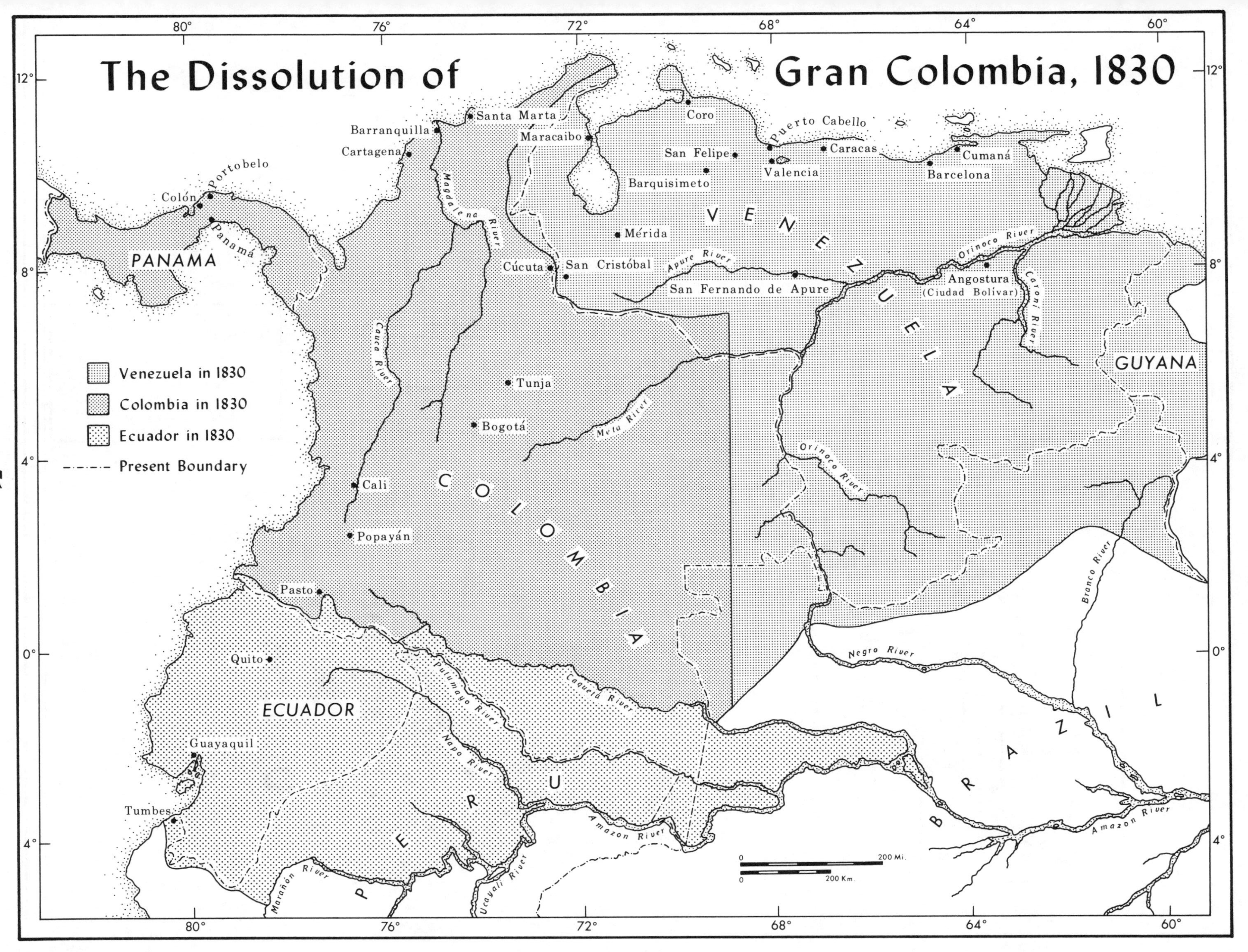

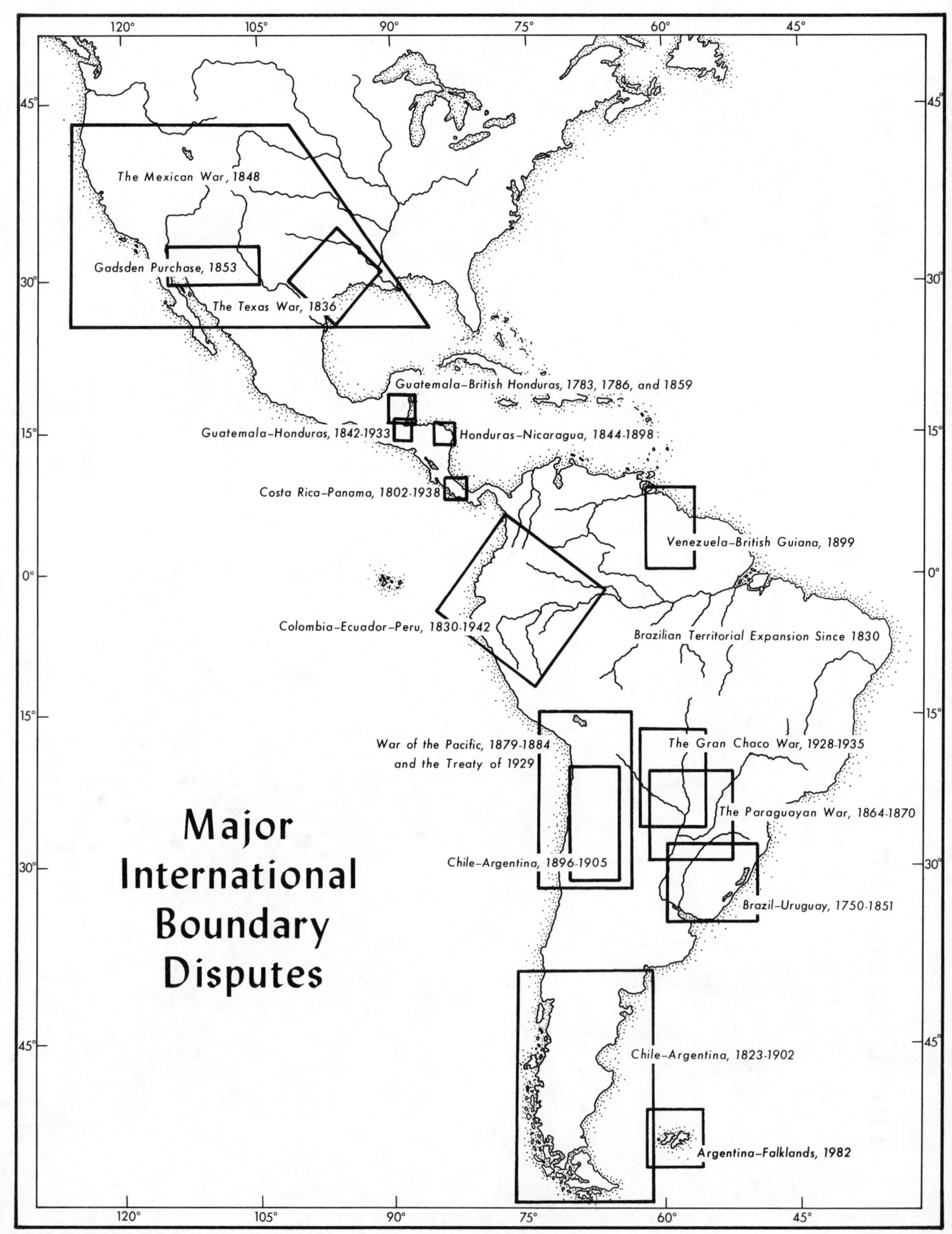

Major International Boundary Disputes
120°
105°
90°
75°
60°
45°
45°
30°
15°
0°
The Mexican War, 1848
Gadsden Purchase, 1853
The Texas War, 1836
Guatemala–British Honduras, 1783, 1786, and 1859
Guatemala–Honduras, 1842-1933
Honduras–Nicaragua, 1844-1898
Costa Rica–Panama, 1802-1938
Venezuela–British Guiana, 1899
Colombia–Ecuador–Peru, 1830-1942
Brazilian Territorial Expansion Since 1830
War of the Pacific, 1879-1884
and the Treaty of 1929
The Gran Chaco War, 1928-1935
The Paraguayan War, 1864-1870
Chile–Argentina, 1896-1905
Brazil–Uruguay, 1750-1851
Chile–Argentina, 1823-1902
Argentina–Falklands, 1982

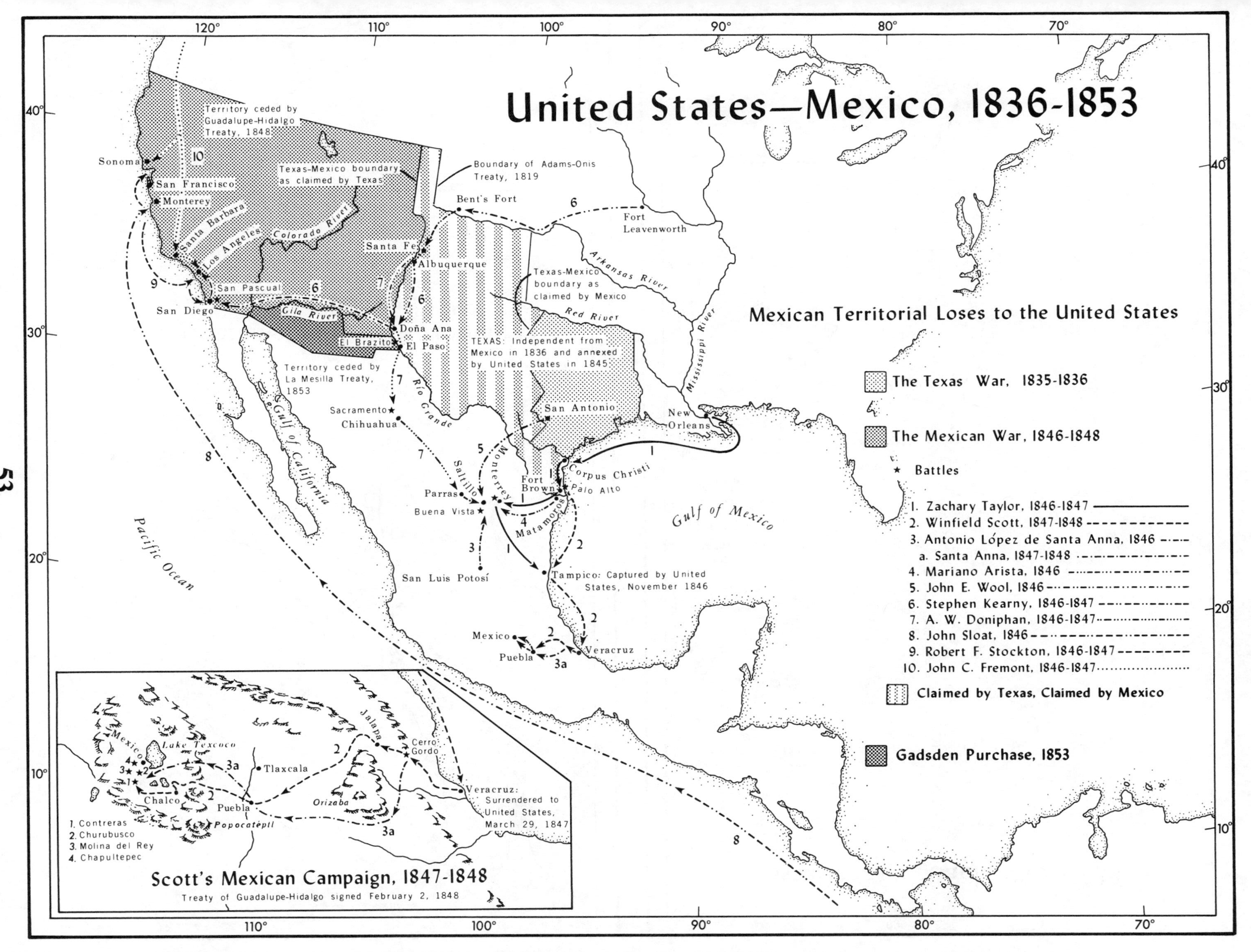
United States—Mexico, 1836-1853
Mexican Territorial Loses to the United States
The Texas War, 1835-1836
The Mexican War, 1846-1848
Battles
1. Zachary Taylor, 1846-1847
2. Winfield Scott, 1847-1848
3. Antonio López de Santa Anna, 1846
a. Santa Anna, 1847-1848
4. Mariano Arista, 1846
5. John E. Wool, 1846
6. Stephen Kearny, 1846-1847
7. A. W. Doniphan, 1846-1847
8. John Sloat, 1846
9. Robert F. Stockton, 1846-1847
10. John C. Fremont, 1846-1847
Claimed by Texas, Claimed by Mexico
Gadsden Purchase, 1853
Territory ceded by Guadalupe-Hidalgo Treaty, 1848
Texas-Mexico boundary as claimed by Texas
Boundary of Adams-Onis Treaty, 1819
Texas-Mexico boundary as claimed by Mexico
TEXAS: Independent from Mexico in 1836 and annexed by United States in 1845
Territory ceded by La Mesilla Treaty, 1853
Tampico: Captured by United States, November 1846
Sonoma
San Francisco
Monterey
Santa Barbara
Los Angeles
San Pascual
San Diego
Colorado River
Gila River
Santa Fe
Albuquerque
Bent's Fort
Fort Leavenworth
Arkansas River
Red River
Mississippi River
Doña Ana
El Brazito
El Paso
Río Grande
Sacramento
Chihuahua
San Antonio
New Orleans
Corpus Christi
Fort Brown
Palo Alto
Matamoros
Monterrey
Saltillo
Parras
Buena Vista
San Luis Potosí
Mexico
Puebla
Veracruz
Gulf of California
Gulf of Mexico
Pacific Ocean
Scott's Mexican Campaign, 1847-1848
Treaty of Guadalupe-Hidalgo signed February 2, 1848
1. Contreras
2. Churubusco
3. Molina del Rey
4. Chapultepec
Lake Texcoco
Mexico
Chalco
Popocatépetl
Tlaxcala
Puebla
Orizaba
Jalapa
Cerro Gordo
Veracruz: Surrendered to United States, March 29, 1847

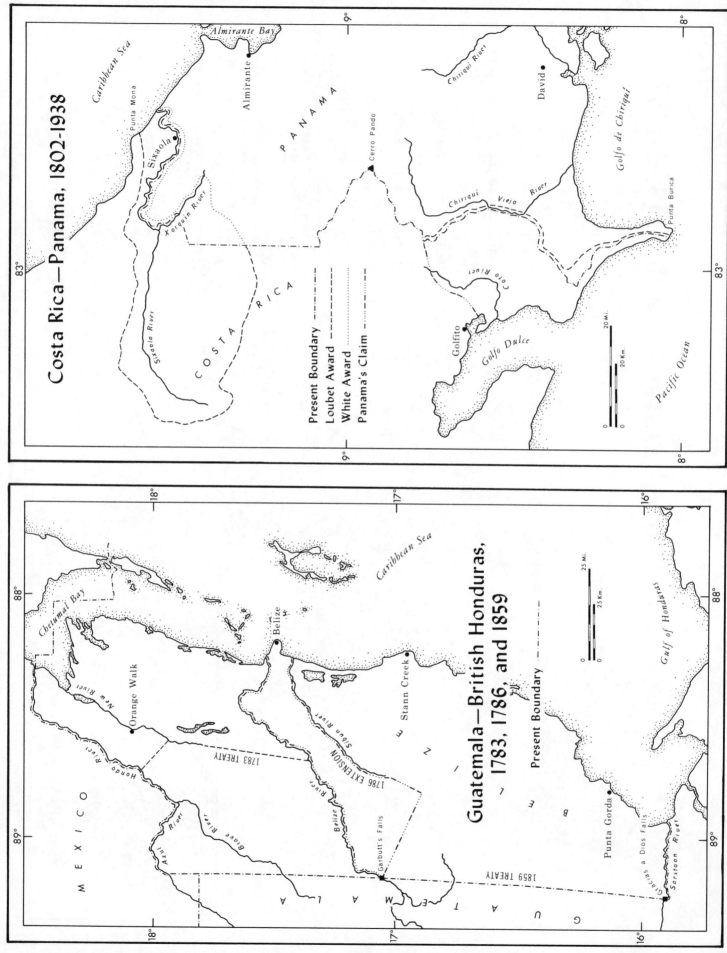

Guatemala—British Honduras, 1783, 1786, and 1859

Present Boundary

MEXICO
GUATEMALA
BELIZE
Hondo River
New River
Azul River
Brave River
Belize River
Sibun River
Sarstoon River
Chetumal Bay
Caribbean Sea
Gulf of Honduras
Orange Walk
Belize
Stann Creek
Punta Gorda
Garbutt's Falls
Gracias a Dios Falls
1783 TREATY
1786 EXTENSION
1859 TREATY
0 25 Mi.
0 25 Km.
89° 88°
18° 17° 16°

Costa Rica—Panama, 1802-1938

Present Boundary
Loubet Award
White Award
Panama's Claim

COSTA RICA
PANAMA
Caribbean Sea
Punta Mona
Sixaola
Sixaola River
Xorquin River
Almirante
Almirante Bay
Cerro Pando
Golfito
Golfo Dulce
Coto River
Chiriqui Viejo River
Chiriqui River
David
Golfo de Chiriqui
Punta Burica
Pacific Ocean
0 20 Mi.
0 20 Km.
83°
9° 8°

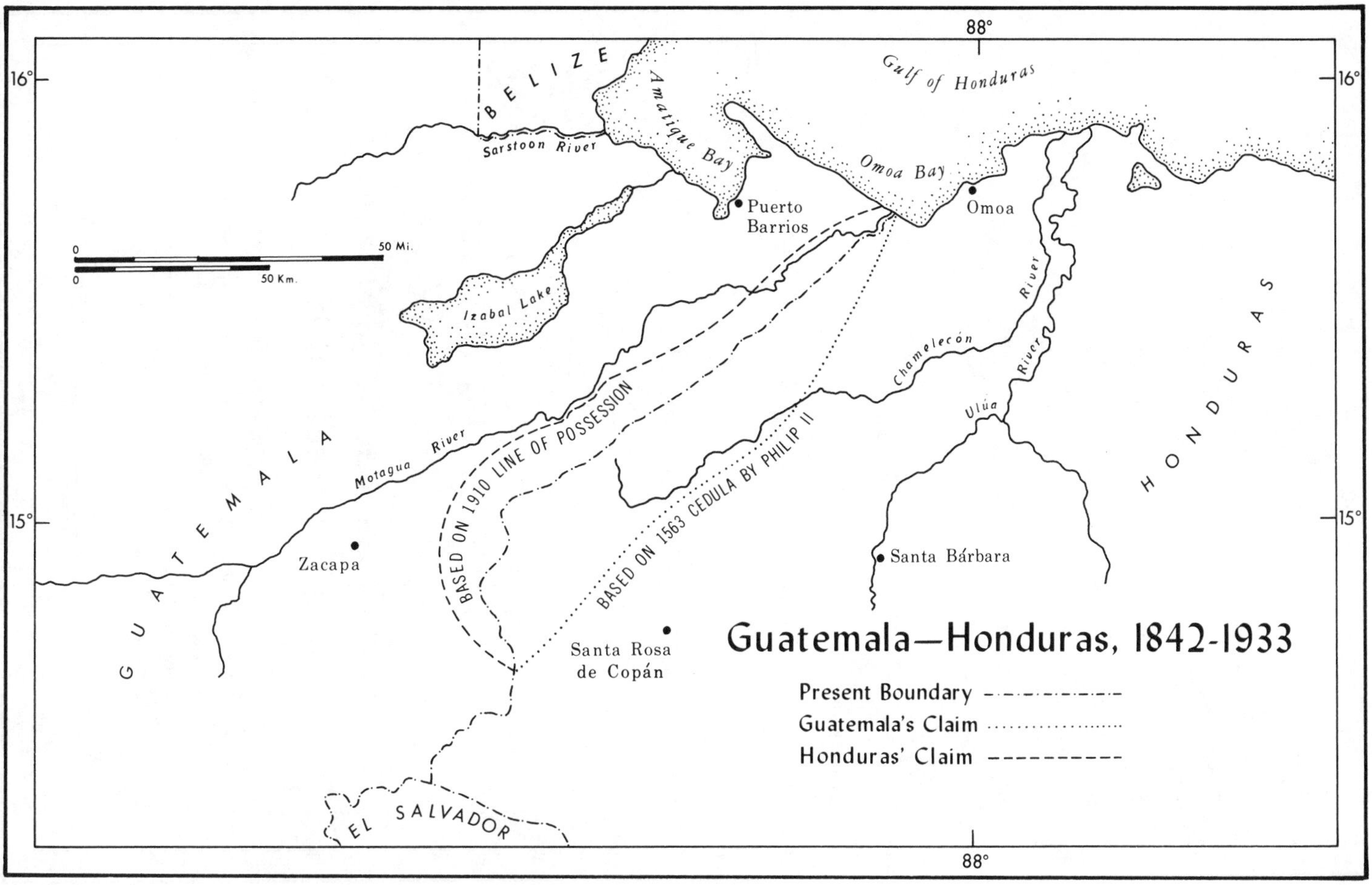

Guatemala—Honduras, 1842-1933

Present Boundary -·-·-·-·-·-
Guatemala's Claim ···············
Honduras' Claim ----------

88°
16°
15°
BELIZE
Gulf of Honduras
Amatique Bay
Sarstoon River
Omoa Bay
Puerto Barrios
Omoa
0 50 Mi.
0 50 Km.
Izabal Lake
HONDURAS
Chamelecón River
Ulúa River
GUATEMALA
Motagua River
BASED ON 1910 LINE OF POSSESSION
BASED ON 1563 CEDULA BY PHILIP II
Zacapa
Santa Bárbara
Santa Rosa de Copán
EL SALVADOR

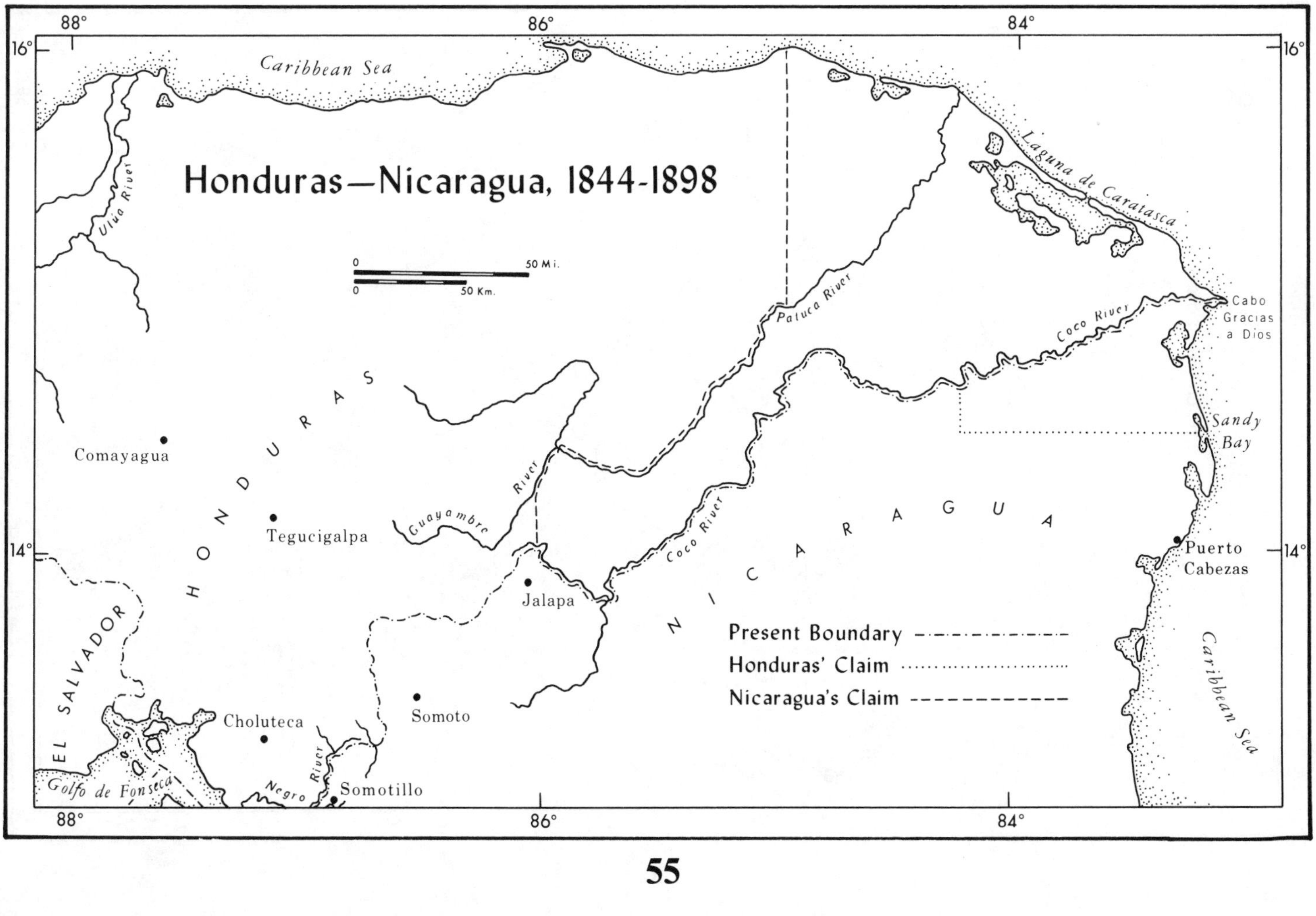

Honduras—Nicaragua, 1844-1898

Present Boundary -·-·-·-·-·-
Honduras' Claim ···············
Nicaragua's Claim ------------

88°
86°
84°
16°
14°
Caribbean Sea
Ulúa River
Laguna de Caratasca
0 50 Mi.
0 50 Km.
Patuca River
Coco River
Cabo Gracias a Dios
HONDURAS
Comayagua
Sandy Bay
Guayambre River
Tegucigalpa
NICARAGUA
Coco River
Puerto Cabezas
Jalapa
EL SALVADOR
Choluteca
Somoto
Golfo de Fonseca
Negro River
Somotillo

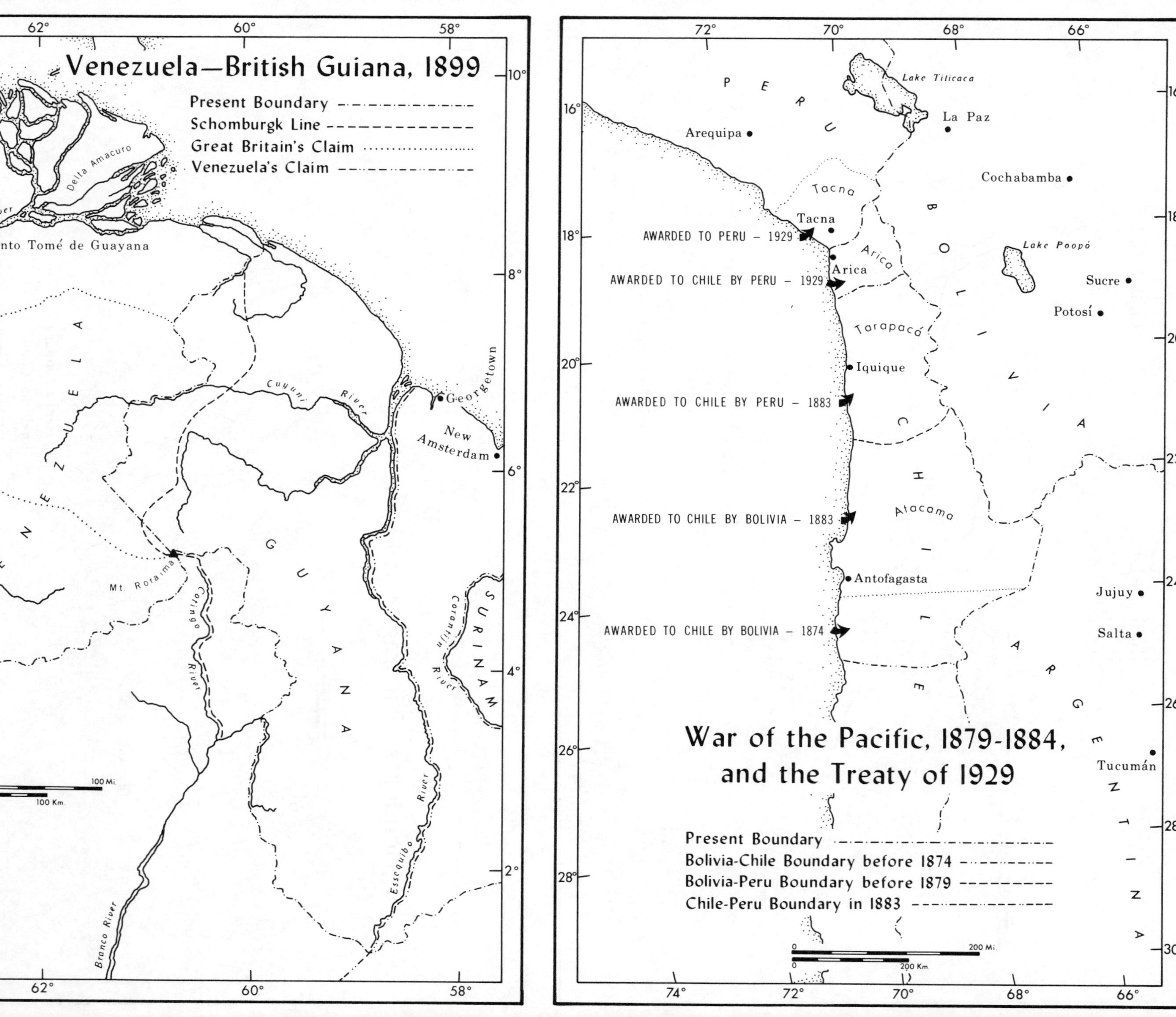
Venezuela—British Guiana, 1899
Present Boundary
Schomburgk Line
Great Britain's Claim
Venezuela's Claim
Delta Amacuro
Orinoco River
Santo Tomé de Guayana
Cuyuni River
Georgetown
New Amsterdam
Caroni River
V E N E Z U E L A
G U Y A N A
Mt. Roraima
Cotingo River
Corantijn River
S U R I N A M
Essequibo River
Branco River
100 Mi.
100 Km.
War of the Pacific, 1879-1884, and the Treaty of 1929
P E R U
Lake Titicaca
La Paz
Arequipa
Cochabamba
Tacna
B O L I V I A
Lake Poopó
Arica
Sucre
Potosí
Tarapacá
Iquique
AWARDED TO PERU – 1929
AWARDED TO CHILE BY PERU – 1929
AWARDED TO CHILE BY PERU – 1883
AWARDED TO CHILE BY BOLIVIA – 1883
AWARDED TO CHILE BY BOLIVIA – 1874
C H I L E
Atacama
Antofagasta
Jujuy
Salta
A R G E N T I N A
Tucumán
Present Boundary
Bolivia-Chile Boundary before 1874
Bolivia-Peru Boundary before 1879
Chile-Peru Boundary in 1883
200 Mi.
200 Km.

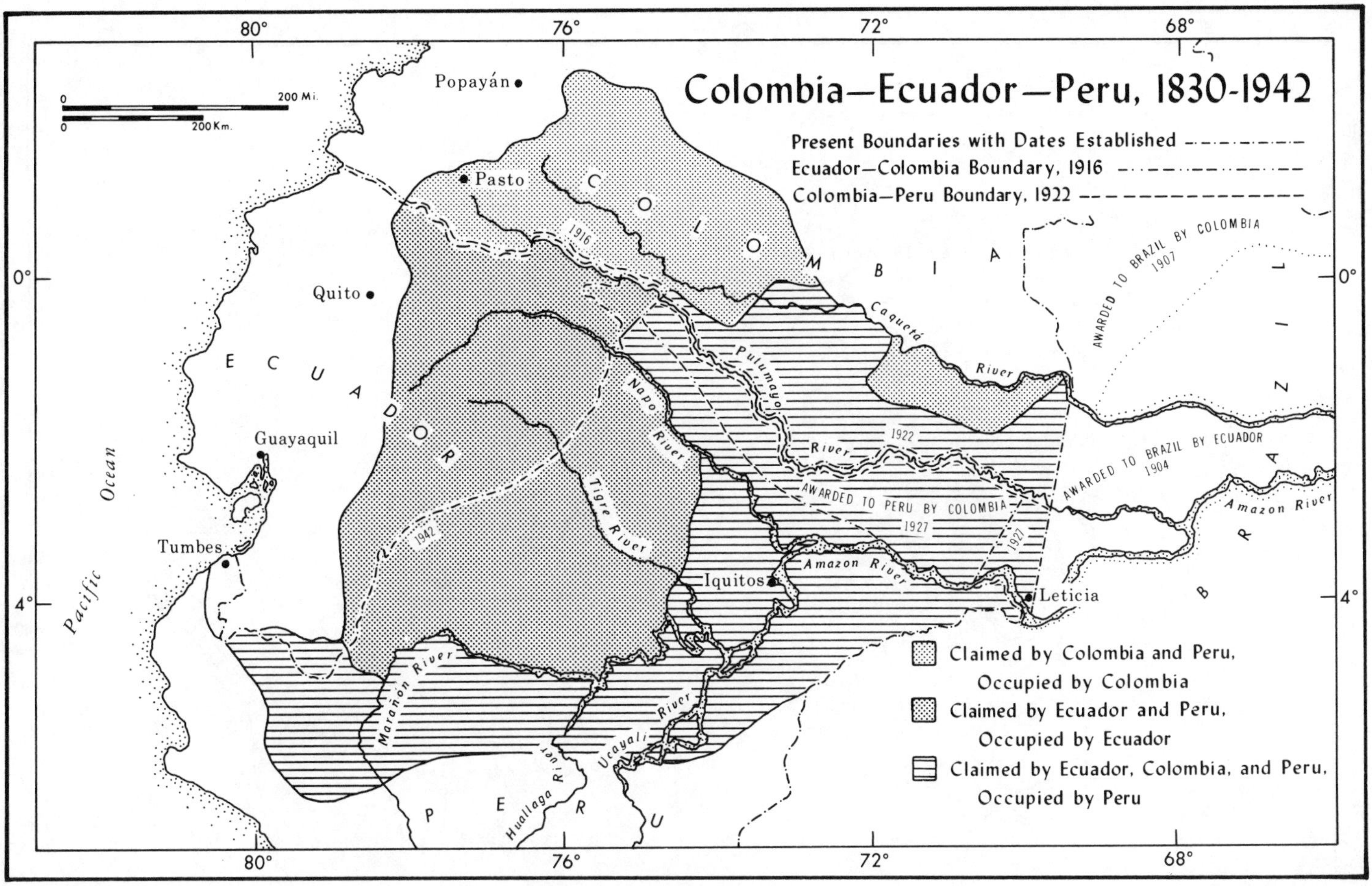

Colombia—Ecuador—Peru, 1830-1942

Present Boundaries with Dates Established
Ecuador—Colombia Boundary, 1916
Colombia—Peru Boundary, 1922

Claimed by Colombia and Peru, Occupied by Colombia
Claimed by Ecuador and Peru, Occupied by Ecuador
Claimed by Ecuador, Colombia, and Peru, Occupied by Peru

0 200 Mi.
0 200 Km.

80° 76° 72° 68°
0° 4°

COLOMBIA
ECUADOR
PERU
BRAZIL
Popayán
Pasto
Quito
Guayaquil
Tumbes
Iquitos
Leticia
Pacific Ocean
Caquetá River
Putumayo River
Napo River
Tigre River
Marañon River
Huallaga River
Ucayali River
Amazon River
1916
1922
1927
1942
AWARDED TO BRAZIL BY COLOMBIA 1907
AWARDED TO BRAZIL BY ECUADOR 1904
AWARDED TO PERU BY COLOMBIA 1927

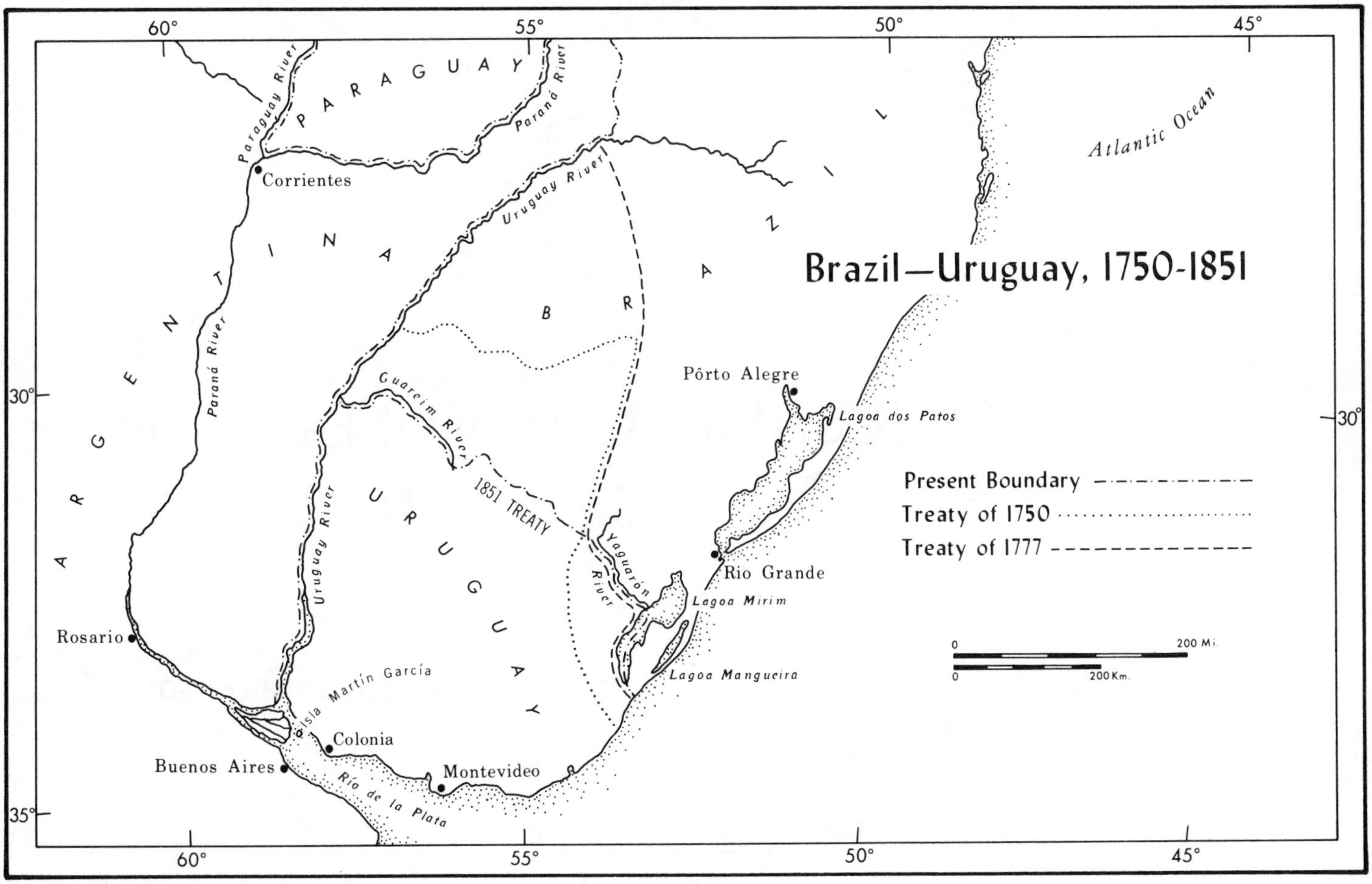

Brazil—Uruguay, 1750-1851

Present Boundary
Treaty of 1750
Treaty of 1777

0 200 Mi.
0 200 Km.

60° 55° 50° 45°
30° 35°

PARAGUAY
ARGENTINA
BRAZIL
URUGUAY
Atlantic Ocean
Paraguay River
Paraná River
Uruguay River
Guareim River
Yaguarón River
1851 TREATY
Corrientes
Pôrto Alegre
Lagoa dos Patos
Rio Grande
Lagoa Mirim
Lagoa Mangueira
Rosario
Isla Martín García
Colonia
Buenos Aires
Montevideo
Río de la Plata

80°
70°
60°
50°
40°
10°
0°
10°
20°
30°
40°
50°
90°
80°
70°
60°
50°
40°
30°
From Venezuela, 1859 and 1905
From Colombia, 1907
From Ecuador, 1904
From Bolivia,
1867 and 1903
From Paraguay, 1872
From Argentina, 1895
From Uruguay, 1851
Brazilian Territorial Expansion
Since 1830
Brazil in 1830
Territory Acquired After 1830

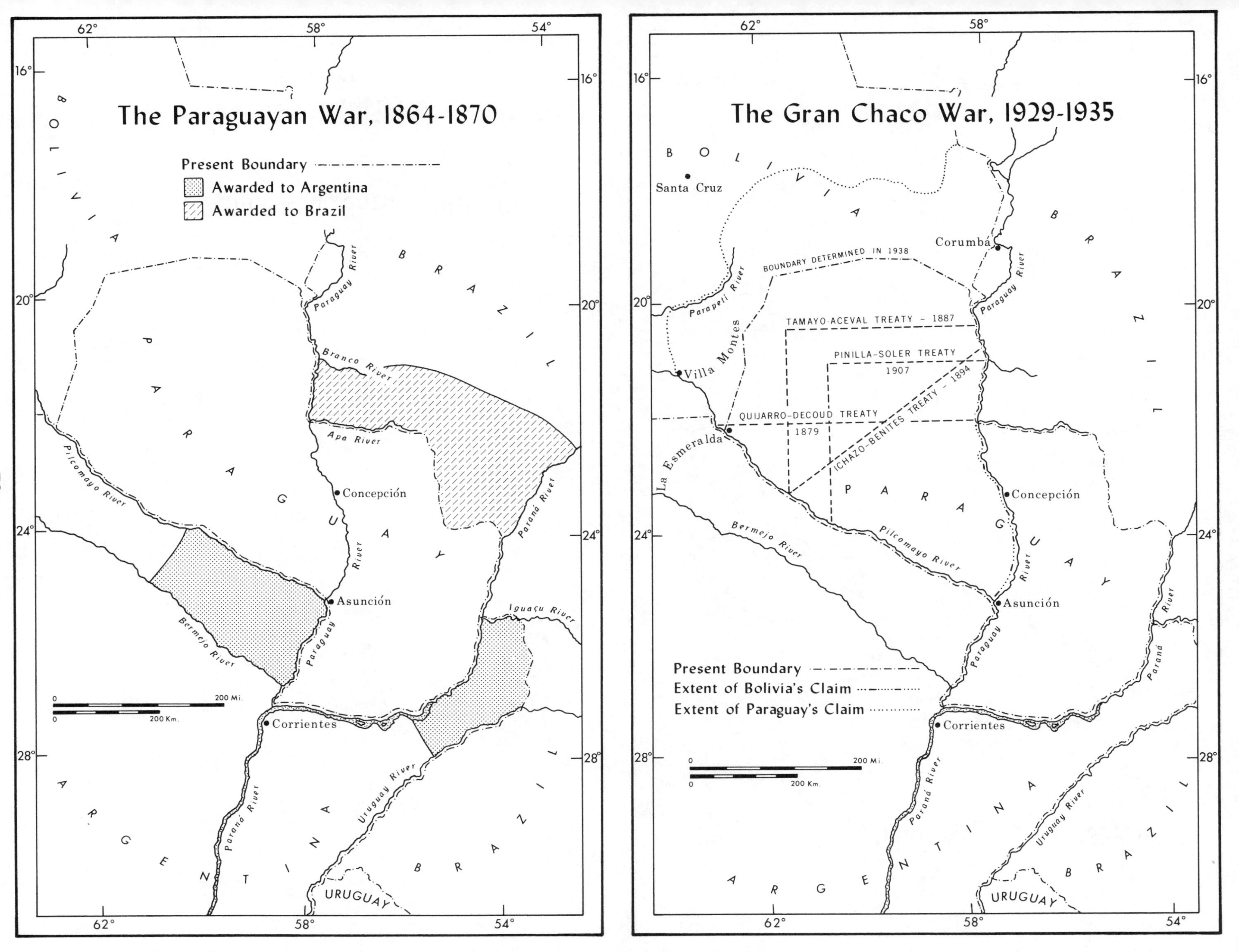
The Paraguayan War, 1864-1870
Present Boundary
Awarded to Argentina
Awarded to Brazil
BOLIVIA
BRAZIL
PARAGUAY
ARGENTINA
URUGUAY
Concepción
Asunción
Corrientes
Paraguay River
Branco River
Apa River
Pilcomayo River
Bermejo River
Paraná River
Iguaçu River
Uruguay River
200 Mi.
200 Km.
The Gran Chaco War, 1929-1935
BOLIVIA
BRAZIL
PARAGUAY
ARGENTINA
URUGUAY
Santa Cruz
Corumbá
Villa Montes
La Esmeralda
Concepción
Asunción
Corrientes
Parapeti River
Paraguay River
Pilcomayo River
Bermejo River
Paraná River
Uruguay River
BOUNDARY DETERMINED IN 1938
TAMAYO-ACEVAL TREATY - 1887
PINILLA-SOLER TREATY 1907
ICHAZO-BENITES TREATY - 1894
QUIJARRO-DECOUD TREATY 1879
Present Boundary
Extent of Bolivia's Claim
Extent of Paraguay's Claim
200 Mi.
200 Km.

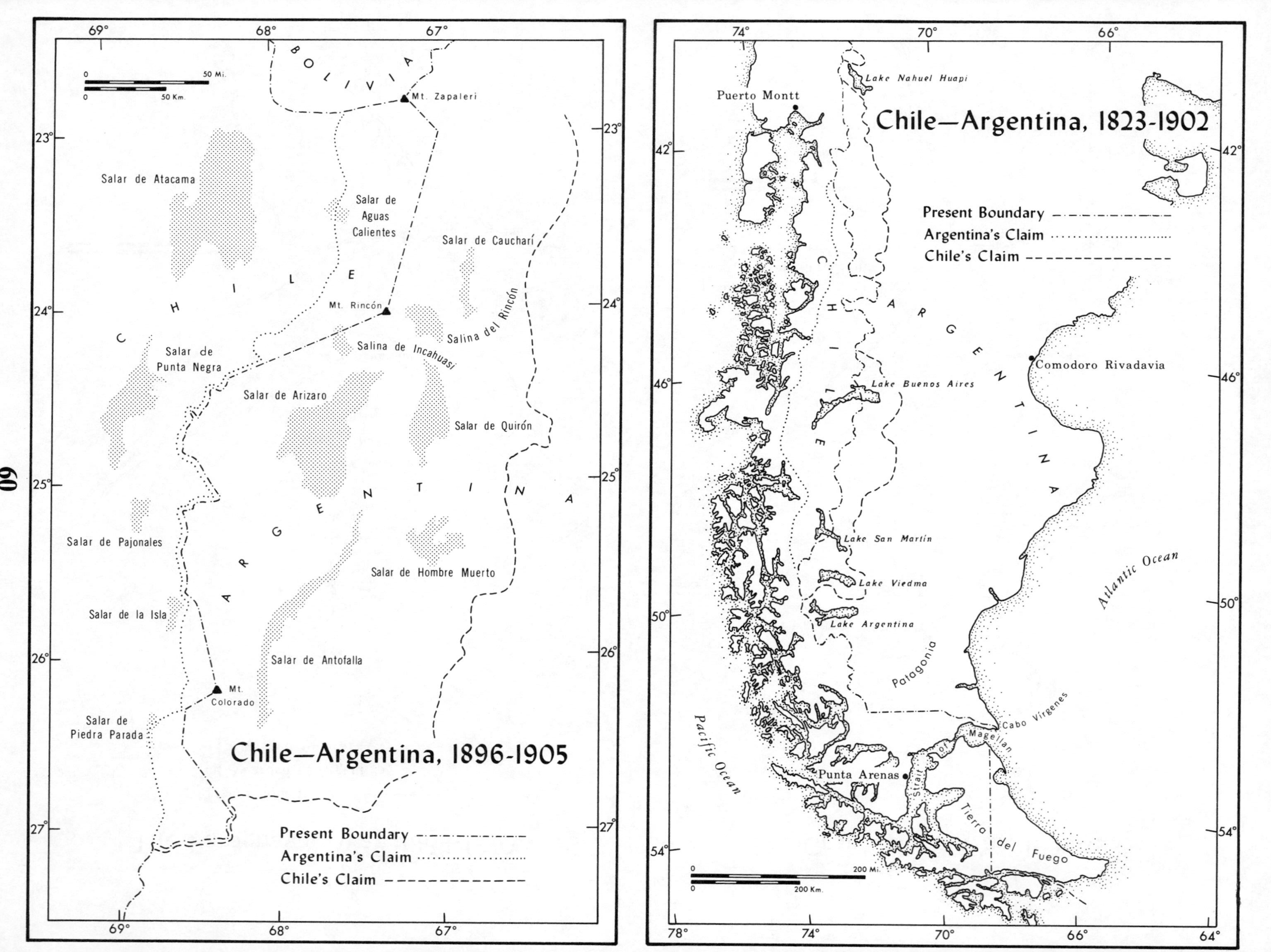

Chile—Argentina, 1896-1905
Present Boundary
Argentina's Claim
Chile's Claim
B O L I V I A
C H I L E
A R G E N T I N A
Mt. Zapaleri
Mt. Rincón
Mt. Colorado
Salar de Atacama
Salar de Aguas Calientes
Salar de Cauchari
Salina del Rincón
Salina de Incahuasi
Salar de Punta Negra
Salar de Arizaro
Salar de Quirón
Salar de Pajonales
Salar de Hombre Muerto
Salar de la Isla
Salar de Antofalla
Salar de Piedra Parada
50 Mi.
50 Km.
Chile—Argentina, 1823-1902
Present Boundary
Argentina's Claim
Chile's Claim
Puerto Montt
Lake Nahuel Huapi
C H I L E
A R G E N T I N A
Comodoro Rivadavia
Lake Buenos Aires
Lake San Martín
Lake Viedma
Lake Argentina
Patagonia
Atlantic Ocean
Pacific Ocean
Cabo Vírgenes
Strait of Magellan
Punta Arenas
Tierra del Fuego
200 Mi.
200 Km.

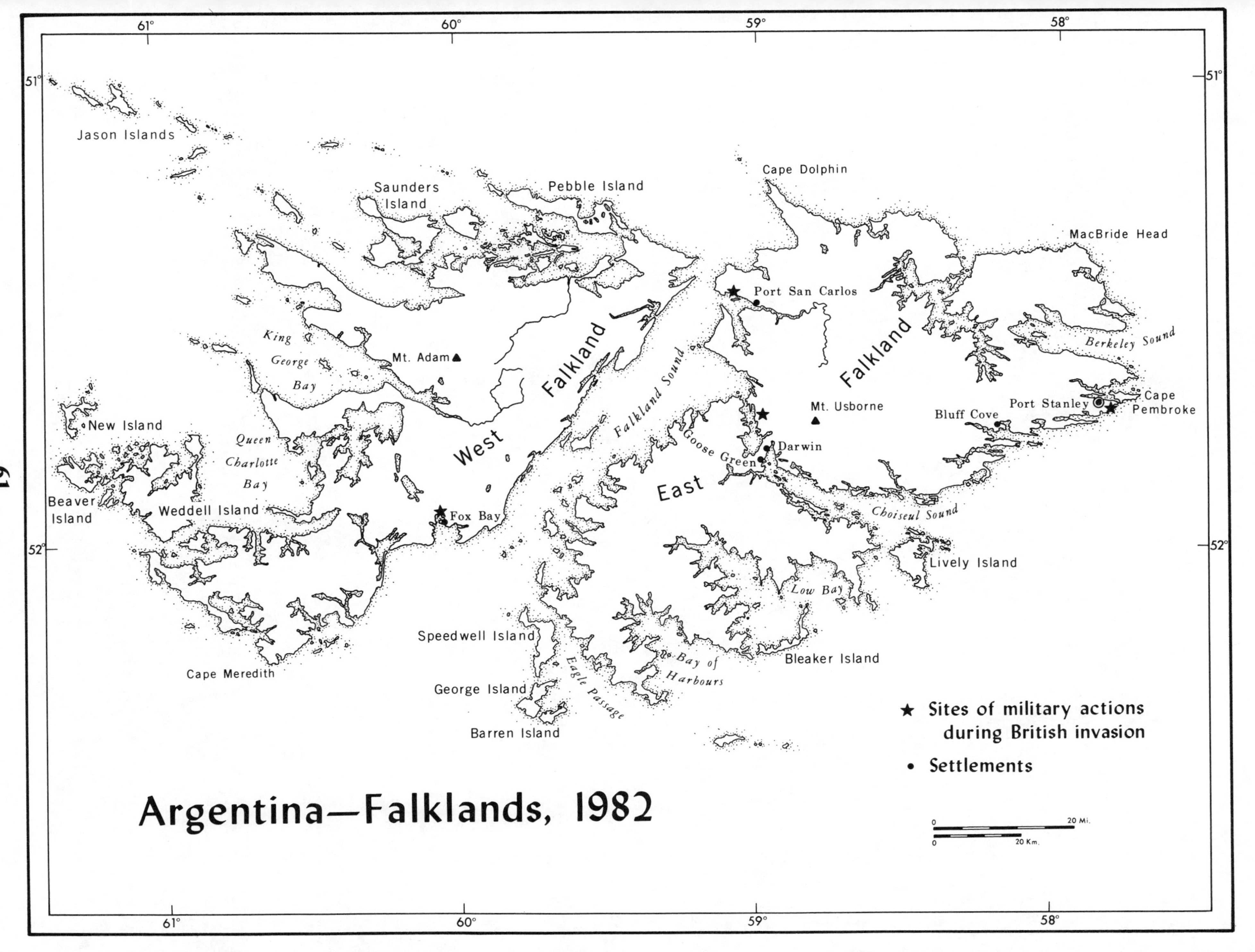
Argentina—Falklands, 1982
★ Sites of military actions during British invasion
• Settlements
0 20 Mi.
0 20 Km.
61°
60°
59°
58°
51°
52°
Jason Islands
Saunders Island
Pebble Island
Cape Dolphin
MacBride Head
Port San Carlos
Berkeley Sound
King George Bay
Mt. Adam
West
Falkland
Falkland Sound
Falkland
Mt. Usborne
Port Stanley
Cape Pembroke
Bluff Cove
New Island
Queen Charlotte Bay
Goose Green
Darwin
East
Beaver Island
Weddell Island
Fox Bay
Choiseul Sound
Lively Island
Low Bay
Speedwell Island
Bay of Harbours
Bleaker Island
Cape Meredith
George Island
Eagle Passage
Barren Island

Latin American International Relations

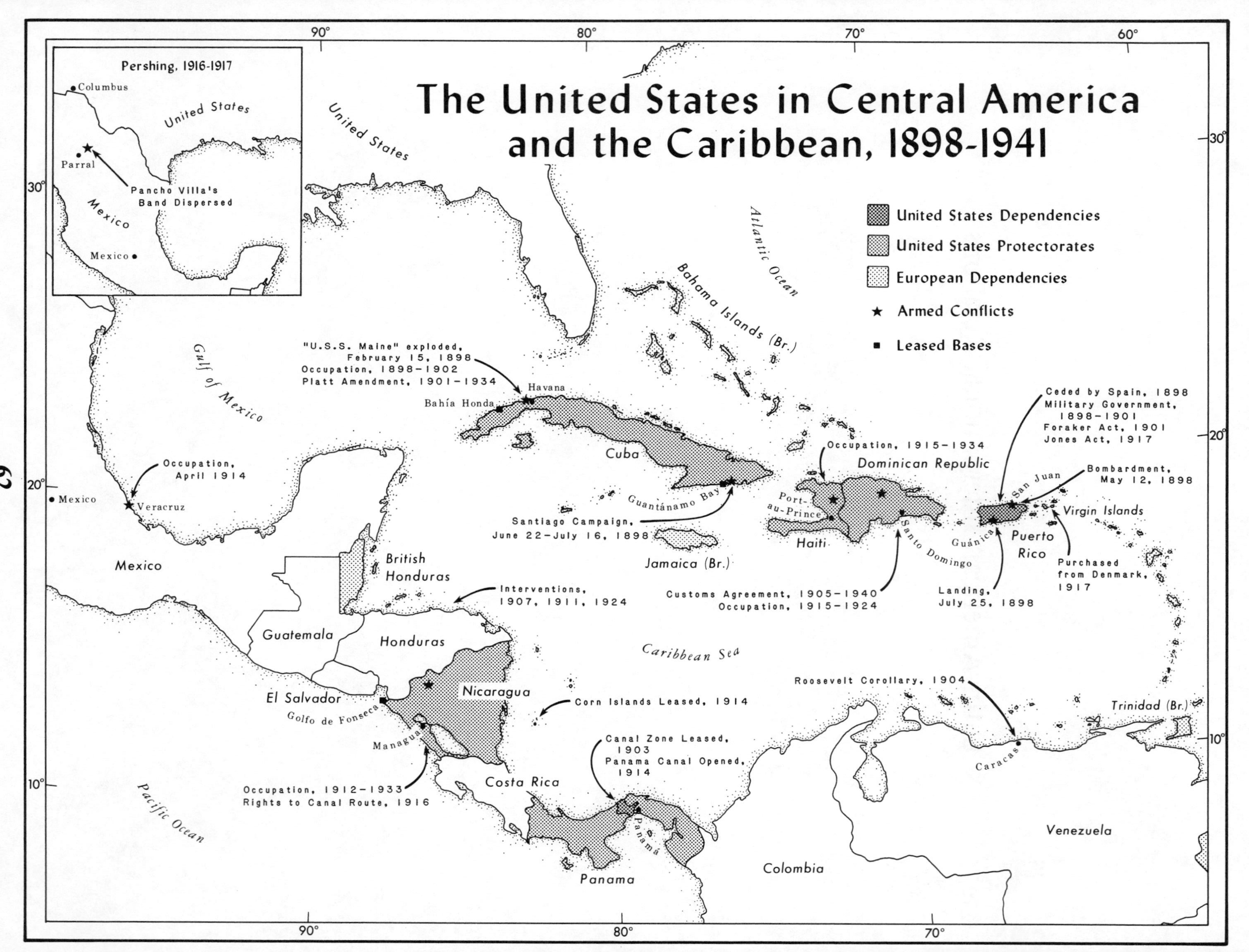

The United States in Central America and the Caribbean, 1898-1941
United States Dependencies
United States Protectorates
European Dependencies
Armed Conflicts
Leased Bases
Pershing, 1916-1917
Columbus
United States
Parral
Pancho Villa's Band Dispersed
Mexico
Mexico
United States
Atlantic Ocean
Bahama Islands (Br.)
Gulf of Mexico
"U.S.S. Maine" exploded, February 15, 1898
Occupation, 1898-1902
Platt Amendment, 1901-1934
Havana
Bahía Honda
Cuba
Guantánamo Bay
Santiago Campaign, June 22-July 16, 1898
Jamaica (Br.)
Occupation, April 1914
Veracruz
Mexico
Mexico
Occupation, 1915-1934
Dominican Republic
Port-au-Prince
Haiti
Santo Domingo
Customs Agreement, 1905-1940
Occupation, 1915-1924
Ceded by Spain, 1898
Military Government, 1898-1901
Foraker Act, 1901
Jones Act, 1917
Bombardment, May 12, 1898
San Juan
Virgin Islands
Guánica
Puerto Rico
Purchased from Denmark, 1917
Landing, July 25, 1898
British Honduras
Interventions, 1907, 1911, 1924
Guatemala
Honduras
Caribbean Sea
El Salvador
Golfo de Fonseca
Nicaragua
Corn Islands Leased, 1914
Managua
Occupation, 1912-1933
Rights to Canal Route, 1916
Costa Rica
Canal Zone Leased, 1903
Panama Canal Opened, 1914
Panamá
Panama
Pacific Ocean
Colombia
Roosevelt Corollary, 1904
Caracas
Venezuela
Trinidad (Br.)
90°
80°
70°
60°
30°
20°
10°

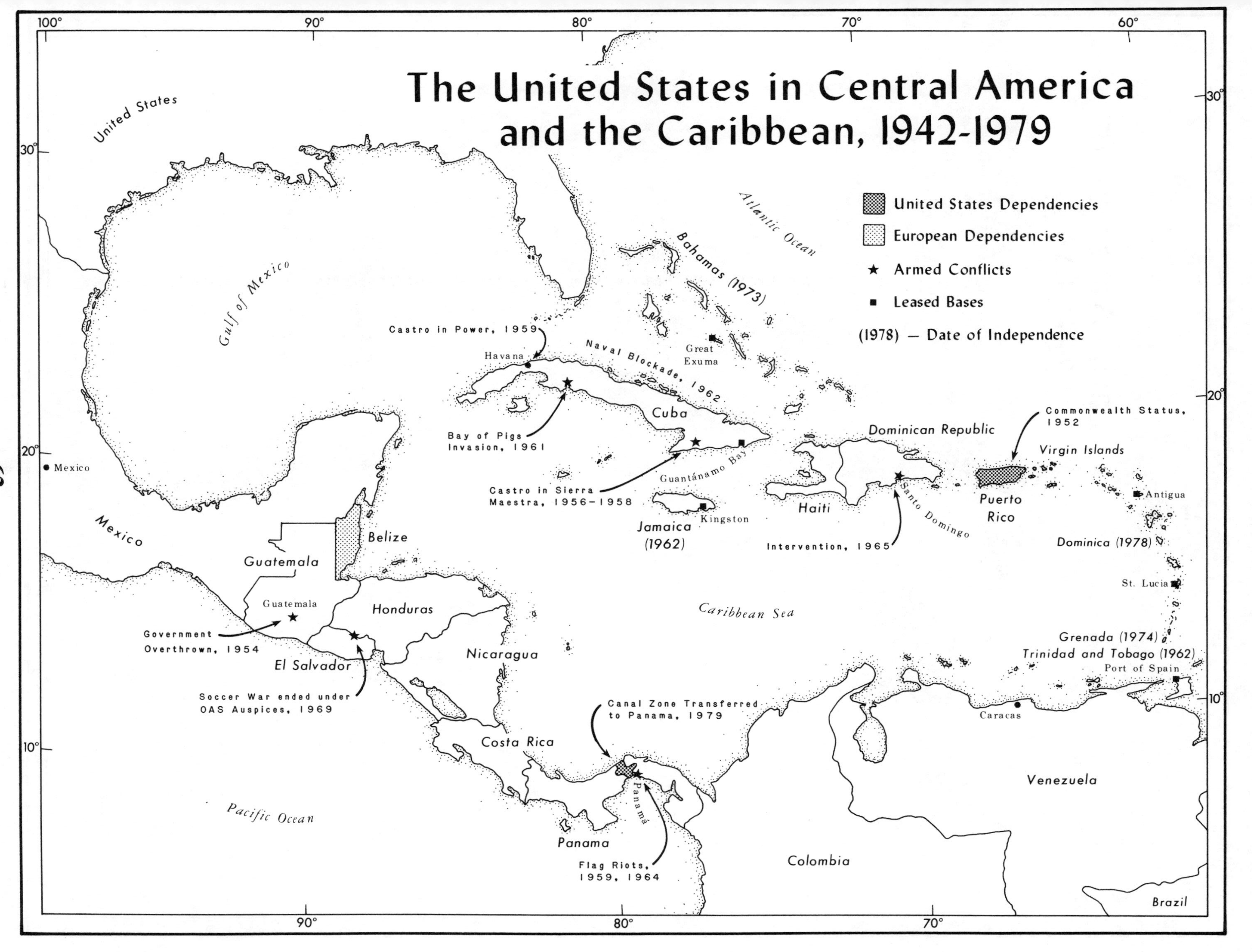
The United States in Central America and the Caribbean, 1942-1979
United States Dependencies
European Dependencies
Armed Conflicts
Leased Bases
(1978) — Date of Independence
United States
Gulf of Mexico
Mexico
Mexico
Atlantic Ocean
Bahamas (1973)
Great Exuma
Castro in Power, 1959
Havana
Naval Blockade, 1962
Cuba
Bay of Pigs Invasion, 1961
Guantánamo Bay
Castro in Sierra Maestra, 1956-1958
Jamaica (1962)
Kingston
Haiti
Dominican Republic
Santo Domingo
Intervention, 1965
Commonwealth Status, 1952
Virgin Islands
Puerto Rico
Antigua
Dominica (1978)
St. Lucia
Grenada (1974)
Trinidad and Tobago (1962)
Port of Spain
Caribbean Sea
Caracas
Venezuela
Belize
Guatemala
Guatemala
Government Overthrown, 1954
Honduras
El Salvador
Soccer War ended under OAS Auspices, 1969
Nicaragua
Costa Rica
Canal Zone Transferred to Panama, 1979
Panamá
Panama
Flag Riots, 1959, 1964
Colombia
Brazil
Pacific Ocean
100°
90°
80°
70°
60°
30°
20°
10°

Latin America in World War I
MEXICO
CUBA, April 1917
DOMINICAN REPUBLIC, April 1917
HONDURAS, July 1918
HAITI, July 1918
GUATEMALA, April 1918
NICARAGUA, March 1918
EL SALVADOR
COSTA RICA, May 1918
PANAMA, April 1918
VENEZUELA
COLOMBIA
ECUADOR, December 1917
BRAZIL, October 1917
PERU, October 1917
BOLIVIA, April 1917
PARAGUAY
CHILE
ARGENTINA
URUGUAY, October 1917
Declared War
Broke Diplomatic Relations
Remained Neutral
110°
100°
90°
80°
70°
60°
50°
40°
30°
120°
20°
0°
10°

Latin America in the League of Nations
MEXICO
CUBA
DOMINICAN REPUBLIC
HAITI
GUATEMALA, 1936
HONDURAS, 1936
EL SALVADOR, 1936
NICARAGUA, 1936
COSTA RICA, 1924
PANAMA
VENEZUELA, 1938
COLOMBIA
ECUADOR
BRAZIL, 1926
PERU, 1936
BOLIVIA
PARAGUAY, 1937
ARGENTINA
URUGUAY
CHILE, 1938
Founding Countries
Countries Admitted after January 1920
Countries Admitted after January 1921
The year in which a country left the League follows its name.
110°
100°
90°
80°
70°
60°
50°
40°
30°
20°
10°
0°
120°

Latin America in World War II
MEXICO, May 1942
CUBA, December 1941
DOMINICAN REPUBLIC, December 1941
HONDURAS, December 1941
GUATEMALA, December 1941
HAITI, December 1941
NICARAGUA, December 1941
EL SALVADOR, December 1941
COSTA RICA, December 1941
VENEZUELA, February 1945
PANAMA, December 1941
COLOMBIA, November 1943
ECUADOR, February 1945
BRAZIL, August 1942
PERU, February 1945
BOLIVIA, April 1943
PARAGUAY, 1945
ARGENTINA, March 1945
CHILE, February 1945
URUGUAY, February 1945
Declared War on Axis
Declared War on Germany only
Declared War on Japan only
Neutral until 1945, Declared War on Axis

Latin American Countries ca 1975

The Countries of Latin America
MEXICO
Mexico City
BELIZE
Belmopan
GUATEMALA
Guatemala
HONDURAS
Tegucigalpa
San Salvador
EL SALVADOR
NICARAGUA
Managua
San José
COSTA RICA
Panamá
PANAMA
Havana
CUBA
HAITI
DOMINICAN REPUBLIC
PUERTO RICO
San Juan
Port-au-Prince
Kingston
JAMAICA
Santo Domingo
LESSER ANTILLES
Port of Spain
TRINIDAD AND TOBAGO
Caracas
VENEZUELA
Georgetown
Paramaribo
Cayenne
GUYANA
SURINAM
FRENCH GUIANA
Bogotá
COLOMBIA
GALAPAGOS ISLANDS
Quito
ECUADOR
PERU
BRAZIL
Lima
BOLIVIA
La Paz
Brasília
PARAGUAY
CHILE
Asunción
ARGENTINA
URUGUAY
Santiago
Buenos Aires
Montevideo
FALKLAND ISLANDS
(Islas Malvinas)
110° 100° 90° 80° 70° 60° 50° 40° 30°
120° 110° 100° 90° 80° 70° 60° 50° 40° 30° 20°
30° 20° 10° 0° 10° 20° 30° 40° 50°

Mexico
Population
MEXICO CITY ★ Over 1,000,000
Puebla ■ 250,000 - 1,000,000
Queretaro ● 100,000 - 250,000
Pachuca ⊙ 25,000 - 100,000
Tlaxcala ○ 0 - 25,000
The national capital is circled.
The state capitals are underlined.
0 300 Mi.
0 300 Km.
Mexicali
Tijuana
BAJA CALIFORNIA
BAJA CALIFORNIA SUR
La Paz
Nogales
SONORA
Hermosillo
Guaymas
Ciudad Juárez
CHIHUAHUA
Chihuahua
SINALOA
Culiacán
Mazatlán
Río Grande
COAHUILA
Nuevo Laredo
Gómez Palacio
Torreón
DURANGO
Durango
Saltillo
NUEVO LEÓN
MONTERREY
Matamoros
TAMAULIPAS
Ciudad Victoria
ZACATECAS
Zacatecas
SAN LUIS POTOSÍ
San Luis Potosí
Tampico
NAYARIT
Tepic
AGUASCALIENTES
Aguascalientes
GUANAJUATO
León
Guanajuato
GUADALAJARA
JALISCO
Colima
COLIMA
Morelia
MICHOACÁN
Chilpancingo
GUERRERO
Acapulco
Jalapa
Veracruz
VERACRUZ
Oaxaca
OAXACA
Villahermosa
TABASCO
CHIAPAS
Grijalva River
Tuxtla Gutiérrez
Mérida
YUCATÁN
Campeche
CAMPECHE
QUINTANA ROO
Ciudad Chetumal
Celaya
Querétaro
QUERÉTARO
HIDALGO
VERACRUZ
Pachuca
Tula
Tulancingo
Huauchinango
PUEBLA
MICHOACÁN
MEXICO
Teotihuacán ruins
Texcoco
TLAXCALA
MEXICO CITY
Toluca
DISTRITO FEDERAL
Xochilmilco
Chalco
Ixtacihuatl
Tlaxcala
Cholula
Puebla
Popocatépetl
Cuernavaca
Atlixco
Tecamachalco
MORELOS
Cuautla
115°
110°
105°
100°
95°
90°
85°
30°
25°
20°
15°

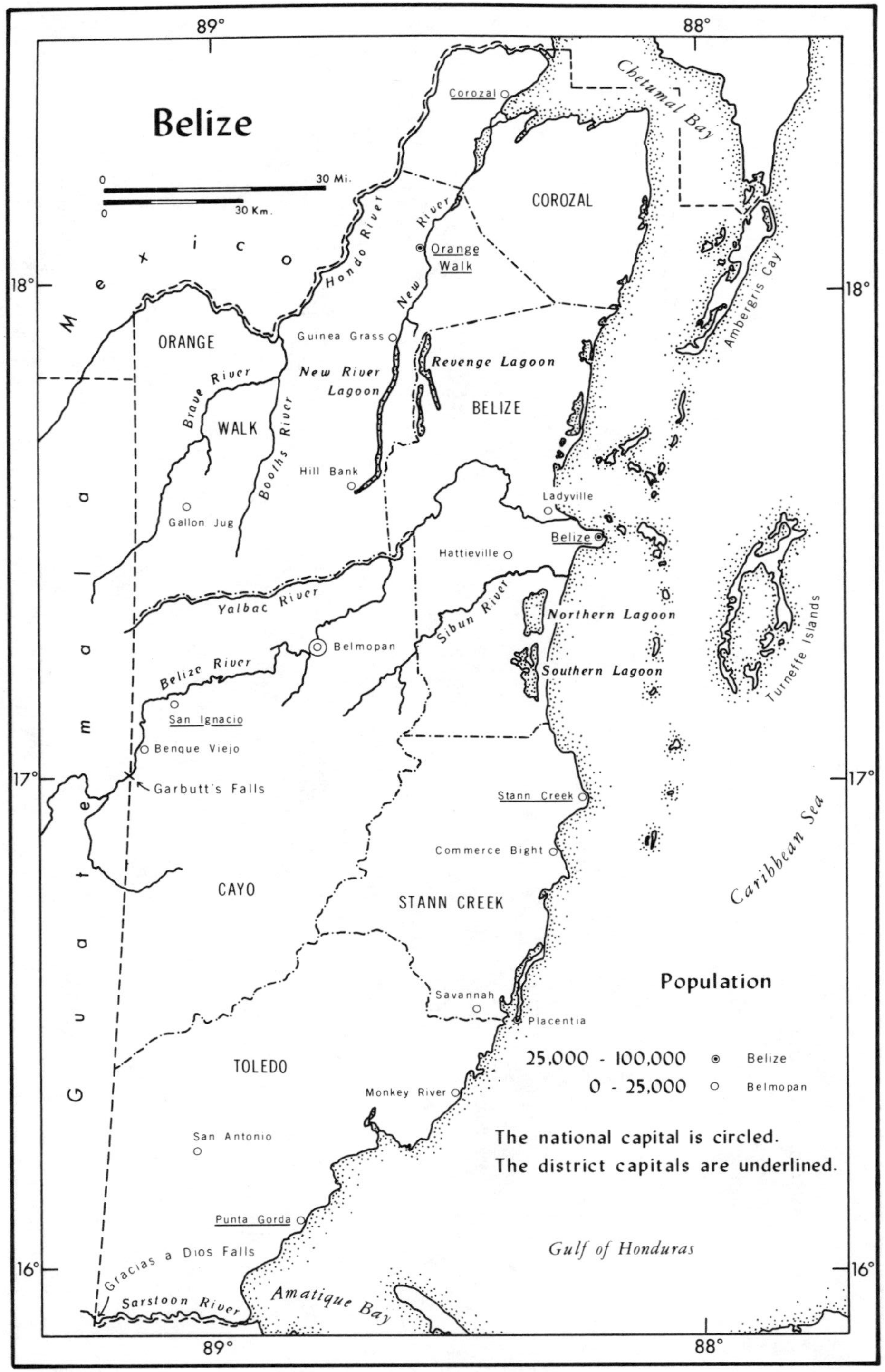

Belize

0 30 Mi.
0 30 Km.

Mexico
Guatemala
Chetumal Bay
Ambergris Cay
Turneffe Islands
Caribbean Sea
Gulf of Honduras
Amatique Bay
COROZAL
ORANGE WALK
BELIZE
CAYO
STANN CREEK
TOLEDO
Corozal
Orange Walk
Guinea Grass
Hill Bank
Gallon Jug
Ladyville
Belize
Hattieville
Belmopan
San Ignacio
Benque Viejo
Garbutt's Falls
Stann Creek
Commerce Bight
Savannah
Placentia
Monkey River
San Antonio
Punta Gorda
Gracias a Dios Falls
Hondo River
New River
New River Lagoon
Revenge Lagoon
Booths River
Brave River
Yalbac River
Belize River
Sibun River
Northern Lagoon
Southern Lagoon
Sarstoon River

Population

25,000 - 100,000	⊙	Belize
0 - 25,000	○	Belmopan

The national capital is circled.
The district capitals are underlined.

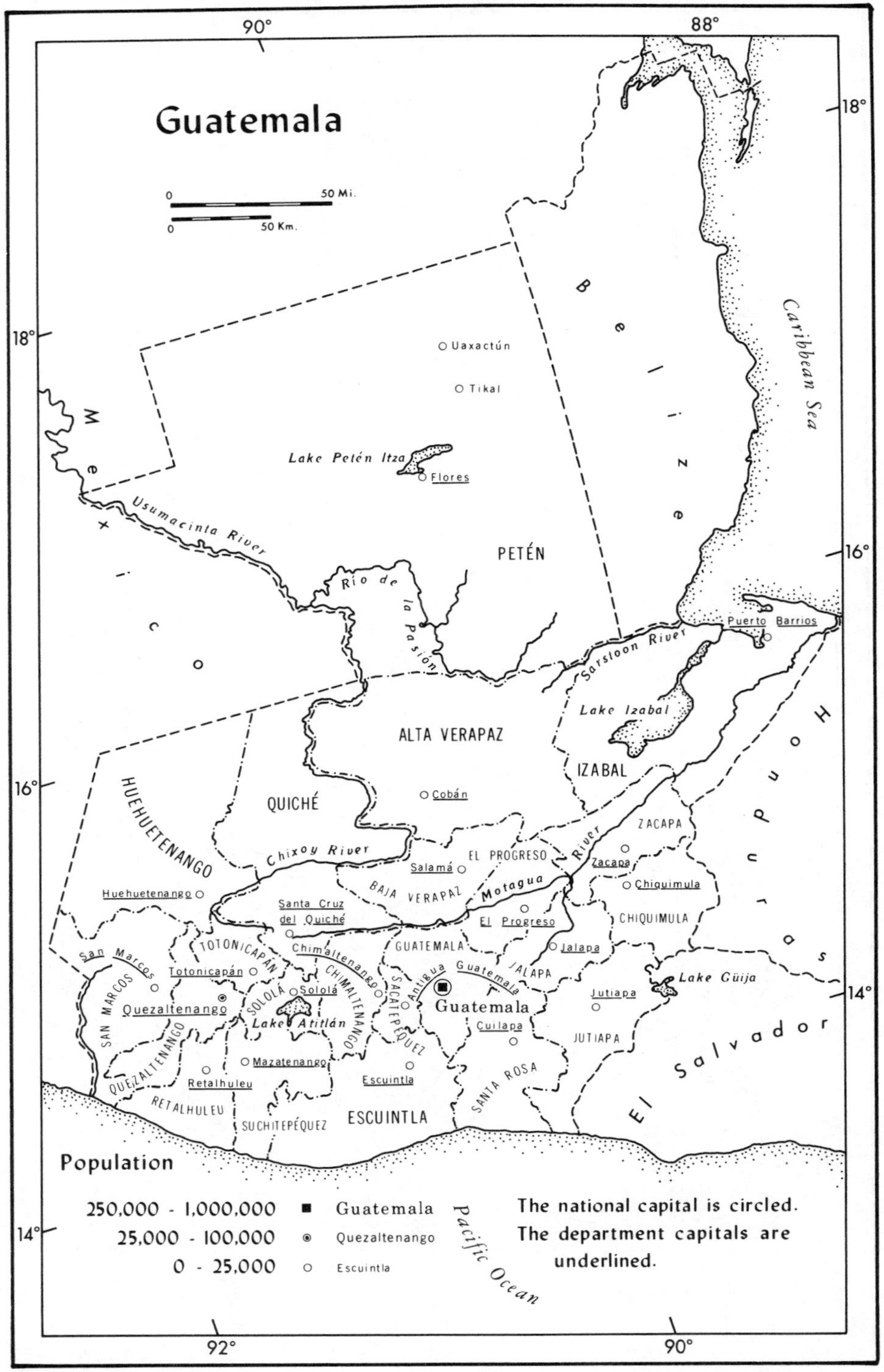

Guatemala

0 50 Mi.
0 50 Km.

Mexico
Belize
Honduras
El Salvador
Caribbean Sea
Pacific Ocean
PETÉN
ALTA VERAPAZ
IZABAL
QUICHÉ
HUEHUETENANGO
EL PROGRESO
BAJA VERAPAZ
ZACAPA
CHIQUIMULA
GUATEMALA
JALAPA
TOTONICAPÁN
CHIMALTENANGO
SOLOLÁ
SACATEPÉQUEZ
SAN MARCOS
QUEZALTENANGO
RETALHULEU
SUCHITEPÉQUEZ
ESCUINTLA
SANTA ROSA
JUTIAPA
Uaxactún
Tikal
Flores
Puerto Barrios
Cobán
Salamá
Zacapa
Chiquimula
Huehuetenango
Santa Cruz del Quiché
El Progreso
Jalapa
San Marcos
Totonicapán
Chimaltenango
Sololá
Guatemala
Antigua Guatemala
Quezaltenango
Jutiapa
Cuilapa
Mazatenango
Retalhuleu
Escuintla
Lake Petén Itza
Lake Izabal
Lake Atitlán
Lake Güija
Usumacinta River
Río de la Pasión
Sarstoon River
Chixoy River
Motagua River

Population

250,000 - 1,000,000	■	Guatemala
25,000 - 100,000	⊙	Quezaltenango
0 - 25,000	○	Escuintla

The national capital is circled.
The department capitals are underlined.

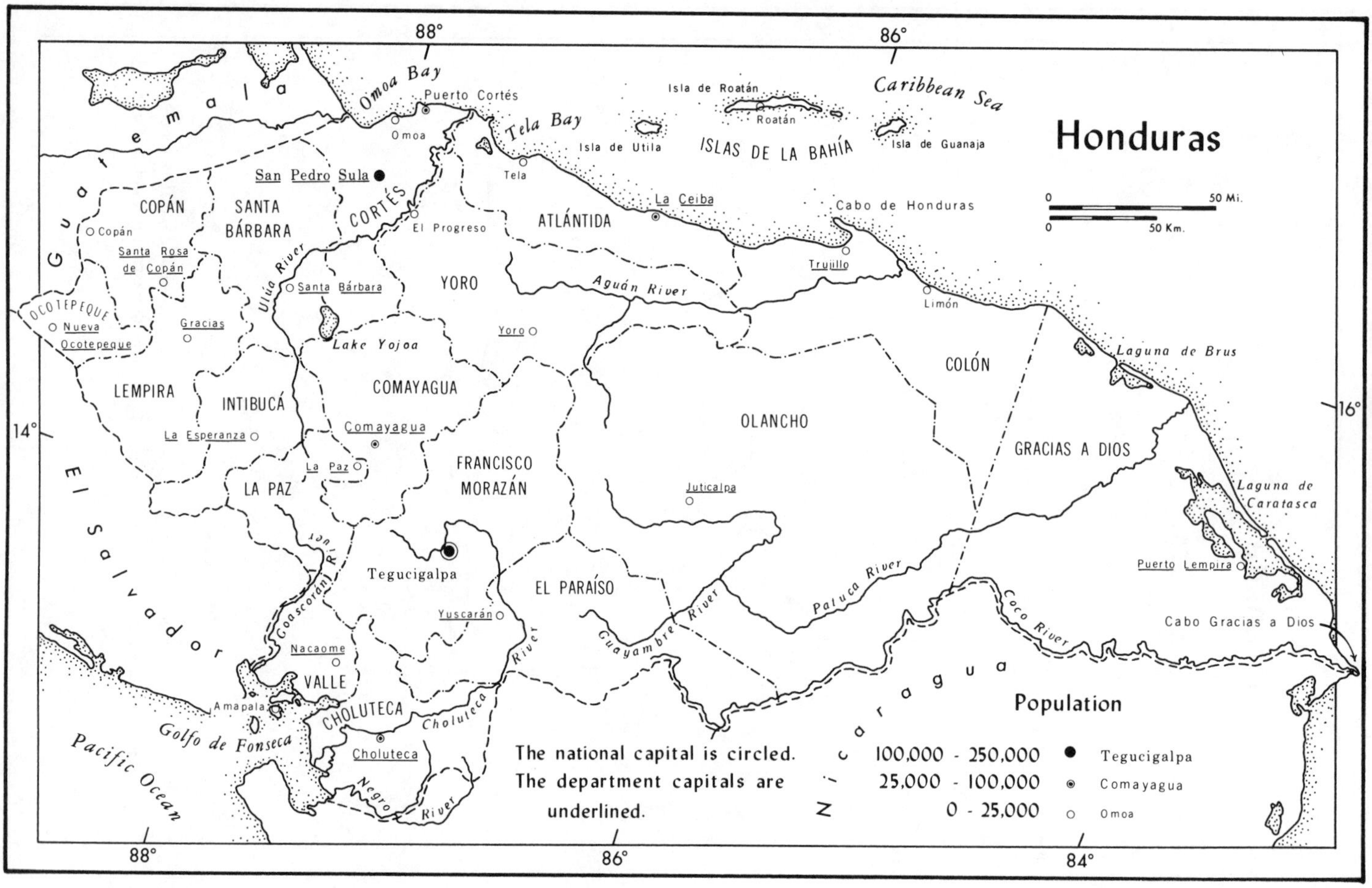

Honduras

0 50 Mi.
0 50 Km.

The national capital is circled.
The department capitals are underlined.

Population

100,000 - 250,000	●	Tegucigalpa
25,000 - 100,000	◉	Comayagua
0 - 25,000	○	Omoa

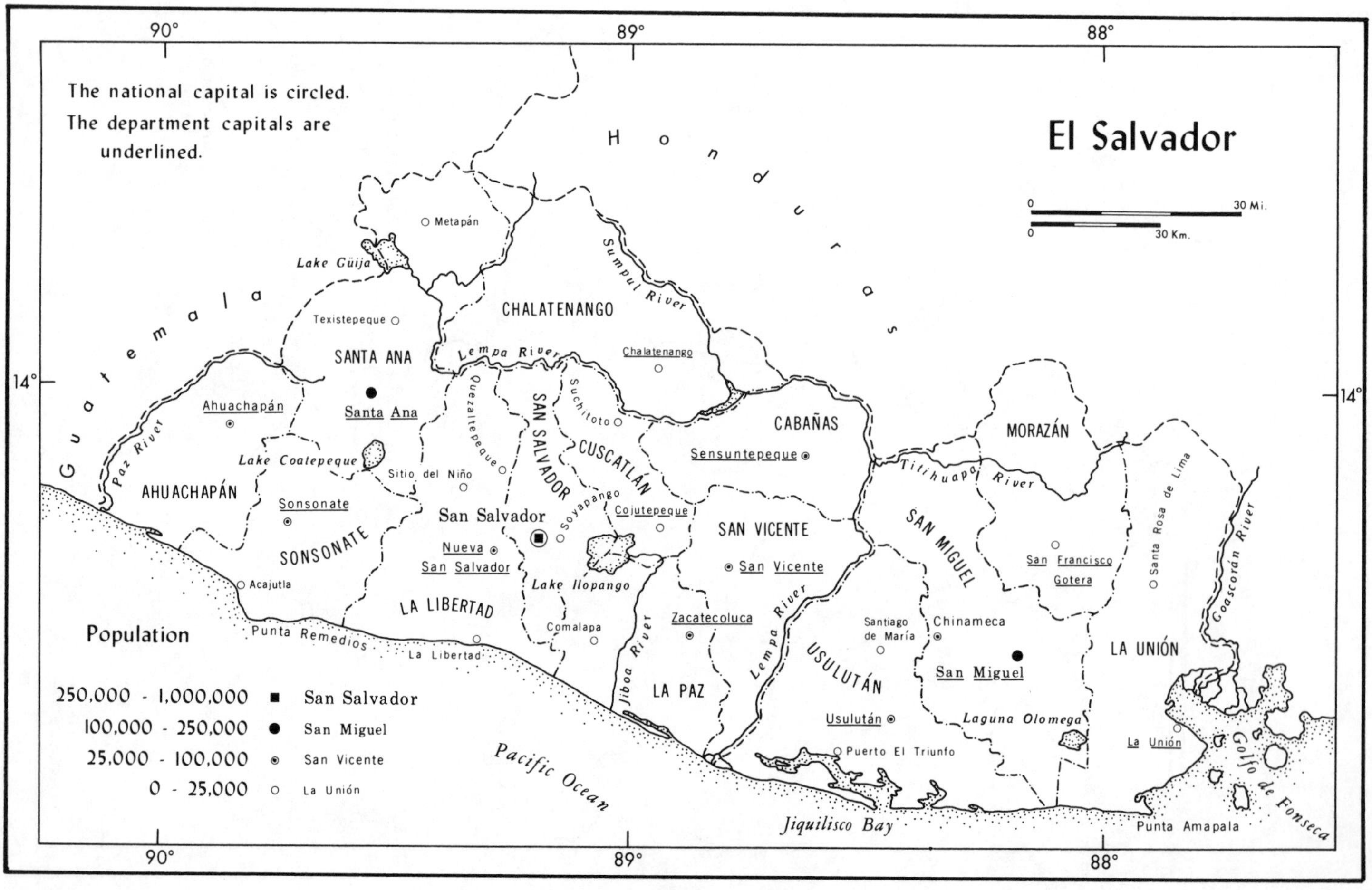

El Salvador

The national capital is circled.
The department capitals are underlined.

0 30 Mi.
0 30 Km.

Population

250,000 - 1,000,000	■	San Salvador
100,000 - 250,000	●	San Miguel
25,000 - 100,000	◉	San Vicente
0 - 25,000	○	La Unión

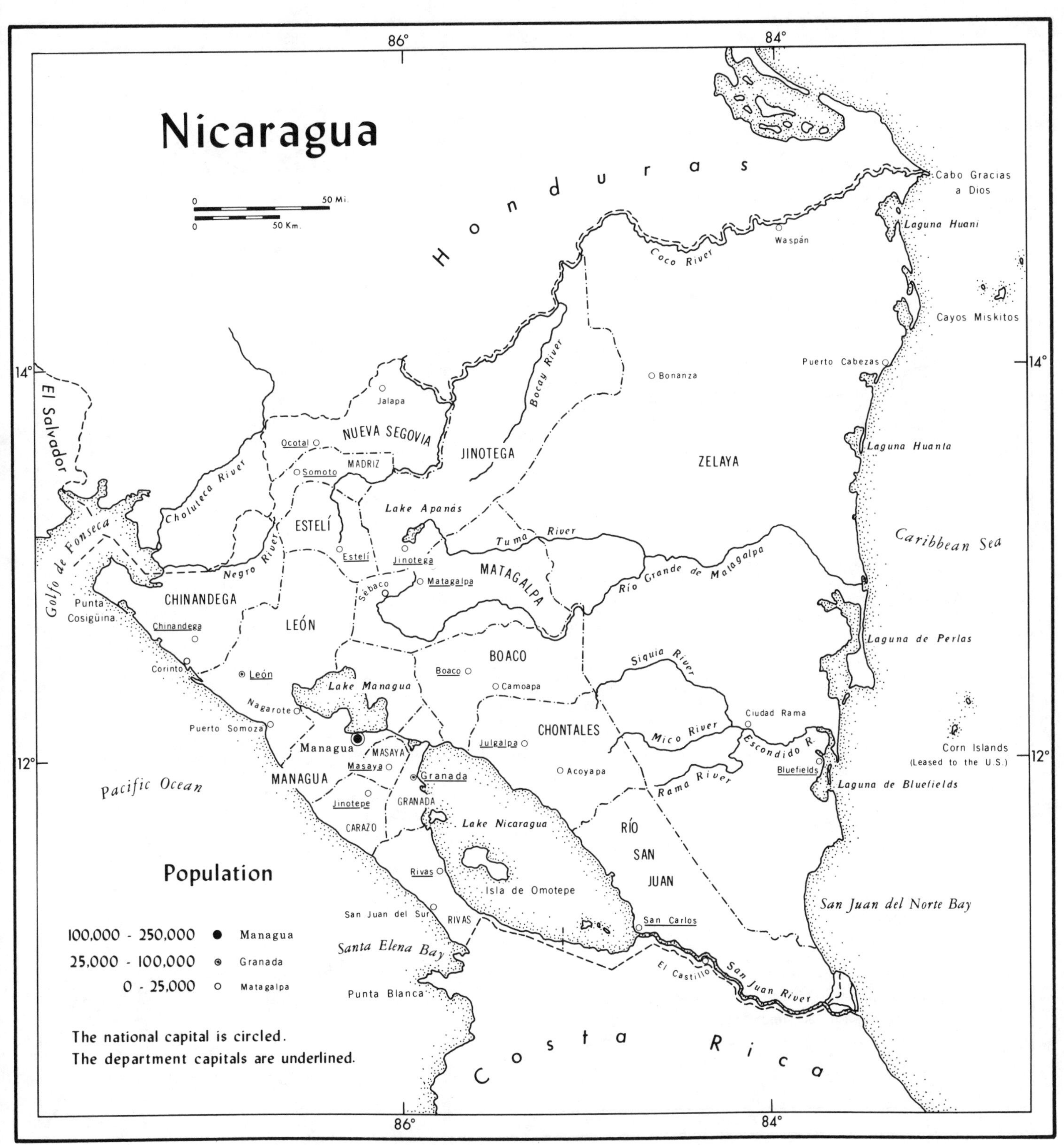

Nicaragua
Honduras
El Salvador
Costa Rica
Pacific Ocean
Caribbean Sea
Population
100,000 - 250,000 Managua
25,000 - 100,000 Granada
0 - 25,000 Matagalpa
The national capital is circled.
The department capitals are underlined.
NUEVA SEGOVIA
MADRIZ
JINOTEGA
ZELAYA
ESTELÍ
CHINANDEGA
LEÓN
MATAGALPA
BOACO
CHONTALES
MANAGUA
MASAYA
GRANADA
CARAZO
RIVAS
RÍO SAN JUAN
Cabo Gracias a Dios
Laguna Huani
Waspán
Coco River
Cayos Miskitos
Puerto Cabezas
Bonanza
Bocay River
Jalapa
Ocotal
Somoto
Laguna Huanta
Choluteca River
Lake Apanás
Golfo de Fonseca
Tuma River
Negro River
Estelí
Jinotega
Río Grande de Matagalpa
Sebaco
Matagalpa
Punta Cosigüina
Chinandega
Laguna de Perlas
Corinto
León
Boaco
Siquia River
Lake Managua
Camoapa
Nagarote
Ciudad Rama
Puerto Somoza
Managua
Mico River
Escondido R.
Corn Islands
(Leased to the U.S.)
Masaya
Julgalpa
Bluefields
Granada
Acoyapa
Rama River
Laguna de Bluefields
Jinotepe
Lake Nicaragua
Rivas
Isla de Omotepe
San Juan del Norte Bay
San Juan del Sur
San Carlos
Santa Elena Bay
El Castillo
San Juan River
Punta Blanca
86°
84°
14°
12°
0
50 Mi.
50 Km.

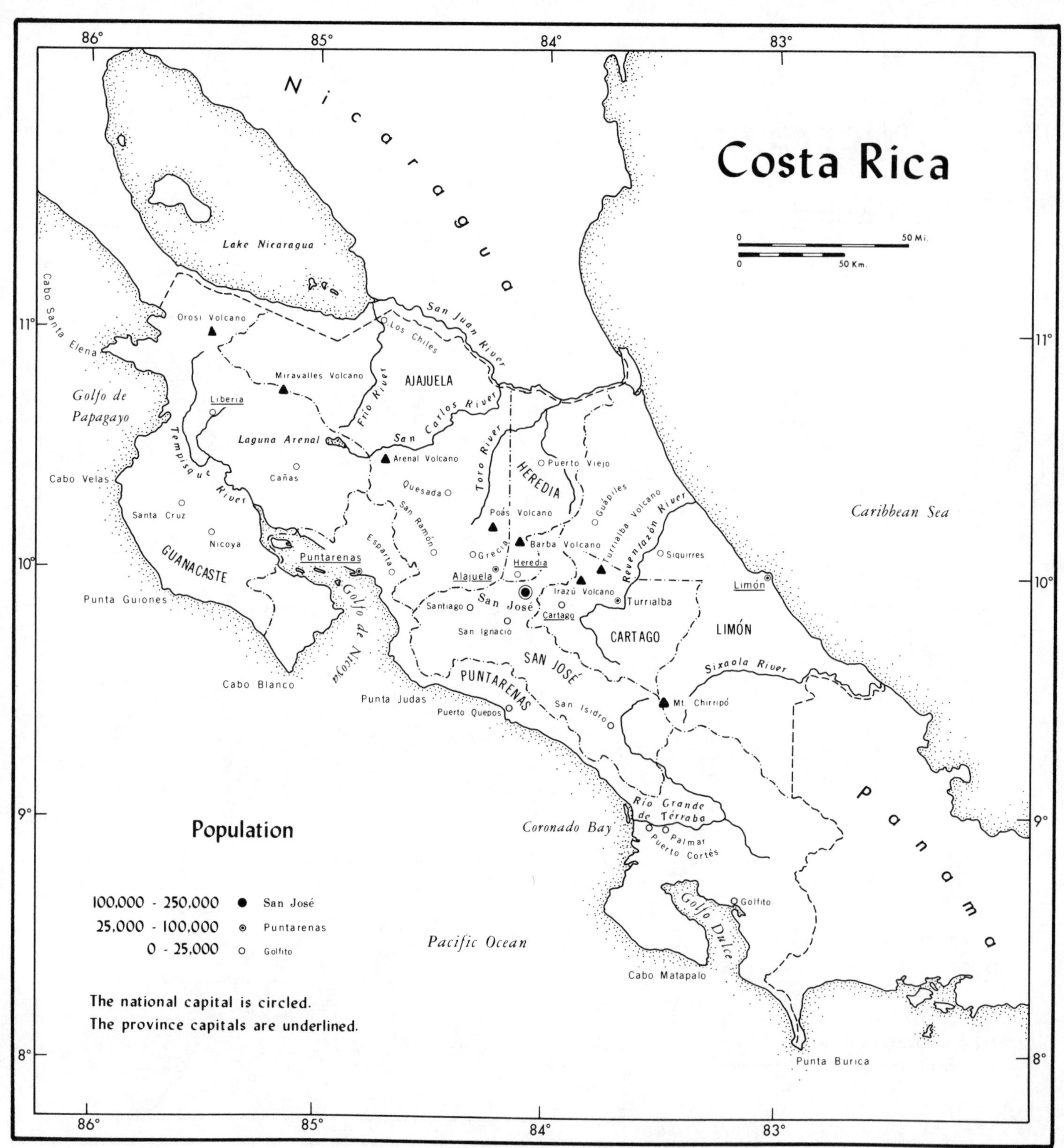
Costa Rica
0
50 Mi.
0
50 Km.
Nicaragua
Lake Nicaragua
San Juan River
Los Chiles
Orosi Volcano
Cabo Santa Elena
Golfo de Papagayo
Miravalles Volcano
Liberia
AJAJUELA
Frío River
San Carlos River
Laguna Arenal
Arenal Volcano
Tempisque River
Cabo Velas
Cañas
Quesada
Santa Cruz
Nicoya
GUANACASTE
Puntarenas
Golfo de Nicoya
Punta Guiones
Cabo Blanco
Toro River
HEREDIA
Puerto Viejo
Poás Volcano
Barba Volcano
San Ramón
Esparta
Grecia
Heredia
Alajuela
San José
Santiago
San Ignacio
Irazú Volcano
Cartago
Turrialba Volcano
Reventazón River
Guápiles
Siquirres
Turrialba
Limón
CARTAGO
LIMÓN
Caribbean Sea
SAN JOSÉ
PUNTARENAS
Punta Judas
Puerto Quepos
San Isidro
Sixaola River
Mt. Chirripó
Río Grande de Térraba
Coronado Bay
Palmar
Puerto Cortés
Panama
Golfito
Golfo Dulce
Pacific Ocean
Cabo Matapalo
Punta Burica
Population
100,000 - 250,000 San José
25,000 - 100,000 Puntarenas
0 - 25,000 Golfito
The national capital is circled.
The province capitals are underlined.

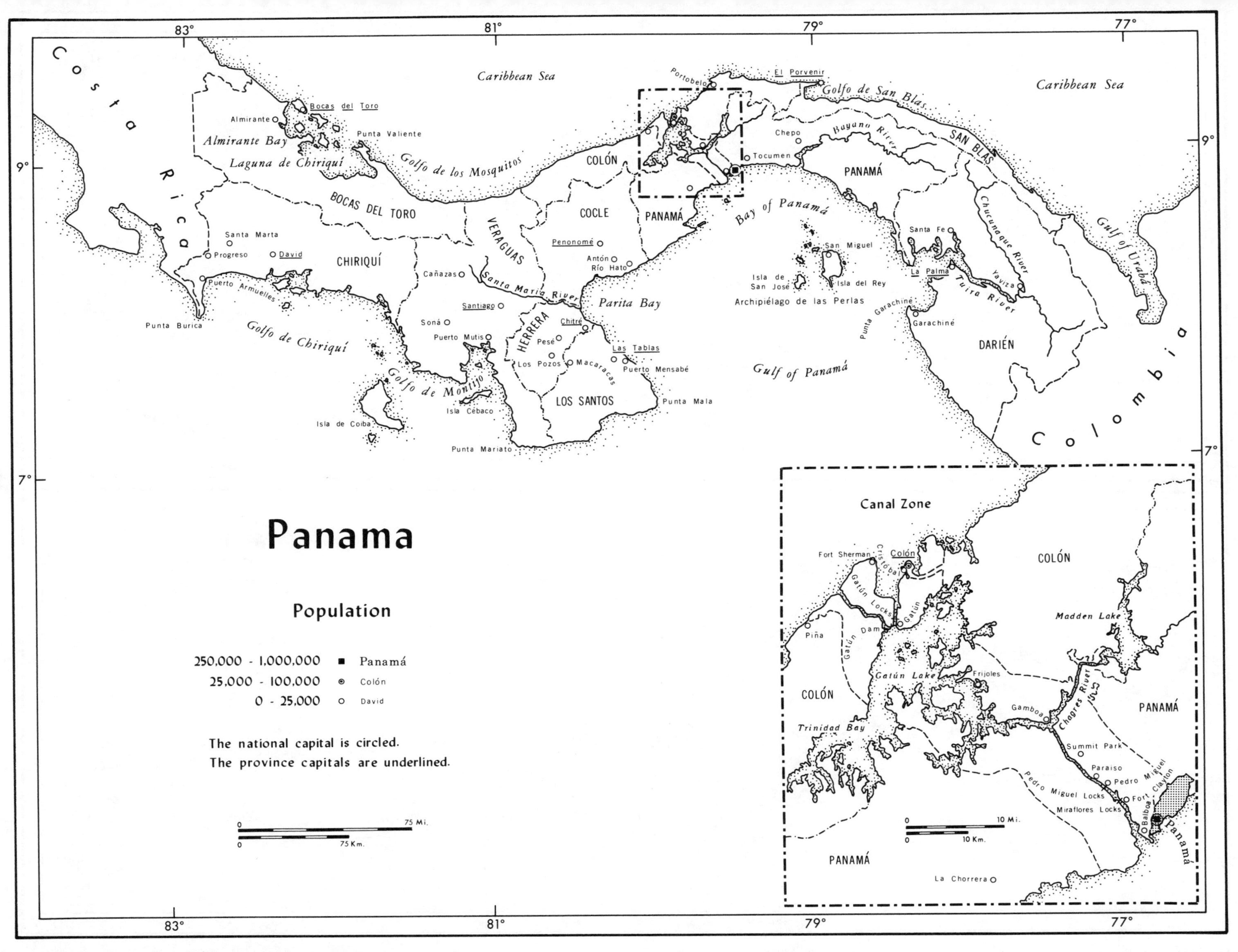

Panama
Population
250,000 - 1,000,000 ■ Panamá
25,000 - 100,000 ⊙ Colón
0 - 25,000 ○ David
The national capital is circled.
The province capitals are underlined.
0 75 Mi.
0 75 Km.
Caribbean Sea
Costa Rica
Colombia
Almirante
Bocas del Toro
Punta Valiente
Almirante Bay
Laguna de Chiriquí
Golfo de los Mosquitos
BOCAS DEL TORO
CHIRIQUÍ
Santa Marta
Progreso
David
Puerto Armuelles
Punta Burica
Golfo de Chiriquí
Isla de Coiba
Golfo de Montijo
Isla Cébaco
Punta Mariato
Cañazas
VERAGUAS
Santiago
Soná
Puerto Mutis
Santa María River
HERRERA
Chitré
Pesé
Los Pozos
Macaracas
LOS SANTOS
Las Tablas
Puerto Mensabé
Punta Mala
COCLE
Penonomé
Antón
Río Hato
Parita Bay
COLÓN
PANAMÁ
Portobelo
El Porvenir
Golfo de San Blas
SAN BLAS
Chepo
Tocumen
Bayano River
Bay of Panamá
San Miguel
Isla del Rey
Isla de San José
Archipiélago de las Perlas
Gulf of Panamá
Punta Garachiné
Garachiné
Santa Fe
La Palma
Tuira River
Yaviza
Chucunaque River
DARIÉN
Gulf of Urabá
Canal Zone
Fort Sherman
Cristóbal
Colón
Gatún Locks
Gatún
Gatún Dam
Piña
Gatún Lake
Frijoles
Madden Lake
Chagres River
Gamboa
Trinidad Bay
Summit Park
Paraiso
Pedro Miguel
Pedro Miguel Locks
Miraflores Locks
Fort Clayton
Balboa
Panamá
La Chorrera
0 10 Mi.
0 10 Km.
83°
81°
79°
77°
9°
7°

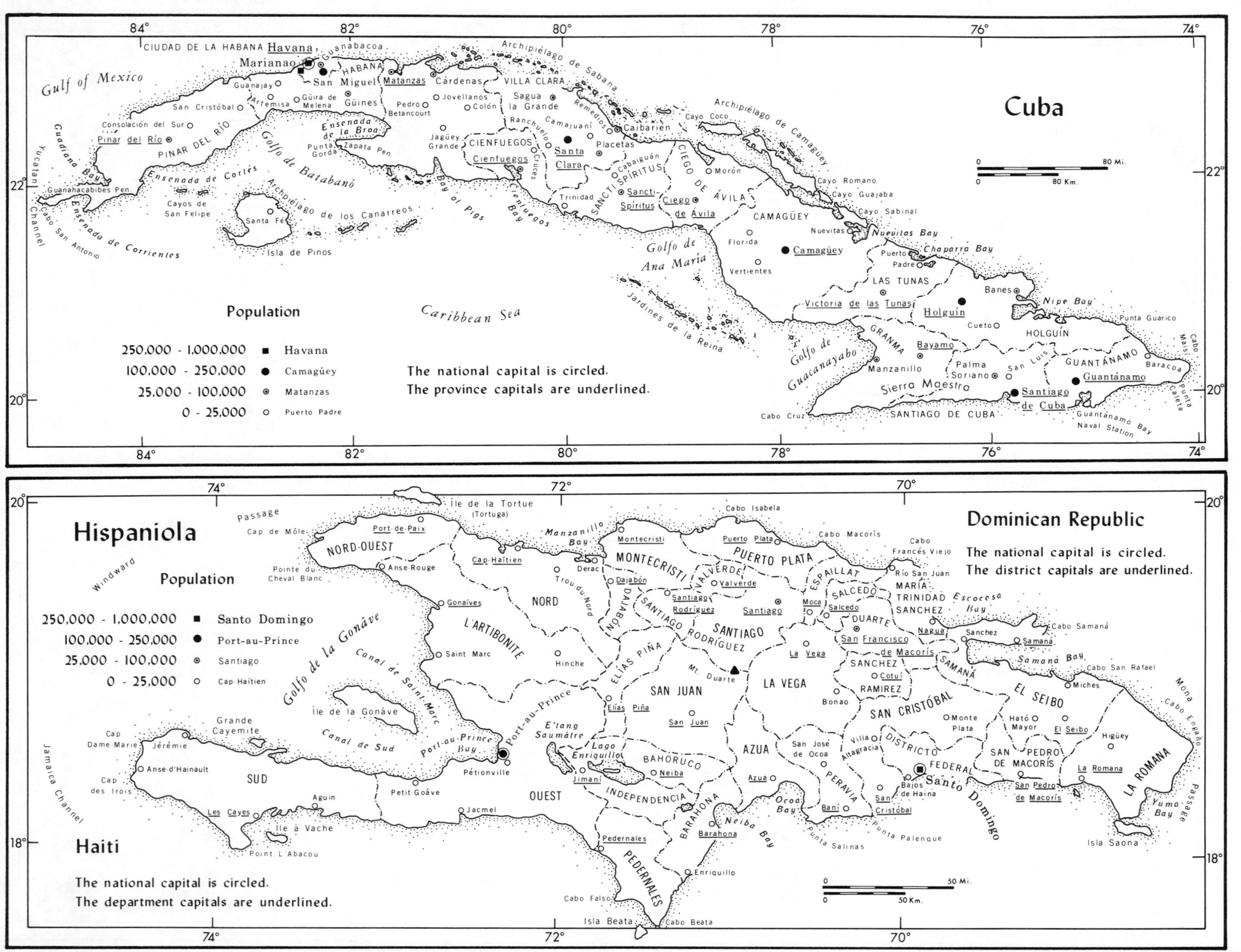
Cuba
The national capital is circled.
The province capitals are underlined.
Population
250,000 - 1,000,000 ■ Havana
100,000 - 250,000 ● Camagüey
25,000 - 100,000 ◉ Matanzas
0 - 25,000 ○ Puerto Padre
Gulf of Mexico
Caribbean Sea
CIUDAD DE LA HABANA
Havana
Marianao
HABANA
San Miguel
Matanzas
VILLA CLARA
Santa Clara
CIENFUEGOS
Cienfuegos
SANCTI SPIRITUS
Sancti-Spíritus
CIEGO DE ÁVILA
Ciego de Ávila
CAMAGÜEY
Camagüey
LAS TUNAS
Victoria de las Tunas
GRANMA
Bayamo
HOLGUÍN
Holguín
SANTIAGO DE CUBA
Santiago de Cuba
GUANTÁNAMO
Guantánamo
PINAR DEL RÍO
Pinar del Río
Isla de Pinos
Golfo de Batabanó
Bay of Pigs
Sierra Maestra
Hispaniola
Population
250,000 - 1,000,000 ■ Santo Domingo
100,000 - 250,000 ● Port-au-Prince
25,000 - 100,000 ◉ Santiago
0 - 25,000 ○ Cap-Haïtien
Dominican Republic
The national capital is circled.
The district capitals are underlined.
Haiti
The national capital is circled.
The department capitals are underlined.
Santo Domingo
Port-au-Prince
Cap-Haïtien
NORD-OUEST
NORD
L'ARTIBONITE
OUEST
SUD
MONTECRISTI
PUERTO PLATA
SANTIAGO
LA VEGA
SAN JUAN
AZUA
BAHORUCO
BARAHONA
PEDERNALES
INDEPENDENCIA
SAN CRISTÓBAL
DISTRICTO FEDERAL
SAN PEDRO DE MACORÍS
EL SEIBO
LA ROMANA
SAMANÁ
Golfo de la Gonâve
Jamaica Channel
Windward Passage
Mona Passage

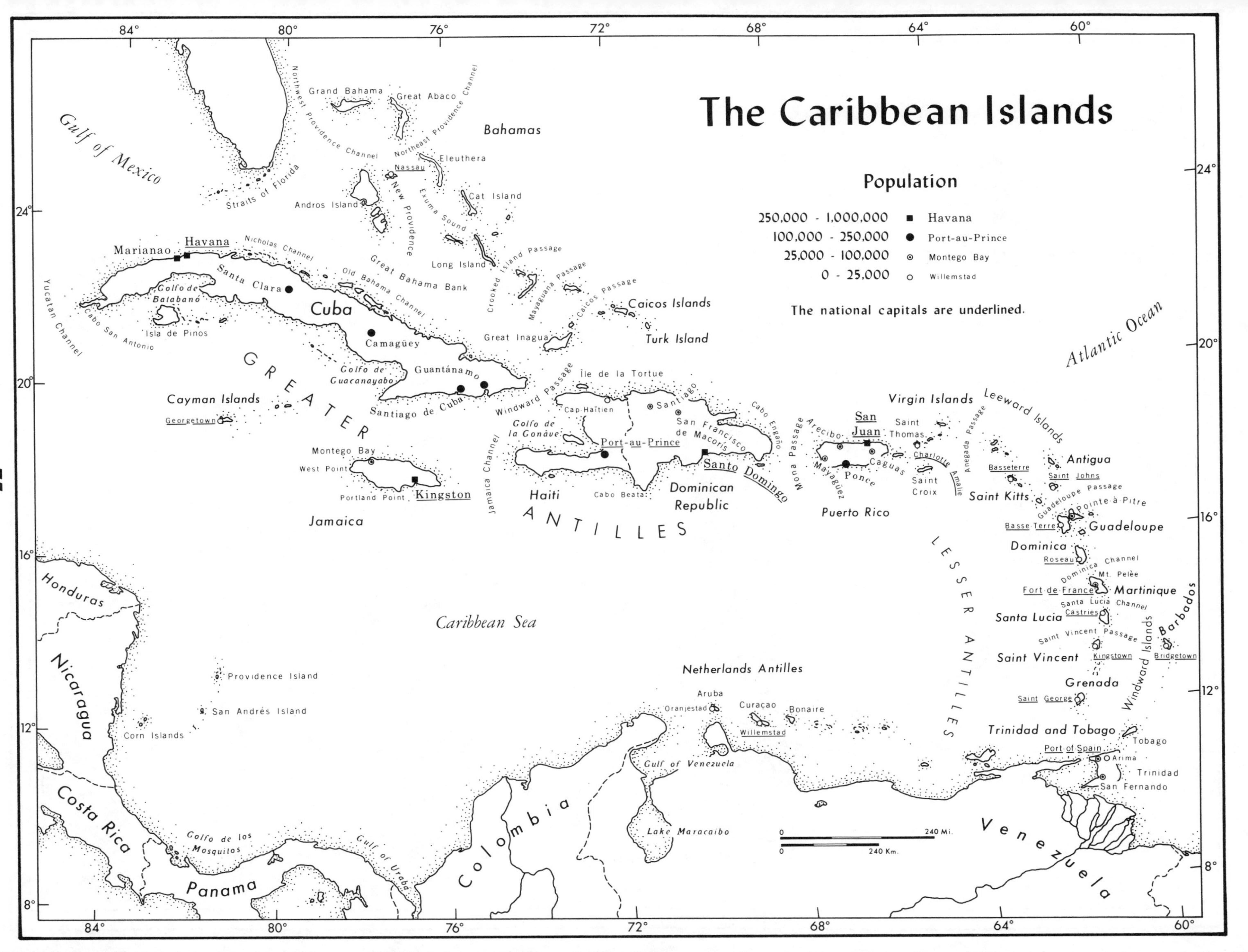

The Caribbean Islands
Population
250,000 - 1,000,000 Havana
100,000 - 250,000 Port-au-Prince
25,000 - 100,000 Montego Bay
0 - 25,000 Willemstad
The national capitals are underlined.
Gulf of Mexico
Atlantic Ocean
Caribbean Sea
Straits of Florida
Northwest Providence Channel
Northeast Providence Channel
Grand Bahama
Great Abaco
Bahamas
Eleuthera
Nassau
New Providence
Andros Island
Exuma Sound
Cat Island
Long Island
Crooked Island Passage
Mayaguana Passage
Caicos Passage
Caicos Islands
Turk Island
Great Inagua
Great Bahama Bank
Old Bahama Channel
Nicholas Channel
Marianao
Havana
Santa Clara
Cuba
Camagüey
Golfo de Batabanó
Isla de Pinos
Cabo San Antonio
Yucatan Channel
Golfo de Guacanayabo
Guantánamo
Santiago de Cuba
Cayman Islands
Georgetown
GREATER ANTILLES
Windward Passage
Île de la Tortue
Cap Haïtien
Santiago
San Francisco de Macoris
Cabo Engaño
Golfo de la Gonâve
Port-au-Prince
Haiti
Cabo Beata
Dominican Republic
Santo Domingo
Jamaica Channel
Montego Bay
West Point
Portland Point
Kingston
Jamaica
Mona Passage
Arecibo
San Juan
Mayagüez
Ponce
Caguas
Puerto Rico
Virgin Islands
Saint Thomas
Charlotte Amalie
Saint Croix
Anegada Passage
Leeward Islands
Antigua
Saint Johns
Basseterre
Saint Kitts
Guadeloupe Passage
Pointe-à-Pitre
Basse Terre
Guadeloupe
Dominica
Roseau
Dominica Channel
Mt. Pelèe
Fort de France
Martinique
Santa Lucia Channel
Castries
Santa Lucia
Saint Vincent Passage
Saint Vincent
Kingstown
Barbados
Bridgetown
Windward Islands
Grenada
Saint George
LESSER ANTILLES
Trinidad and Tobago
Tobago
Port of Spain
Arima
Trinidad
San Fernando
Netherlands Antilles
Aruba
Oranjestad
Curaçao
Willemstad
Bonaire
Gulf of Venezuela
Lake Maracaibo
Venezuela
Colombia
Gulf of Urabá
Panama
Golfo de los Mosquitos
Costa Rica
Nicaragua
Honduras
Providence Island
San Andrés Island
Corn Islands
0 240 Mi.
0 240 Km.
84°
80°
76°
72°
68°
64°
60°
24°
20°
16°
12°
8°

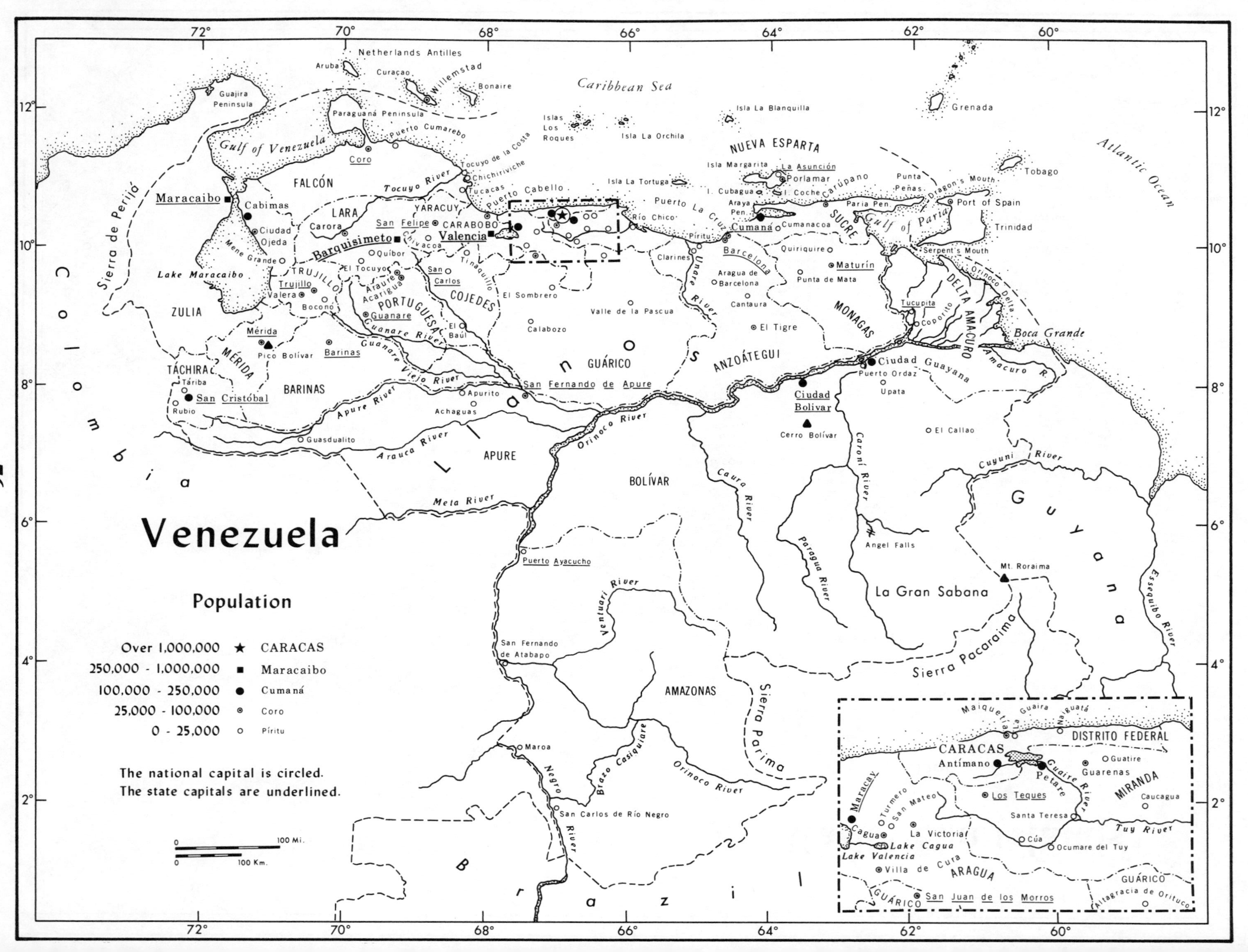

Venezuela
Population
Over 1,000,000 ★ CARACAS
250,000 - 1,000,000 ■ Maracaibo
100,000 - 250,000 ● Cumaná
25,000 - 100,000 ⊙ Coro
0 - 25,000 ○ Píritu
The national capital is circled.
The state capitals are underlined.
100 Mi.
100 Km.
Atlantic Ocean
Caribbean Sea
Colombia
Brazil
Guyana
Llanos
Tobago
Trinidad
Grenada
Port of Spain
Dragon's Mouth
Serpent's Mouth
Gulf of Paria
Boca Grande
Orinoco Delta
Amacuro R.
Essequibo River
Cuyuni River
Mt. Roraima
Sierra Pacaraima
La Gran Sabana
Angel Falls
Caroní River
Paragua River
Caura River
Sierra Parima
Orinoco River
Brazo Casiquiare
Ventuari River
Negro River
Meta River
Arauca River
Apure River
Guanare Viejo River
Guanare River
Unare River
Tocuyo River
Tuy River
Guaire River
Lake Valencia
Lake Cagua
Lake Maracaibo
Gulf of Venezuela
Sierra de Perijá
Guajira Peninsula
Paraguaná Peninsula
Netherlands Antilles
Aruba
Curaçao
Bonaire
Willemstad
Islas Los Roques
Isla La Orchila
Isla La Tortuga
Isla La Blanquilla
Isla Margarita
I. Cubagua
I. Coche
Tocuyo de la Costa
Chichiriviche
Tucacas
Puerto Cabello
Puerto Cumarebo
Coro
FALCÓN
ZULIA
Maracaibo
Cabimas
Ciudad Ojeda
Mene Grande
LARA
Carora
Barquisimeto
Quíbor
El Tocuyo
YARACUY
San Felipe
Chivacoa
CARABOBO
Valencia
COJEDES
San Carlos
Tinaquillo
PORTUGUESA
Acarigua
Araure
Guanare
TRUJILLO
Trujillo
Valera
Boconó
MÉRIDA
Mérida
Pico Bolívar
TÁCHIRA
San Cristóbal
Táriba
Rubio
BARINAS
Barinas
Guasdualito
APURE
San Fernando de Apure
Apurito
Achaguas
El Baúl
GUÁRICO
Calabozo
El Sombrero
Valle de la Pascua
ANZOÁTEGUI
Barcelona
Aragua de Barcelona
Cantaura
El Tigre
Clarines
Píritu
Puerto La Cruz
Río Chico
NUEVA ESPARTA
La Asunción
Porlamar
SUCRE
Cumaná
Araya Pen.
Cumanacoa
Carúpano
Paria Pen.
Punta Peñas
MONAGAS
Maturín
Quiriquire
Punta de Mata
DELTA AMACURO
Tucupita
Coporito
Ciudad Guayana
Puerto Ordaz
Upata
El Callao
Ciudad Bolívar
Cerro Bolívar
BOLÍVAR
AMAZONAS
Puerto Ayacucho
San Fernando de Atabapo
Maroa
San Carlos de Río Negro
DISTRITO FEDERAL
Maiquetía
La Guaira
Naiguatá
CARACAS
Antímano
Petare
Guatire
Guarenas
Caucagua
MIRANDA
Los Teques
Santa Teresa
Cúa
Ocumare del Tuy
Altagracia de Orituco
GUÁRICO
ARAGUA
Maracay
Turmero
San Mateo
La Victoria
Cagua
Villa de Cura
San Juan de los Morros
12°
10°
8°
6°
4°
2°
60°
62°
64°
66°
68°
70°
72°

Colombia
Caribbean Sea
Pacific Ocean
Punta Gallinas
Guajira Peninsula
Punta Espada
Gulf of Venezuela
Ríohacha
Santa Marta
Barranquilla
ATLÁNTICO
Sabanalarga
Ciénaga
Cartagena
LA GUAJIRA
MAGDALENA
Valledupar
Sierra de Perijá
Plato
Augustín Codazzi
Gulf of Morrosquillo
SUCRE
Sincelejo
Magangué
EL CESAR
Gulf of Urabá
Panama
Gulf of Panamá
Sahagún
Montería
CÓRDOBA
BOLÍVAR
NORTE DE SANTANDER
Ocaña
Cúcuta
Pamplona
Cauca River
Magdalena River
Barrancabermeja
Bucaramanga
Arauca River
Arauca
ARAUCA
Punta Marzo
Gulf of Cupica
Atrato River
ANTIOQUIA
Yarumal
Puerto Berrío
SANTANDER
San Gil
Socorro
Bello
Itagüí
Medellín
Envigado
Punta Solano
Quibdó
Gulf of Tibugá
Chiquinquirá
Duitama
Sogamoso
Casanare River
Puerto Carreno
Orinoco River
Cabo Corrientes
CHOCÓ
RISARALDA
Sta. Rosa de Cabal
La Dorada
CALDA
Manizales
CUNDINAMARCA
Facatativá
Zipaquirá
Tunja
BOYACÁ
VICHADA
Puerto Nariño
Pereira
Cartago
Armenia
QUINDÍO
Ibagué
BOGOTÁ
Meta River
San José de Ocuné
Vichada River
Punta Charambirá
Girardot
Espinal
Fusagasugá
Villavicencio
Puerto López
Buenaventura
Tuluá
Buga
VALLE DEL CAUCA
TOLIMA
Acacías
Guamal
San Martín
Gulf of Tortugas
Palmira
Cali
META
Guaviare River
Isla Gorgona
Punta Guascama
Puerto Tejada
Santander
CAUCA
HUILA
Neivo
Chafurray
Inirida River
Victorino
Santa Rosa
San José de Guaviare
GUAINÍA
Popayán
Guainía River
Anćon de Sardinas Bay
NARIÑO
Garzón
San Vicente de Caguán
Puerto Rico
Calamar
Miraflores
San Felipe
Tumaco
Túquerres
Pitalito
Florencia
VAUPÉS
Içana River
Pasto
Belén
Vaupés River
Mocoa
Puerto Umbría
Tres Esquinas
Apaporis River
Mitú
Ipiales
Mira River
Puerto Asís
PUTUMAYO
CAQUETÁ
Lérida
Uaupés River
Negro River
Population
Over 1,000,000 ★ BOGOTÁ
250,000 - 1,000,000 ■ Medellín
100,000 - 250,000 ● Cartagena
25,000 - 100,000 ◎ Popayán
0 - 25,000 ○ Leticia
La Chorrera
Caquetá River
Putumayo River
AMAZONAS
Arica
Santa Clara
Napo River
The national capital is circled.
The department capitals are underlined
Amazon River
Tarapacá
0 150 Mi.
0 150 Km.
Leticia
Yavarí River
Ecuador
Peru
Brazil
Venezuela
78° 76° 74° 72° 70° 68° 66°
12° 10° 8° 6° 4° 2° 0° 2° 4°

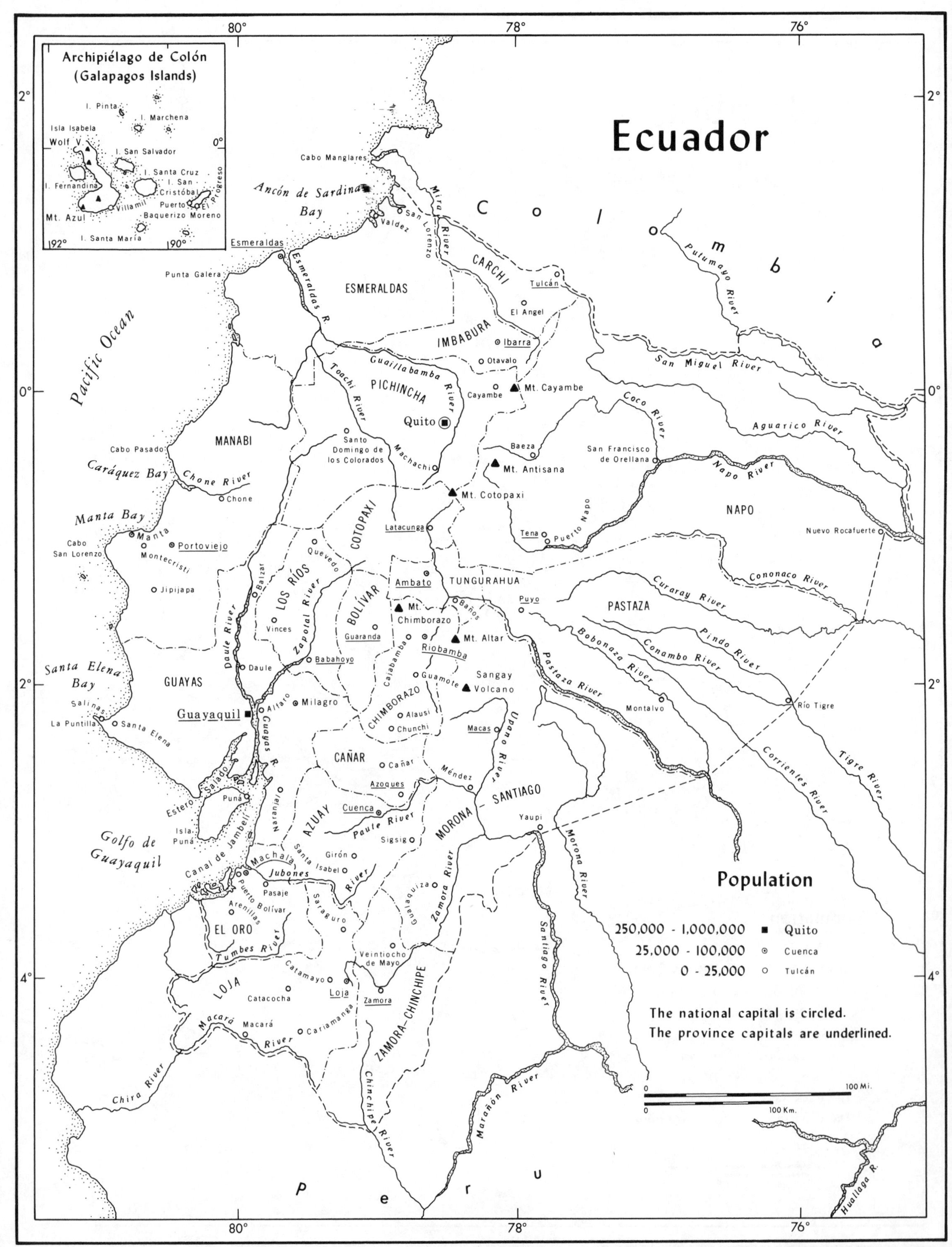
Ecuador
Archipiélago de Colón
(Galapagos Islands)
I. Pinta
I. Marchena
Isla Isabela
Wolf V.
I. San Salvador
I. Santa Cruz
I. Fernandina
I. San Cristóbal
Puerto Baquerizo Moreno
El Progreso
Villamil
Mt. Azul
I. Santa María
Colombia
Pacific Ocean
Peru
ESMERALDAS
CARCHI
IMBABURA
PICHINCHA
MANABI
COTOPAXI
LOS RÍOS
BOLÍVAR
TUNGURAHUA
GUAYAS
CHIMBORAZO
CAÑAR
AZUAY
EL ORO
LOJA
MORONA
SANTIAGO
ZAMORA-CHINCHIPE
NAPO
PASTAZA
Quito
Guayaquil
Cuenca
Tulcán
Esmeraldas
Ibarra
Portoviejo
Latacunga
Ambato
Riobamba
Guaranda
Babahoyo
Azogues
Machala
Loja
Zamora
Macas
Tena
Puyo
Population
250,000 - 1,000,000 Quito
25,000 - 100,000 Cuenca
0 - 25,000 Tulcán
The national capital is circled.
The province capitals are underlined.
100 Mi.
100 Km.

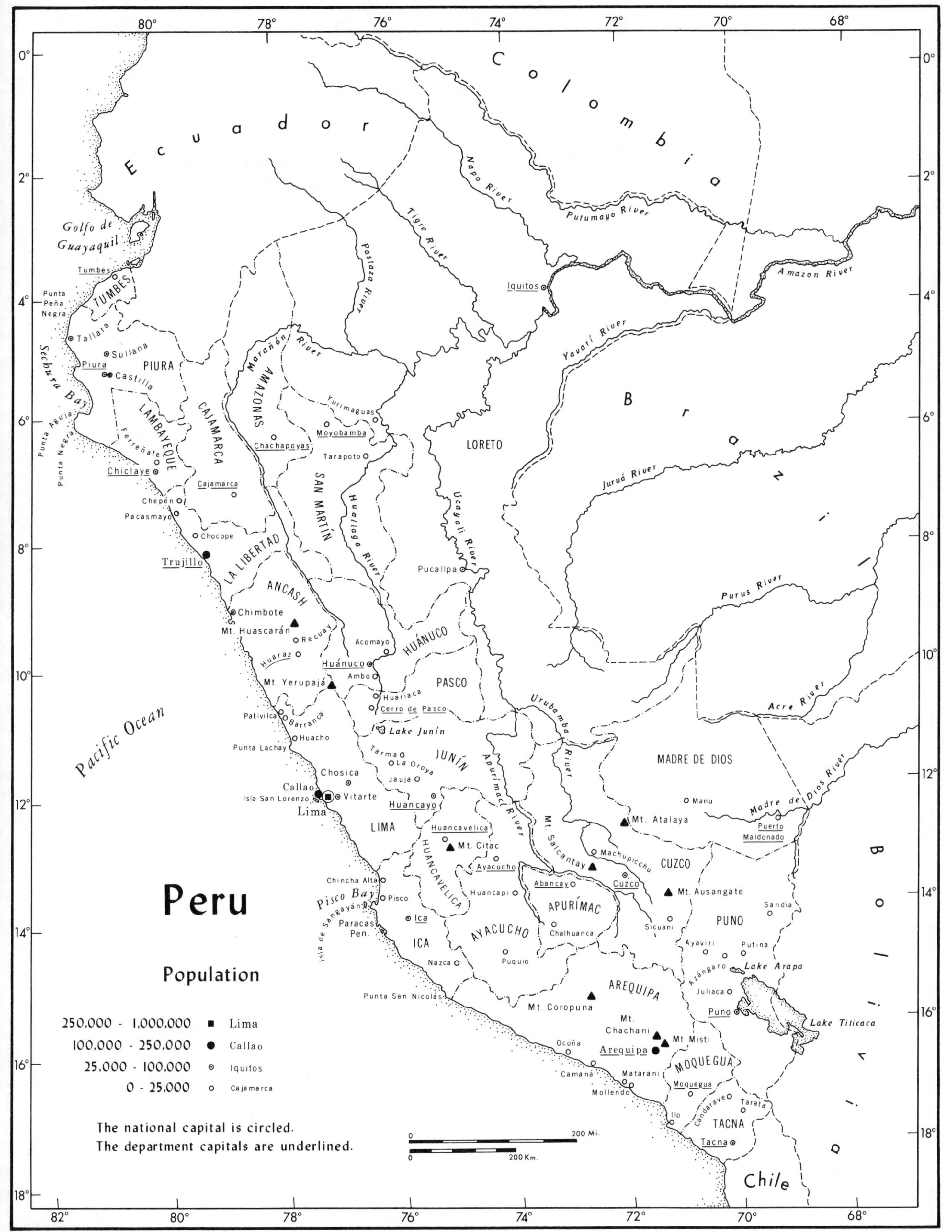
Peru
Population
250,000 - 1,000,000 ■ Lima
100,000 - 250,000 ● Callao
25,000 - 100,000 ⊙ Iquitos
0 - 25,000 ○ Cajamarca
The national capital is circled.
The department capitals are underlined.
Ecuador
Colombia
Brazil
Bolivia
Chile
Pacific Ocean
Golfo de Guayaquil
Sechura Bay
Pisco Bay
TUMBES
PIURA
LAMBAYEQUE
CAJAMARCA
AMAZONAS
SAN MARTÍN
LORETO
LA LIBERTAD
ANCASH
HUÁNUCO
PASCO
JUNÍN
LIMA
HUANCAVELICA
ICA
AYACUCHO
APURÍMAC
CUZCO
MADRE DE DIOS
PUNO
AREQUIPA
MOQUEGUA
TACNA
Napo River
Putumayo River
Tigre River
Pastaza River
Amazon River
Marañón River
Yavarí River
Juruá River
Ucayali River
Huallaga River
Purus River
Acre River
Urubamba River
Apurímac River
Madre de Dios River
Lake Junín
Lake Arapa
Lake Titicaca
Tumbes
Punta Peña Negra
Tallara
Sullana
Piura
Castilla
Punta Aguja
Punta Negra
Ferreñafe
Chiclaye
Cajamarca
Chepén
Pacasmayo
Chocope
Trujillo
Chimbote
Mt. Huascarán
Recuay
Huaraz
Mt. Yerupajá
Pativilca
Barranca
Huacho
Punta Lachay
Chosica
Callao
Isla San Lorenzo
Lima
Vitarte
Yurimaguas
Moyobamba
Chachapoyas
Tarapoto
Iquitos
Pucallpa
Acomayo
Huánuco
Ambo
Huariaca
Cerro de Pasco
Tarma
La Oroya
Jauja
Huancayo
Huancavelica
Mt. Citac
Ayacucho
Huancapi
Abancay
Chalhuanca
Puquio
Chincha Alta
Pisco
Isla de Sangayán
Paracas Pen.
Ica
Nazca
Punta San Nicolás
Mt. Atalaya
Manu
Puerto Maldonado
Mt. Salcantay
Machupicchu
Cuzco
Mt. Ausangate
Sicuani
Sandia
Ayaviri
Putina
Azángaro
Juliaca
Puno
Mt. Coropuna
Mt. Chachani
Mt. Misti
Arequipa
Ocoña
Camaná
Matarani
Mollendo
Moquegua
Ilo
Candarave
Tarata
Tacna
0 200 Mi.
0 200 Km.
80° 78° 76° 74° 72° 70° 68°
82° 80° 78° 76° 74° 72° 70° 68°
0° 2° 4° 6° 8° 10° 12° 14° 16° 18°

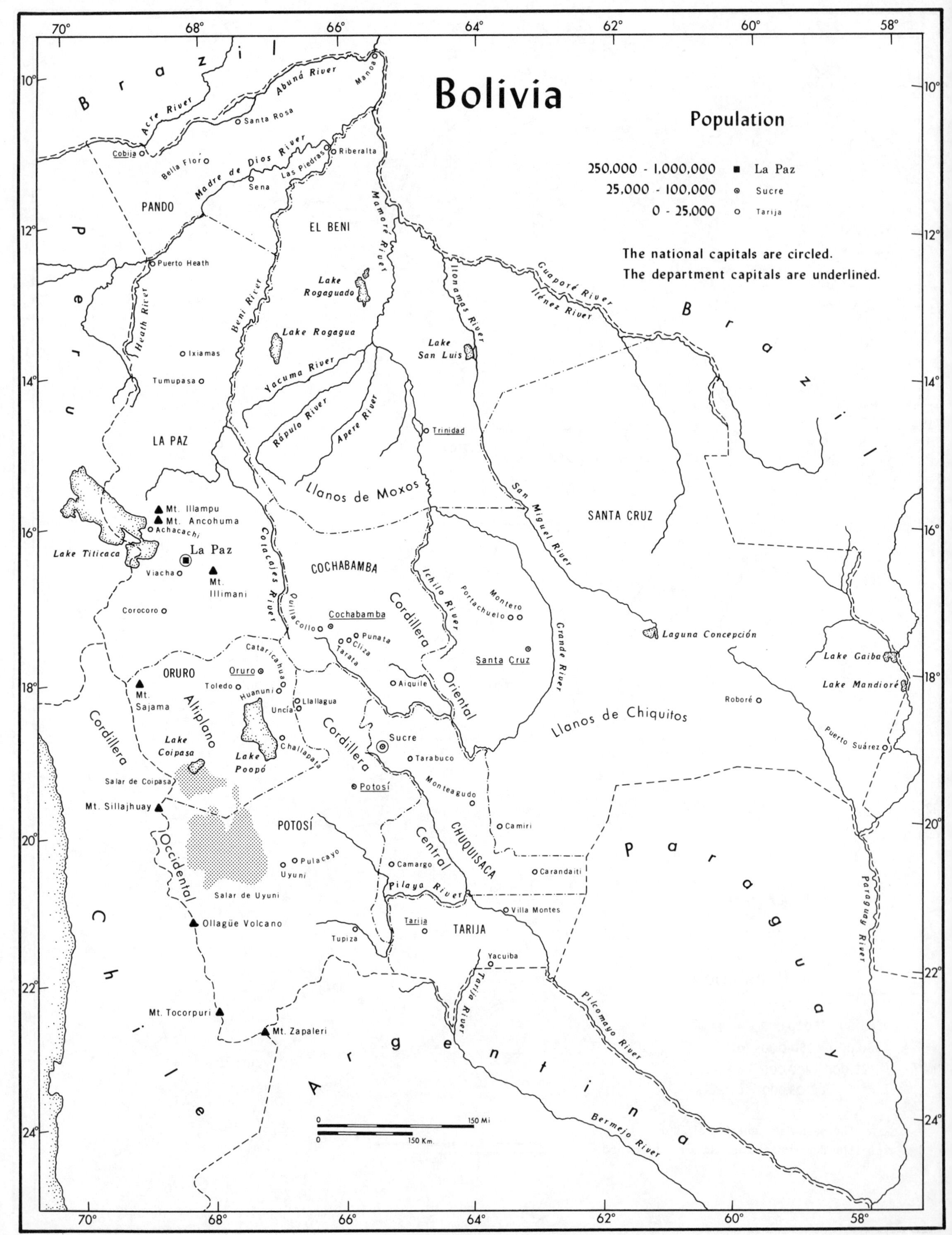
Bolivia
Population
250,000 - 1,000,000 ■ La Paz
25,000 - 100,000 ⊙ Sucre
0 - 25,000 ○ Tarija
The national capitals are circled.
The department capitals are underlined.
Brazil
Peru
Chile
Argentina
Paraguay
PANDO
EL BENI
LA PAZ
COCHABAMBA
SANTA CRUZ
ORURO
POTOSÍ
CHUQUISACA
TARIJA
Acre River
Abuná River
Madre de Dios River
Mamoré River
Beni River
Heath River
Yacuma River
Rápulo River
Apere River
Itonamas River
Guaporé River
Iténez River
San Miguel River
Ichilo River
Grande River
Colacajes River
Pilaya River
Tarija River
Pilcomayo River
Bermejo River
Paraguay River
Lake Rogaguado
Lake Rogagua
Lake San Luis
Lake Titicaca
Lake Coipasa
Lake Poopó
Laguna Concepción
Lake Gaiba
Lake Mandioré
Llanos de Moxos
Llanos de Chiquitos
Cordillera Oriental
Cordillera Central
Cordillera Occidental
Altiplano
Salar de Coipasa
Salar de Uyuni
Mt. Illampu
Mt. Ancohuma
Mt. Illimani
Mt. Sajama
Mt. Sillajhuay
Ollagüe Volcano
Mt. Tocorpuri
Mt. Zapaleri
Manoa
Santa Rosa
Cobija
Bella Flor
Riberalta
Las Piedras
Sena
Puerto Heath
Ixiamas
Tumupasa
Trinidad
Achacachi
La Paz
Viacha
Corocoro
Quillacollo
Cochabamba
Punata
Cliza
Tarata
Aiquile
Portachuelo
Montero
Santa Cruz
Catarichahua
Oruro
Toledo
Huanuni
Llallagua
Uncía
Challapata
Sucre
Tarabuco
Potosí
Monteagudo
Camiri
Pulacayo
Uyuni
Camargo
Carandaiti
Villa Montes
Tarija
Tupiza
Yacuiba
Roboré
Puerto Suárez
0 150 Mi
0 150 Km.
70° 68° 66° 64° 62° 60° 58°
10° 12° 14° 16° 18° 20° 22° 24°

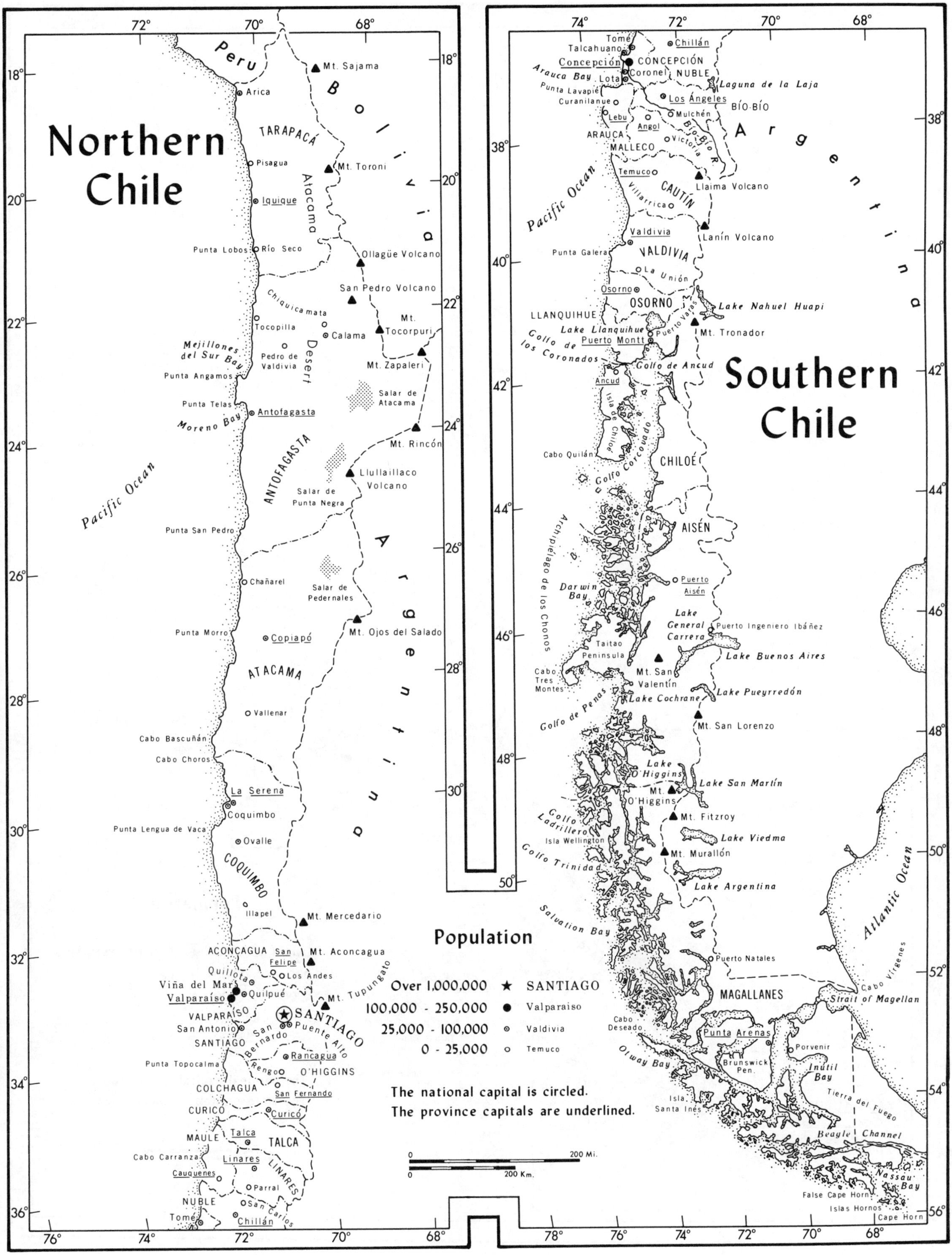
Northern Chile
Southern Chile
Population
Over 1,000,000 ★ SANTIAGO
100,000 - 250,000 ● Valparaiso
25,000 - 100,000 ◎ Valdivia
0 - 25,000 ○ Temuco
The national capital is circled.
The province capitals are underlined.
0 200 Mi.
0 200 Km.
Peru
Bolivia
Argentina
Pacific Ocean
Atlantic Ocean
TARAPACÁ
ANTOFAGASTA
ATACAMA
COQUIMBO
ACONCAGUA
VALPARAÍSO
SANTIAGO
O'HIGGINS
COLCHAGUA
CURICÓ
MAULE
TALCA
LINARES
ÑUBLE
CONCEPCIÓN
ARAUCO
BÍO-BÍO
MALLECO
CAUTÍN
VALDIVIA
OSORNO
LLANQUIHUE
CHILOÉ
AISÉN
MAGALLANES
Arica
Pisagua
Iquique
Punta Lobos
Río Seco
Tocopilla
Chuquicamata
Calama
Pedro de Valdivia
Mejillones del Sur Bay
Punta Angamos
Punta Telas
Antofagasta
Moreno Bay
Atacama Desert
Salar de Atacama
Salar de Punta Negra
Salar de Pedernales
Punta San Pedro
Chañarel
Punta Morro
Copiapó
Vallenar
Cabo Bascuñán
Cabo Choros
La Serena
Coquimbo
Punta Lengua de Vaca
Ovalle
Illapel
San Felipe
Los Andes
Quillota
Viña del Mar
Valparaíso
Quilpué
San Antonio
San Bernardo
Puente Alto
Punta Topocalma
Rancagua
Rengo
San Fernando
Curicó
Talca
Cabo Carranza
Linares
Cauquenes
Parral
San Carlos
Chillán
Tomé
Mt. Sajama
Mt. Toroni
Ollagüe Volcano
San Pedro Volcano
Mt. Tocorpuri
Mt. Zapaleri
Mt. Rincón
Llullaillaco Volcano
Mt. Ojos del Salado
Mt. Mercedario
Mt. Aconcagua
Mt. Tupungato
Talcahuano
Concepción
Arauca Bay
Lota
Coronel
Punta Lavapié
Curanilanue
Lebu
Angol
Los Ángeles
Mulchén
Laguna de la Laja
Bío-Bío R.
Victoria
Temuco
Llaima Volcano
Villarrica
Lanín Volcano
Valdivia
Punta Galera
La Unión
Osorno
Lake Nahuel Huapi
Puerto Varas
Lake Llanquihue
Puerto Montt
Mt. Tronador
Golfo de los Coronados
Golfo de Ancud
Ancud
Isla de Chiloé
Golfo Corcovado
Cabo Quilán
Archipiélago de los Chonos
Puerto Aisén
Darwin Bay
Lake General Carrera
Puerto Ingeniero Ibáñez
Lake Buenos Aires
Taitao Peninsula
Cabo Tres Montes
Mt. San Valentín
Golfo de Penas
Lake Cochrane
Lake Pueyrredón
Mt. San Lorenzo
Lake O'Higgins
Mt. O'Higgins
Lake San Martín
Golfo Ladrillero
Mt. Fitzroy
Isla Wellington
Lake Viedma
Golfo Trinidad
Mt. Murallón
Lake Argentina
Salvation Bay
Puerto Natales
Cabo Vírgenes
Strait of Magellan
Punta Arenas
Cabo Deseado
Porvenir
Otway Bay
Brunswick Pen.
Inútil Bay
Isla Santa Inés
Tierra del Fuego
Beagle Channel
Nassau Bay
False Cape Horn
Islas Hornos
Cape Horn

Brazil
Atlantic Ocean
Population
Over 1,000,000 ★ RIO DE JANEIRO
250,000 - 1,000,000 ■ Belo Horizonte
100,000 - 250,000 ● Brasília
25,000 - 100,000 ◎ Ilhéus
0 - 25,000 ○ Pôrto Velho
The national capital is circled.
The state capitals are underlined.
Colombia
Venezuela
Guyana
Surinam
French Guiana
Peru
Bolivia
Paraguay
Argentina
Uruguay
RORAIMA
AMAPÁ
PARÁ
AMAZONAS
ACRE
RONDÔNIA
MATO GROSSO
GOIÁS
MARANHÃO
PIAUÍ
CEARÁ
RIO GRANDE DO NORTE
PARAÍBA
PERNAMBUCO
ALAGOAS
SERGIPE
BAHIA
MINAS GERAIS
ESPÍRITO SANTO
RIO DE JANEIRO
SÃO PAULO
PARANÁ
SANTA CATARINA
RIO GRANDE DO SUL
DISTRITO FEDERAL
Manaus
Belém
São Luís
Fortaleza
Teresina
Natal
João Pessoa
Recife
Maceió
Aracaju
Salvador
Brasília
Goiânia
Cuiabá
Pôrto Velho
Rio Branco
Boa Vista
Macapá
Vitória
Curitiba
Florianópolis
Pôrto Alegre
Belo Horizonte
SÃO PAULO
RIO DE JANEIRO
Amazon River
Negro River
Orinoco River
Caquetá River
Putumayo River
Javarí River
Juruá River
Purus River
Madeira River
Tapajós River
Xingu River
Tocantins River
Araguaia River
São Francisco River
Paraná River
Paraguay River
Uruguay River
Grande River
Furnas Dam
Represa de Furnas
Guanabara Bay
Ilha Grande Bay
Marajó Bay
São Marcos Bay
Lagoa dos Patos
Lagoa Mirim
Cabo Orange
Cabo Frio
Cabo de São Tomé
450 Mi.
450 Km.
70°
60°
50°
40°
0°
10°
20°
30°

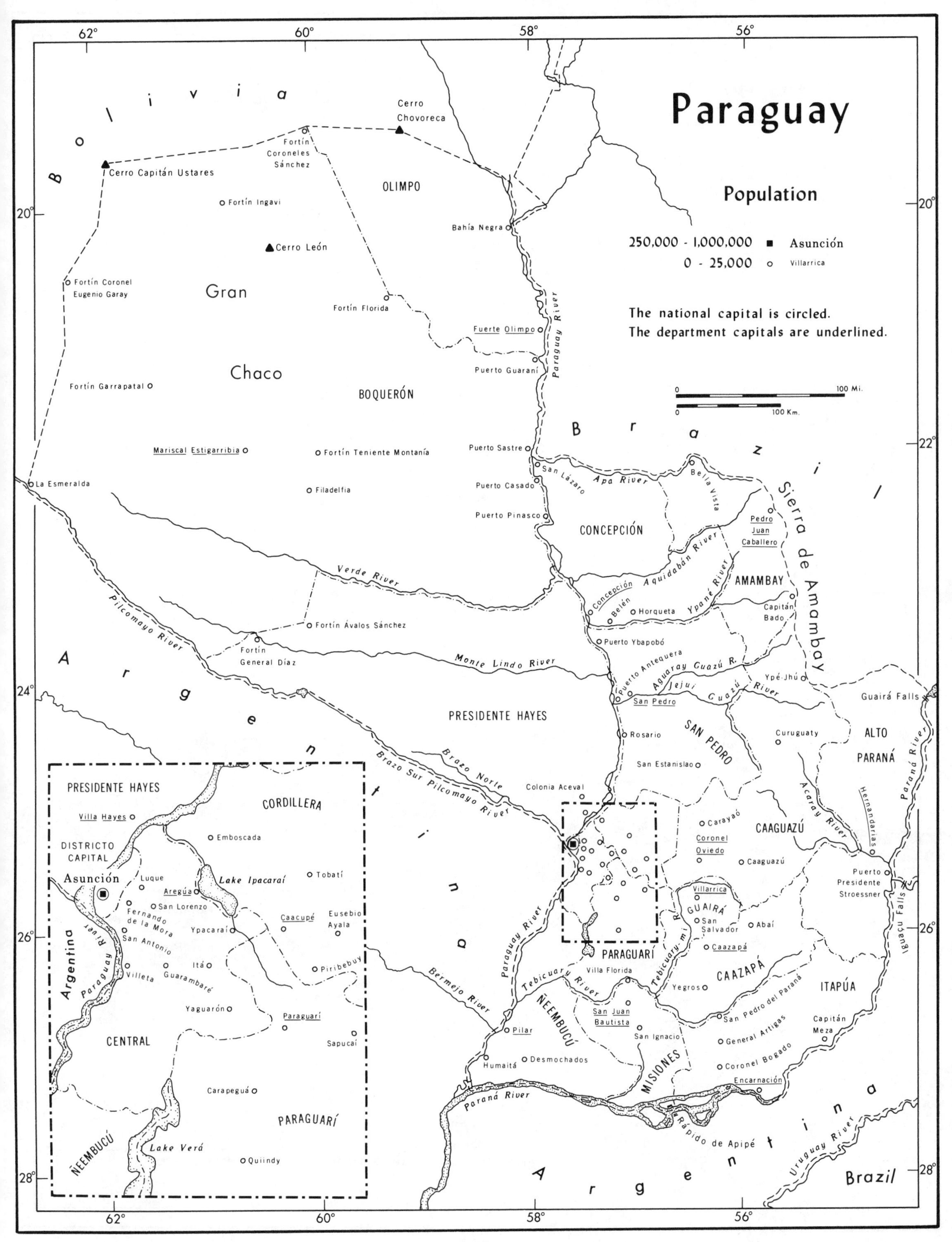

Paraguay
Population
250,000 - 1,000,000 ■ Asunción
0 - 25,000 ○ Villarrica
The national capital is circled.
The department capitals are underlined.
100 Mi.
100 Km.
Bolivia
Brazil
Argentina
Gran Chaco
OLIMPO
BOQUERÓN
PRESIDENTE HAYES
CONCEPCIÓN
AMAMBAY
SAN PEDRO
ALTO PARANÁ
CAAGUAZÚ
GUAIRÁ
CAAZAPÁ
ITAPÚA
PARAGUARÍ
ÑEEMBUCÚ
MISIONES
CORDILLERA
DISTRICTO CAPITAL
CENTRAL
Cerro Chovoreca
Cerro Capitán Ustares
Fortín Coroneles Sánchez
Fortín Ingavi
Cerro León
Bahía Negra
Fortín Coronel Eugenio Garay
Fortín Florida
Fuerte Olimpo
Puerto Guaraní
Fortín Garrapatal
Mariscal Estigarribia
Fortín Teniente Montanía
Puerto Sastre
La Esmeralda
Filadelfia
San Lázaro
Puerto Casado
Puerto Pinasco
Bella Vista
Pedro Juan Caballero
Sierra de Amambay
Apa River
Aquidabán River
Ypané River
Verde River
Pilcomayo River
Concepción
Belén
Horqueta
Capitán Bado
Fortín Ávalos Sánchez
Fortín General Díaz
Monte Lindo River
Puerto Ybapobó
Puerto Antequera
Aguaray Guazú R.
Jejuí Guazú River
Ypé-Jhú
Guairá Falls
San Pedro
Rosario
Curuguaty
San Estanislao
Brazo Norte
Brazo Sur Pilcomayo River
Colonia Aceval
Carayaó
Coronel Oviedo
Caaguazú
Acaray River
Hernandarias
Paraná River
Puerto Presidente Stroessner
Iguaçu Falls
Villarrica
San Salvador
Abaí
Caazapá
Tebicuary-mí R.
Paraguay River
Bermejo River
Tebicuary River
Villa Florida
Yegros
San Pedro del Paraná
Pilar
San Juan Bautista
San Ignacio
General Artigas
Capitán Meza
Humaitá
Desmochados
Coronel Bogado
Encarnación
Rápido de Apipé
Uruguay River
Villa Hayes
Emboscada
Asunción
Luque
Areguá
Lake Ipacaraí
Tobatí
Fernando de la Mora
San Lorenzo
San Antonio
Ypacaraí
Caacupé
Eusebio Ayala
Villeta
Itá
Guarambaré
Piribebuy
Yaguarón
Paraguarí
Sapucaí
Carapeguá
Lake Verá
Quiindy

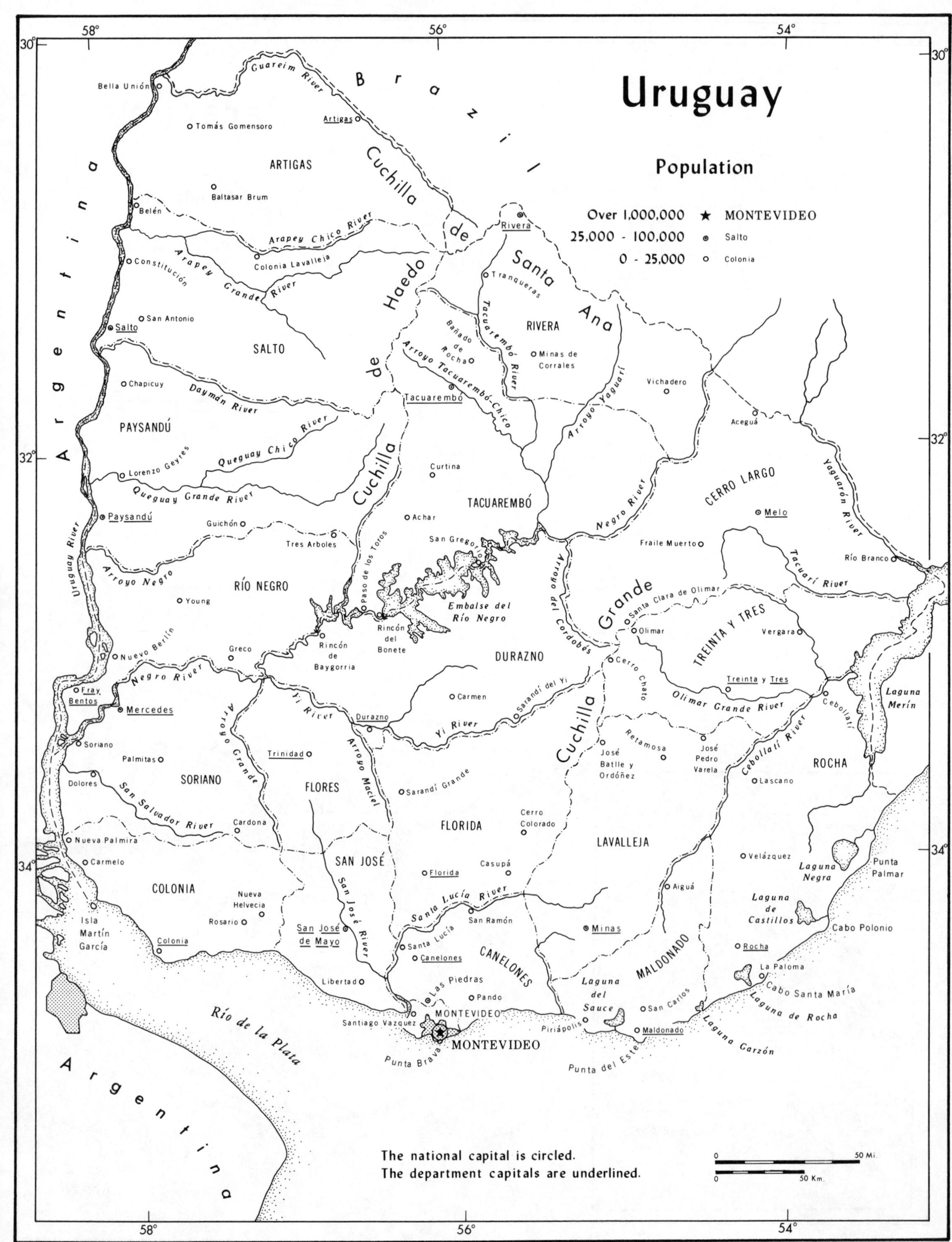

The national capital is circled.
The department capitals are underlined.

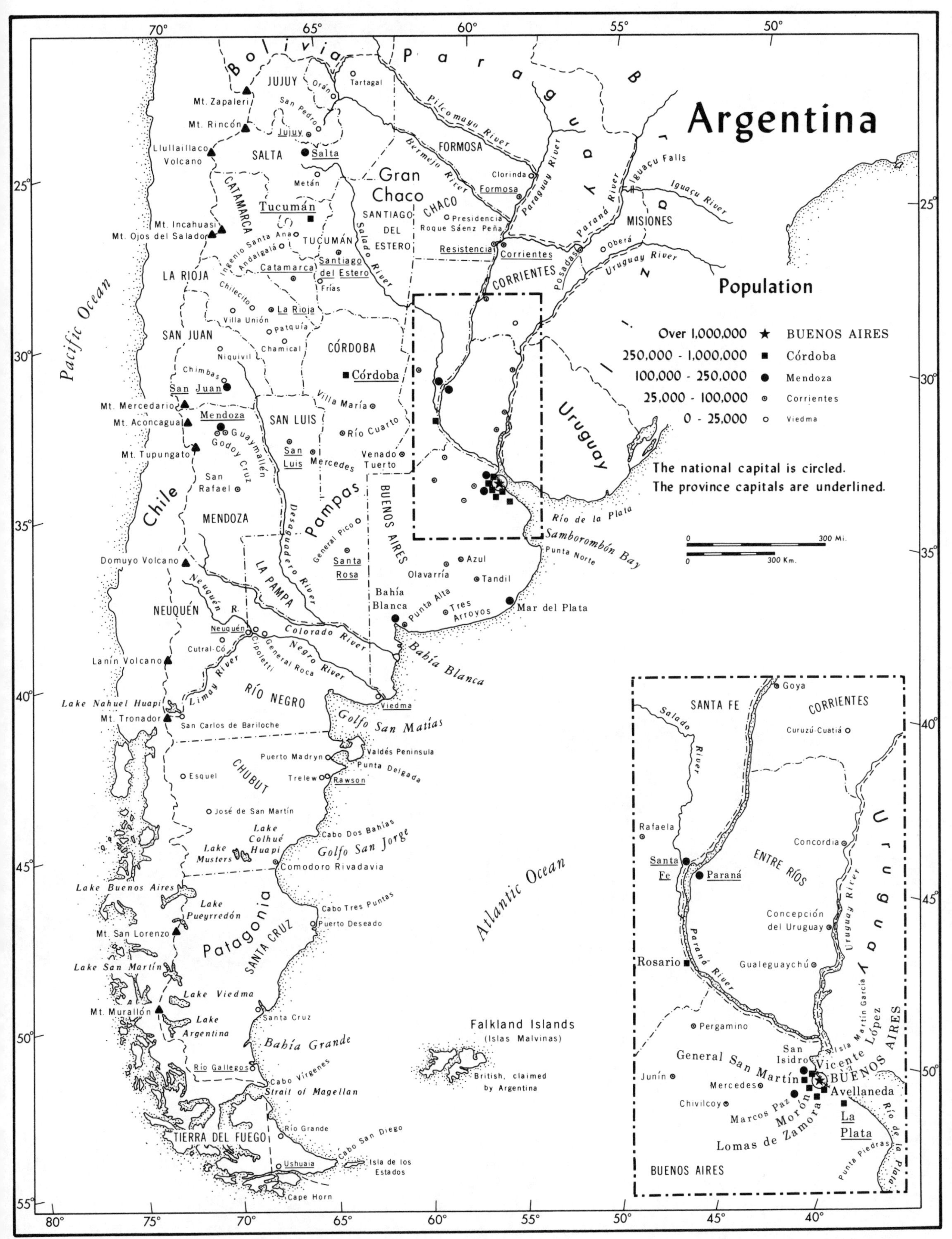
Argentina
Population
Over 1,000,000 ★ BUENOS AIRES
250,000 - 1,000,000 ■ Córdoba
100,000 - 250,000 ● Mendoza
25,000 - 100,000 ◎ Corrientes
0 - 25,000 ○ Viedma
The national capital is circled.
The province capitals are underlined.
300 Mi.
300 Km.
Bolivia
Paraguay
Brazil
Uruguay
Chile
Pacific Ocean
Atlantic Ocean
JUJUY
SALTA
FORMOSA
CATAMARCA
TUCUMÁN
SANTIAGO DEL ESTERO
CHACO
MISIONES
CORRIENTES
LA RIOJA
SAN JUAN
CÓRDOBA
SANTA FE
ENTRE RÍOS
SAN LUIS
MENDOZA
LA PAMPA
BUENOS AIRES
NEUQUÉN
RÍO NEGRO
CHUBUT
SANTA CRUZ
TIERRA DEL FUEGO
Gran Chaco
Pampas
Patagonia
Tucumán
Salta
Jujuy
Catamarca
Santiago del Estero
La Rioja
San Juan
Mendoza
Córdoba
San Luis
Santa Rosa
Formosa
Resistencia
Corrientes
Posadas
Neuquén
Viedma
Rawson
Río Gallegos
Ushuaia
Mt. Zapaleri
Mt. Rincón
Llullaillaco Volcano
Mt. Incahuasi
Mt. Ojos del Salado
Mt. Mercedario
Mt. Aconcagua
Mt. Tupungato
Domuyo Volcano
Lanín Volcano
Mt. Tronador
Mt. San Lorenzo
Mt. Murallón
Lake Nahuel Huapi
Lake Colhué Huapi
Lake Musters
Lake Buenos Aires
Lake Pueyrredón
Lake San Martín
Lake Viedma
Lake Argentina
Pilcomayo River
Bermejo River
Paraguay River
Paraná River
Iguaçu Falls
Iguaçu River
Uruguay River
Salado River
Desaguadero River
Colorado River
Negro River
Neuquén R.
Limay River
Río de la Plata
Samborombón Bay
Punta Norte
Bahía Blanca
Golfo San Matías
Valdés Peninsula
Punta Delgada
Golfo San Jorge
Cabo Dos Bahías
Cabo Tres Puntas
Bahía Grande
Cabo Vírgenes
Strait of Magellan
Cabo San Diego
Isla de los Estados
Cape Horn
Falkland Islands (Islas Malvinas)
British, claimed by Argentina
Orán
Tartagal
San Pedro
Metán
Clorinda
Presidencia Roque Sáenz Peña
Oberá
Andalgalá
Santa Ana
Ingenio Santa Ana
Frías
Chilecito
Villa Unión
Patquía
Chamical
Niquivil
Chimbas
Villa María
Río Cuarto
Venado Tuerto
Mercedes
Guaymallén
Godoy Cruz
San Rafael
General Pico
Azul
Olavarría
Tandil
Tres Arroyos
Punta Alta
Mar del Plata
Cutral-Có
Cipolletti
General Roca
San Carlos de Bariloche
Puerto Madryn
Trelew
Esquel
José de San Martín
Comodoro Rivadavia
Puerto Deseado
Santa Cruz
Río Grande
Goya
Curuzú-Cuatiá
Rafaela
Santa Fe
Paraná
Concordia
Concepción del Uruguay
Rosario
Gualeguaychú
Pergamino
Junín
Mercedes
Chivilcoy
San Isidro
General San Martín
Vicente López
Isla Martín García
BUENOS AIRES
Avellaneda
Morón
Marcos Paz
Lomas de Zamora
La Plata
Punta Piedras
70°
65°
60°
55°
50°
25°
30°
35°
40°
45°
75°
80°

Latin American Population

Life Expectancy at Birth, 1978

Country	Years
ARGENTINA	71
BOLIVIA	52
BRAZIL	62
CHILE	67
COLOMBIA	62
COSTA RICA	70
CUBA	72
DOMINICAN REP.	60
ECUADOR	60
EL SALVADOR	63
GUATEMALA	57
HAITI	51
HONDURAS	57
MEXICO	65
NICARAGUA	55
PANAMA	70
PARAGUAY	63
PERU	56
URUGUAY	71
VENEZUELA	66

Source: World Development Report, 1980.

Years

41 - 55

55 - 68

Over 68

Population Estimates, 1900

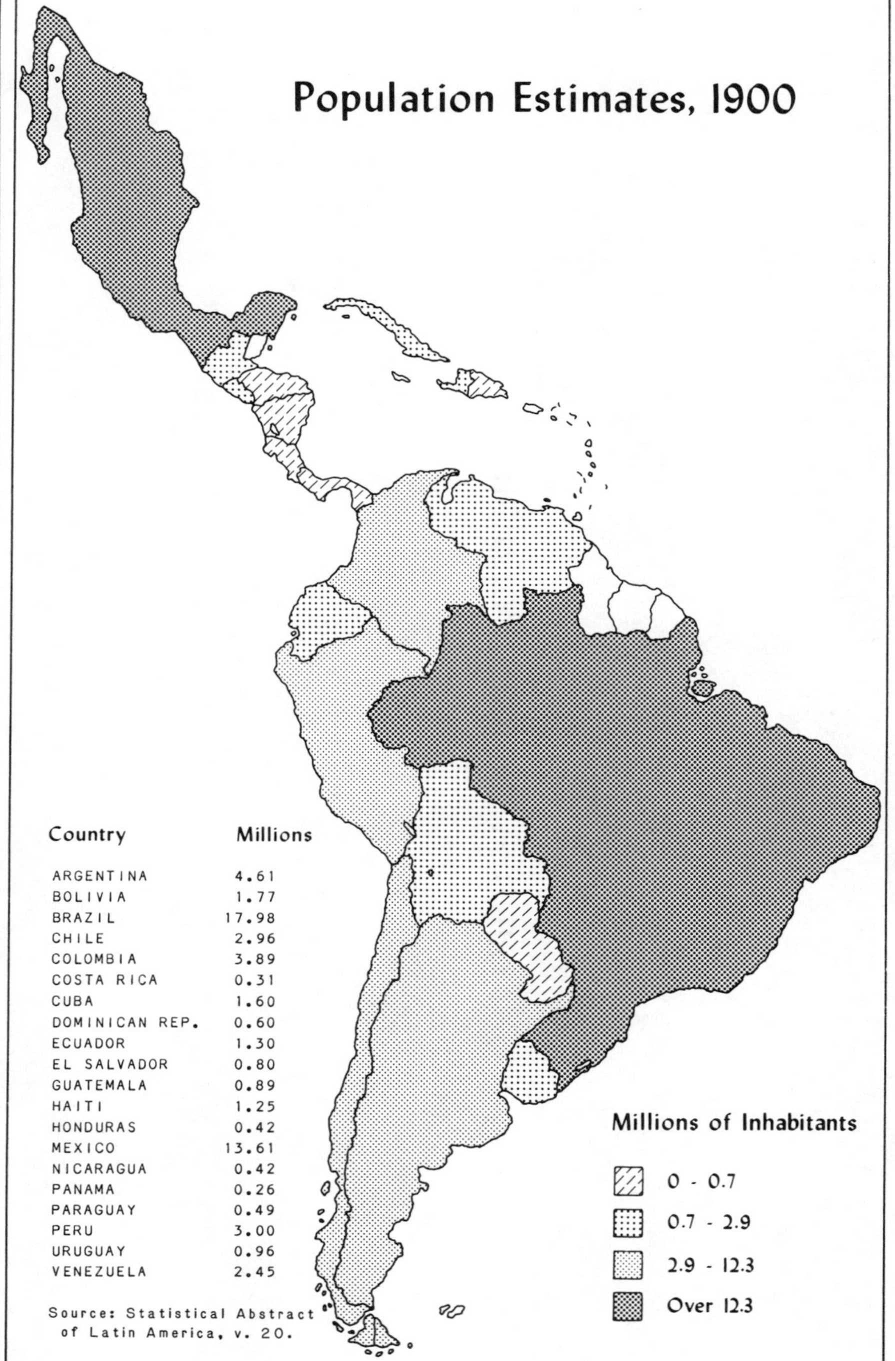

Country	Millions
ARGENTINA	4.61
BOLIVIA	1.77
BRAZIL	17.98
CHILE	2.96
COLOMBIA	3.89
COSTA RICA	0.31
CUBA	1.60
DOMINICAN REP.	0.60
ECUADOR	1.30
EL SALVADOR	0.80
GUATEMALA	0.89
HAITI	1.25
HONDURAS	0.42
MEXICO	13.61
NICARAGUA	0.42
PANAMA	0.26
PARAGUAY	0.49
PERU	3.00
URUGUAY	0.96
VENEZUELA	2.45

Source: Statistical Abstract of Latin America, v. 20.

Millions of Inhabitants

0 - 0.7

0.7 - 2.9

2.9 - 12.3

Over 12.3

Population Estimates, 1950

Country	Millions
ARGENTINA	17.07
BOLIVIA	3.01
BRAZIL	52.18
CHILE	6.07
COLOMBIA	11.33
COSTA RICA	0.80
CUBA	5.51
DOMINICAN REP.	2.24
ECUADOR	3.20
EL SALVADOR	1.86
GUATEMALA	2.81
HAITI	3.39
HONDURAS	1.43
MEXICO	25.78
NICARAGUA	1.06
PANAMA	0.80
PARAGUAY	1.40
PERU	7.97
URUGUAY	2.20
VENEZUELA	4.97

Source: Statistical Abstract of Latin America, v. 20.

Millions of Inhabitants

0 - 2
2 - 8
8 - 36
Over 36

Population Estimates, 1980

Country	Millions
ARGENTINA	27.10
BOLIVIA	6.20
BRAZIL	126.40
CHILE	11.50
COLOMBIA	30.20
COSTA RICA	2.30
CUBA	10.60
DOMINICAN REP.	6.10
ECUADOR	8.30
EL SALVADOR	4.80
GUATEMALA	7.10
HAITI	6.70
HONDURAS	3.60
MEXICO	70.00
NICARAGUA	2.70
PANAMA	1.90
PARAGUAY	3.10
PERU	17.70
URUGUAY	3.20
VENEZUELA	14.10

Source: Statistical Abstract of Latin America, v. 20.

Millions of Inhabitants

0 - 5
5 - 20
20 - 86
Over 86

Population Density, 1978

Country	Inhabitants/ Km^2
ARGENTINA	9.54
BOLIVIA	4.82
BRAZIL	14.04
CHILE	14.13
COLOMBIA	22.48
COSTA RICA	41.18
CUBA	84.35
DOMINICAN REP.	104.08
ECUADOR	27.46
EL SALVADOR	204.76
GUATEMALA	60.55
HAITI	171.43
HONDURAS	30.36
MEXICO	33.15
NICARAGUA	19.23
PANAMA	23.68
PARAGUAY	7.13
PERU	13.07
URUGUAY	16.48
VENEZUELA	15.35

Source: World Development Report, 1980.

Inhabitants/Km^2

- 0 - 8
- 8 - 33
- 33 - 140
- Over 140

Average Annual Growth of Urban Population in Towns over 20,000, 1960-1977

Country	Percent/Year
ARGENTINA	2.30
BOLIVIA	3.10
BRAZIL	4.80
CHILE	2.90
COLOMBIA	5.10
COSTA RICA	4.90
CUBA	1.30
DOMINICAN REP.	6.00
ECUADOR	4.60
EL SALVADOR	3.80
GUATEMALA	2.20
HAITI	3.90
HONDURAS	4.60
MEXICO	5.00
NICARAGUA	5.10
PANAMA	4.40
PARAGUAY	3.10
PERU	5.20
URUGUAY	0.80
VENEZUELA	4.10

Source: Statistical Abstract of Latin America, v. 20.

Percent/Year

- 0 - 1%
- 1 - 2%
- 2 - 3%
- 3 - 5%
- 5 - 6%
- Over 6%

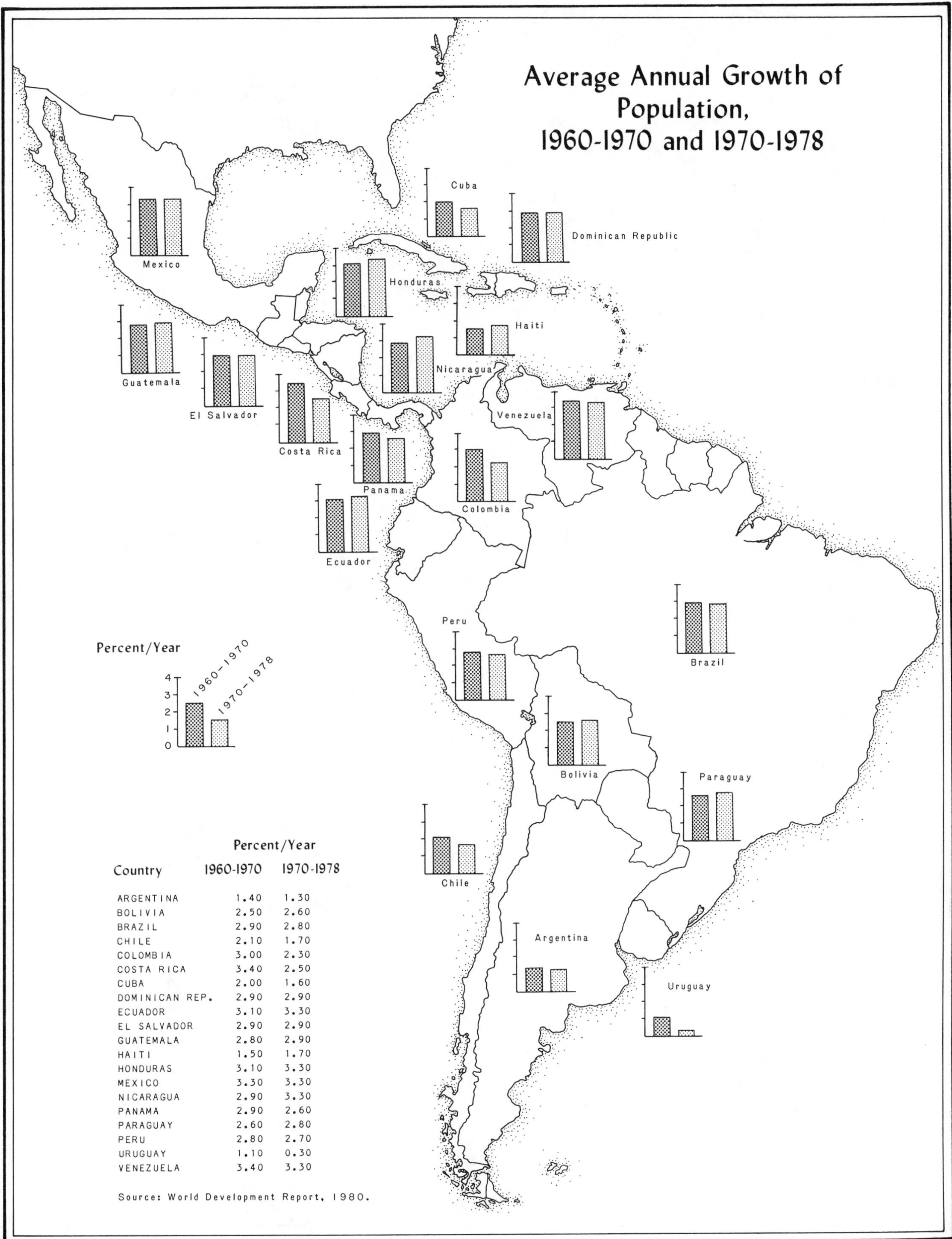

Country	Percent/Year 1960-1970	1970-1978
ARGENTINA	1.40	1.30
BOLIVIA	2.50	2.60
BRAZIL	2.90	2.80
CHILE	2.10	1.70
COLOMBIA	3.00	2.30
COSTA RICA	3.40	2.50
CUBA	2.00	1.60
DOMINICAN REP.	2.90	2.90
ECUADOR	3.10	3.30
EL SALVADOR	2.90	2.90
GUATEMALA	2.80	2.90
HAITI	1.50	1.70
HONDURAS	3.10	3.30
MEXICO	3.30	3.30
NICARAGUA	2.90	3.30
PANAMA	2.90	2.60
PARAGUAY	2.60	2.80
PERU	2.80	2.70
URUGUAY	1.10	0.30
VENEZUELA	3.40	3.30

Source: World Development Report, 1980.

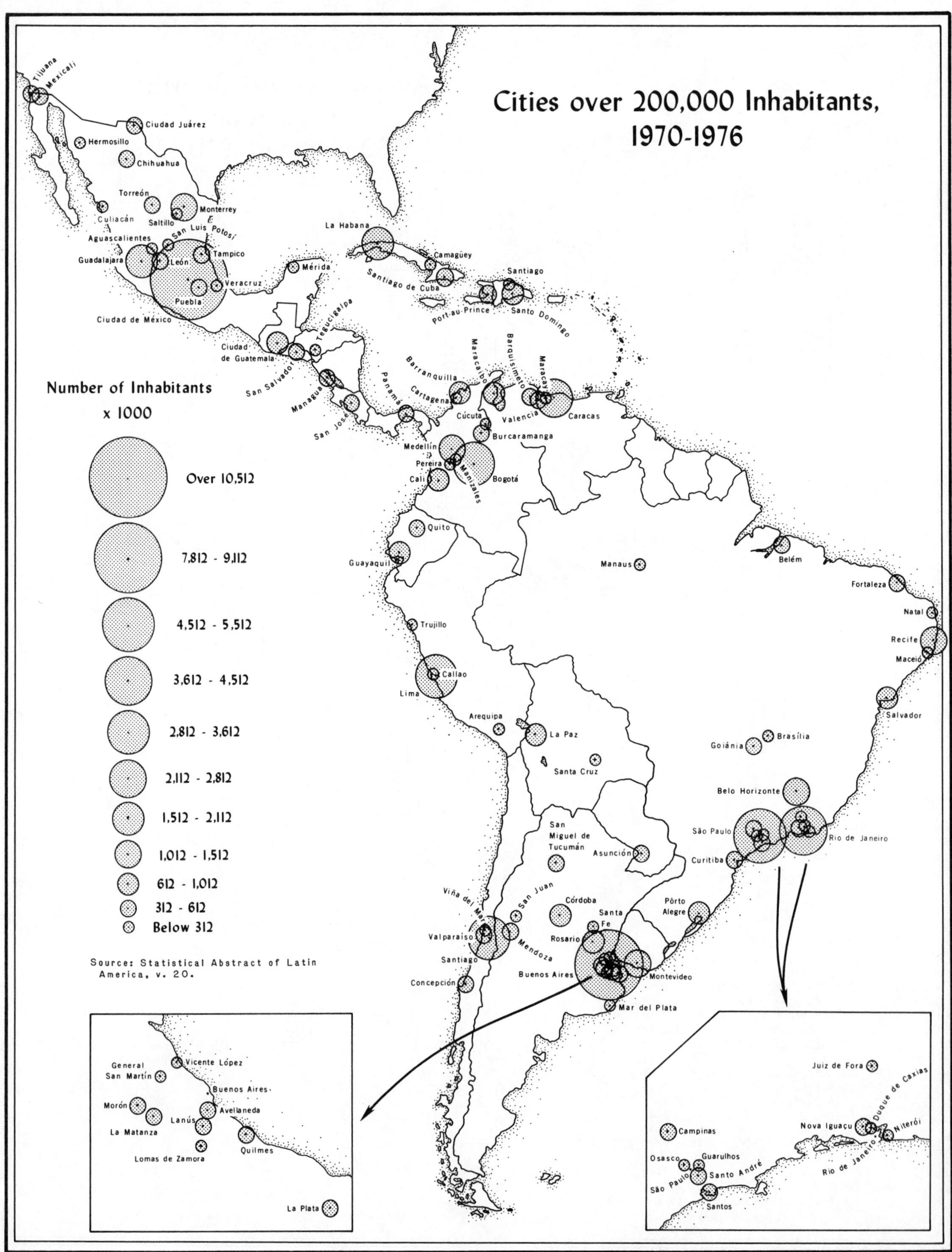
Cities over 200,000 Inhabitants, 1970-1976
Number of Inhabitants x 1000
Over 10,512
7,812 - 9,112
4,512 - 5,512
3,612 - 4,512
2,812 - 3,612
2,112 - 2,812
1,512 - 2,112
1,012 - 1,512
612 - 1,012
312 - 612
Below 312
Source: Statistical Abstract of Latin America, v. 20.
Tijuana
Mexicali
Ciudad Juárez
Hermosillo
Chihuahua
Torreón
Monterrey
Culiacán
Saltillo
San Luis Potosí
Aguascalientes
Guadalajara
León
Tampico
Veracruz
Puebla
Ciudad de México
Mérida
La Habana
Camagüey
Santiago de Cuba
Santiago
Port-au-Prince
Santo Domingo
Tegucigalpa
Ciudad de Guatemala
San Salvador
Managua
San José
Panamá
Barranquilla
Cartagena
Maracaibo
Barquisimeto
Maracay
Valencia
Caracas
Cúcuta
Burcaramanga
Medellín
Pereira
Manizales
Bogotá
Cali
Quito
Guayaquil
Manaus
Belém
Fortaleza
Natal
Recife
Maceió
Trujillo
Callao
Lima
Salvador
Arequipa
La Paz
Santa Cruz
Brasília
Goiânia
Belo Horizonte
São Paulo
Rio de Janeiro
Curitiba
San Miguel de Tucumán
Asunción
Viña del Mar
San Juan
Córdoba
Santa Fe
Pôrto Alegre
Valparaíso
Mendoza
Rosario
Santiago
Buenos Aires
Montevideo
Concepción
Mar del Plata
General San Martín
Vicente López
Buenos Aires
Morón
Avellaneda
Lanús
La Matanza
Lomas de Zamora
Quilmes
La Plata
Juiz de Fora
Duque de Caxias
Campinas
Nova Iguaçu
Niterói
Osasco
Guarulhos
Santo André
São Paulo
Rio de Janeiro
Santos

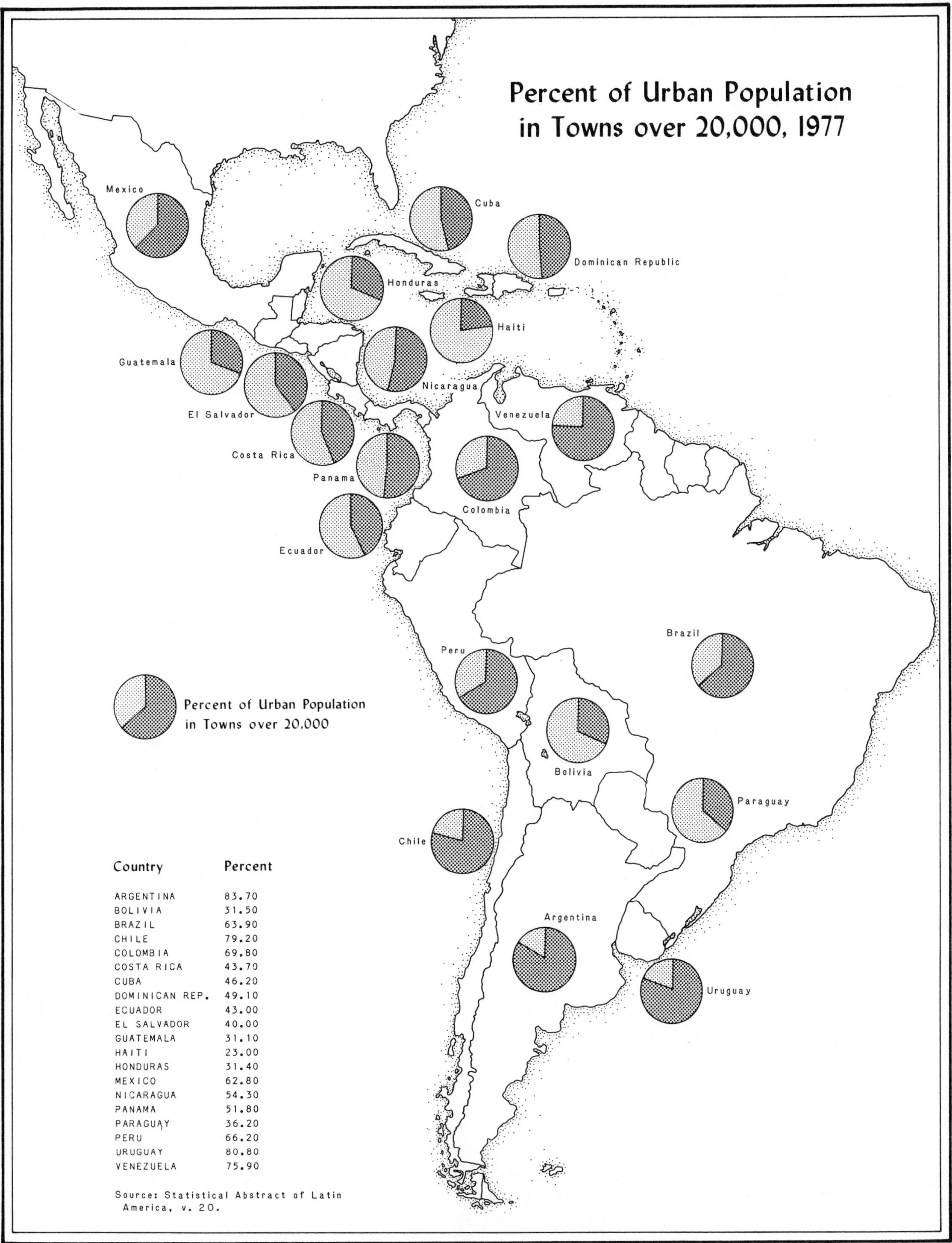

Country	Percent
ARGENTINA	83.70
BOLIVIA	31.50
BRAZIL	63.90
CHILE	79.20
COLOMBIA	69.80
COSTA RICA	43.70
CUBA	46.20
DOMINICAN REP.	49.10
ECUADOR	43.00
EL SALVADOR	40.00
GUATEMALA	31.10
HAITI	23.00
HONDURAS	31.40
MEXICO	62.80
NICARAGUA	54.30
PANAMA	51.80
PARAGUAY	36.20
PERU	66.20
URUGUAY	80.80
VENEZUELA	75.90

Source: Statistical Abstract of Latin America, v. 20.

Latin American Economies and Society

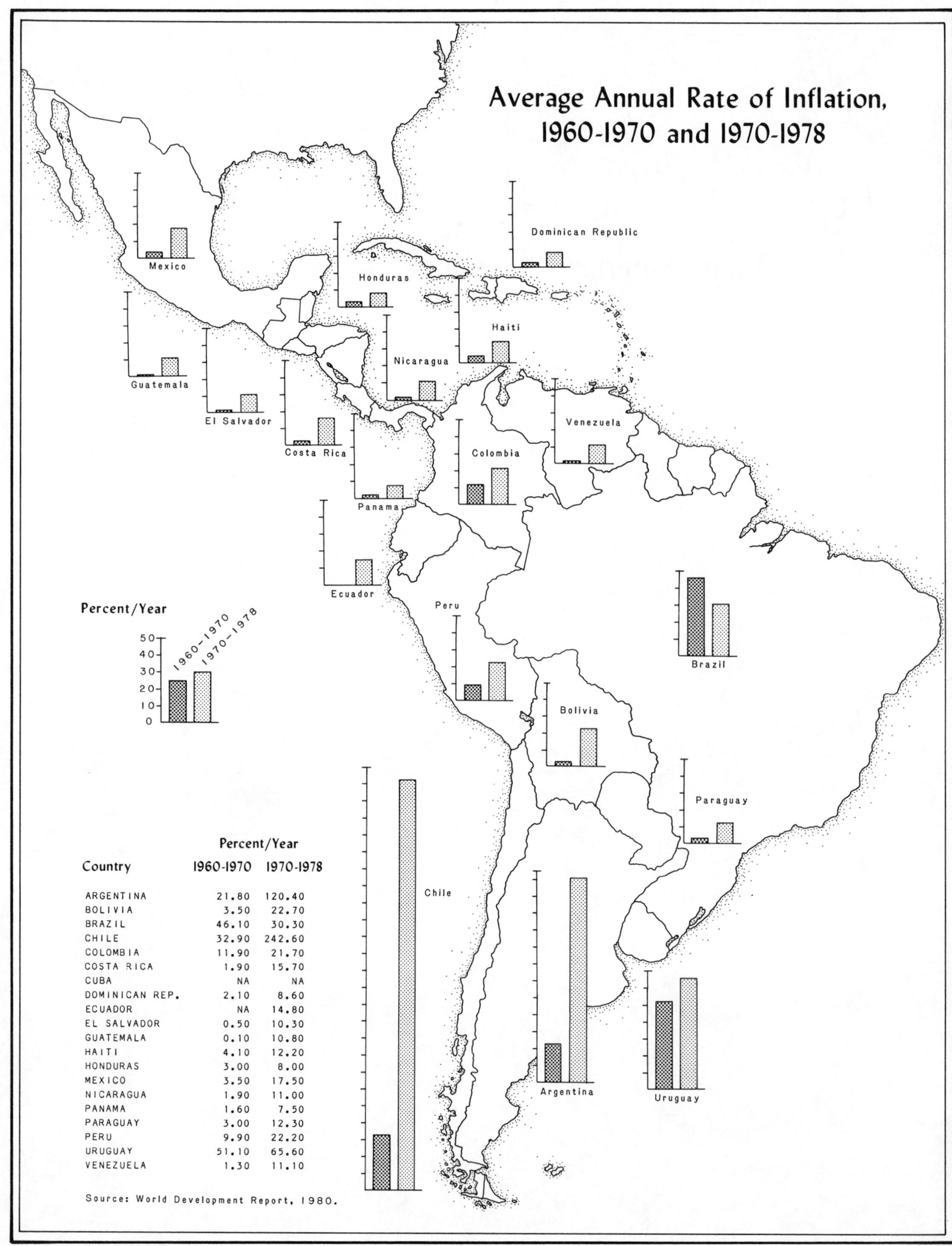

Country	Percent/Year 1960-1970	1970-1978
ARGENTINA	21.80	120.40
BOLIVIA	3.50	22.70
BRAZIL	46.10	30.30
CHILE	32.90	242.60
COLOMBIA	11.90	21.70
COSTA RICA	1.90	15.70
CUBA	NA	NA
DOMINICAN REP.	2.10	8.60
ECUADOR	NA	14.80
EL SALVADOR	0.50	10.30
GUATEMALA	0.10	10.80
HAITI	4.10	12.20
HONDURAS	3.00	8.00
MEXICO	3.50	17.50
NICARAGUA	1.90	11.00
PANAMA	1.60	7.50
PARAGUAY	3.00	12.30
PERU	9.90	22.20
URUGUAY	51.10	65.60
VENEZUELA	1.30	11.10

Source: World Development Report, 1980.

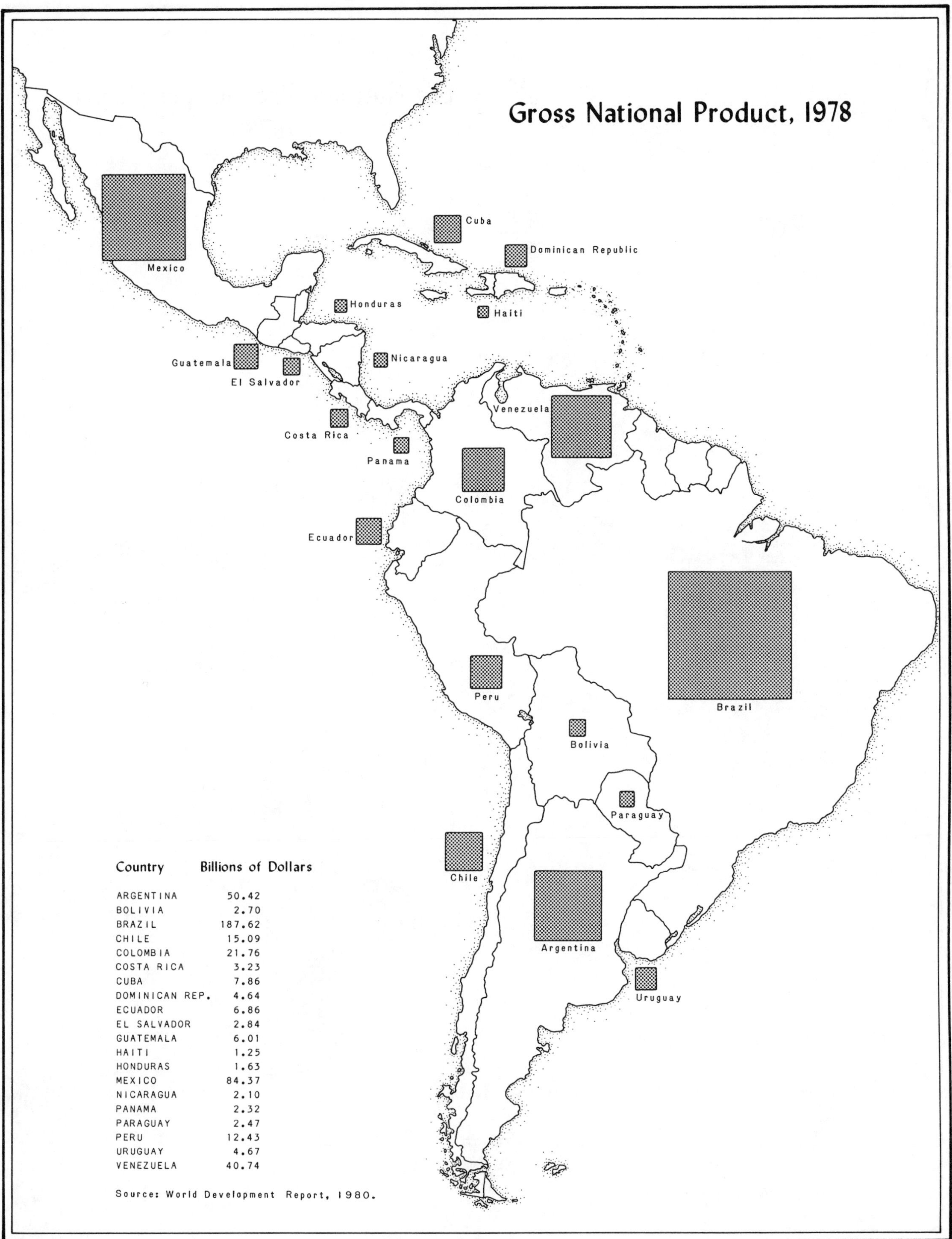

Country	Billions of Dollars
ARGENTINA	50.42
BOLIVIA	2.70
BRAZIL	187.62
CHILE	15.09
COLOMBIA	21.76
COSTA RICA	3.23
CUBA	7.86
DOMINICAN REP.	4.64
ECUADOR	6.86
EL SALVADOR	2.84
GUATEMALA	6.01
HAITI	1.25
HONDURAS	1.63
MEXICO	84.37
NICARAGUA	2.10
PANAMA	2.32
PARAGUAY	2.47
PERU	12.43
URUGUAY	4.67
VENEZUELA	40.74

Source: World Development Report, 1980.

Gross National Product per Capita, 1978

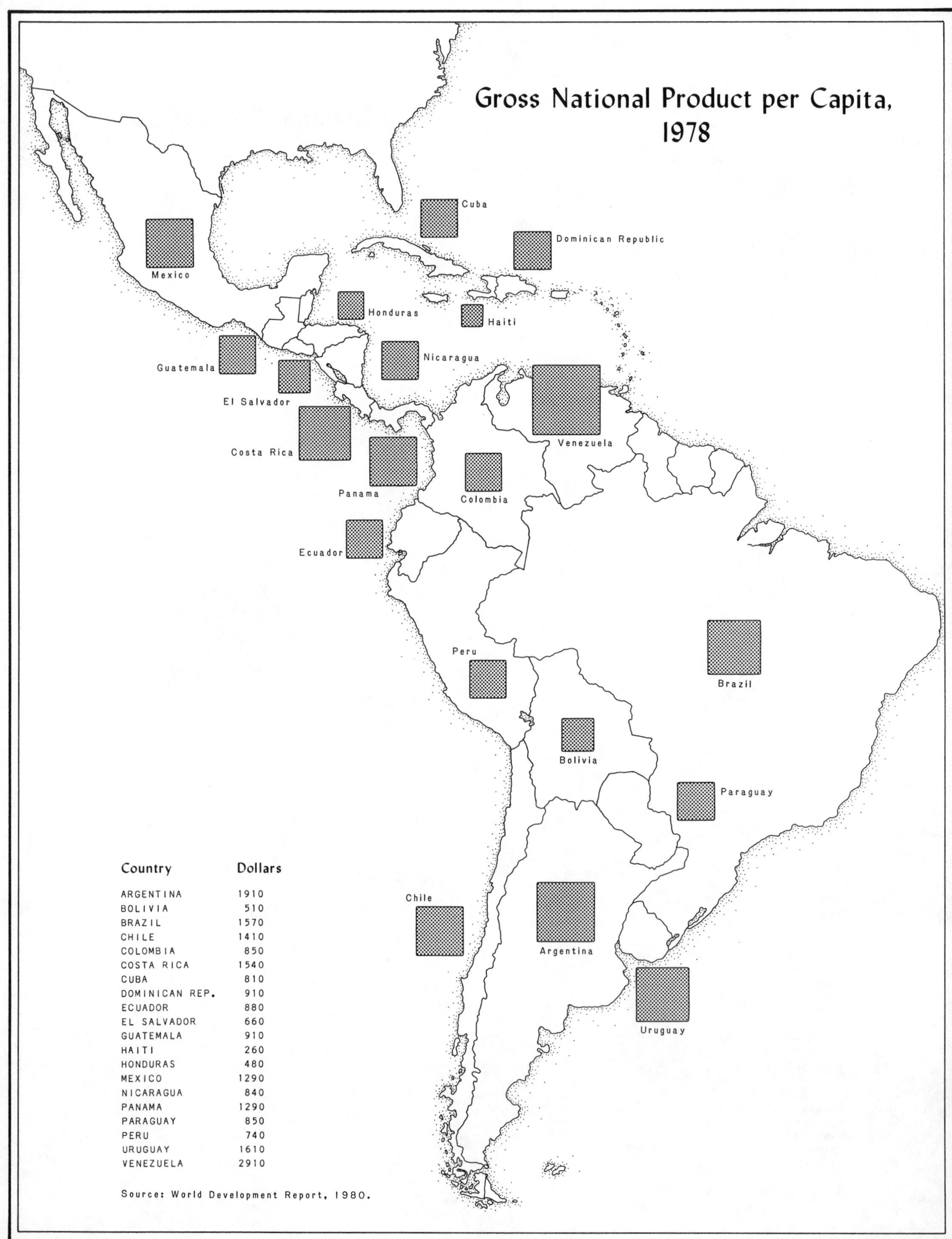

Country	Dollars
ARGENTINA	1910
BOLIVIA	510
BRAZIL	1570
CHILE	1410
COLOMBIA	850
COSTA RICA	1540
CUBA	810
DOMINICAN REP.	910
ECUADOR	880
EL SALVADOR	660
GUATEMALA	910
HAITI	260
HONDURAS	480
MEXICO	1290
NICARAGUA	840
PANAMA	1290
PARAGUAY	850
PERU	740
URUGUAY	1610
VENEZUELA	2910

Source: World Development Report, 1980.

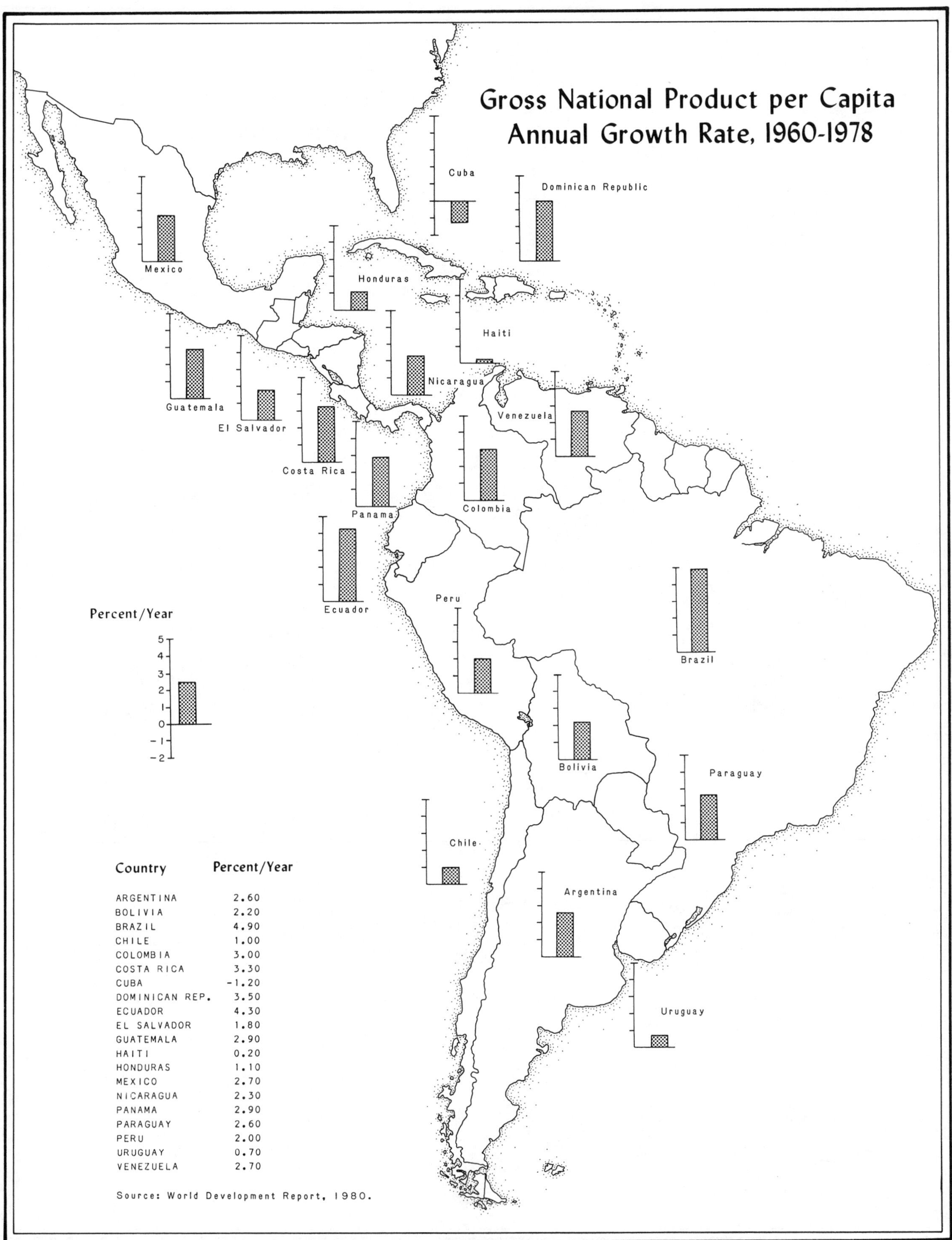

Gross National Product per Capita
Annual Growth Rate, 1960-1978
Cuba
Dominican Republic
Mexico
Honduras
Haiti
Guatemala
El Salvador
Nicaragua
Costa Rica
Venezuela
Colombia
Panama
Ecuador
Peru
Brazil
Percent/Year
5
4
3
2
1
0
-1
-2
Bolivia
Paraguay
Chile
Argentina
Uruguay
Country
Percent/Year
ARGENTINA 2.60
BOLIVIA 2.20
BRAZIL 4.90
CHILE 1.00
COLOMBIA 3.00
COSTA RICA 3.30
CUBA -1.20
DOMINICAN REP. 3.50
ECUADOR 4.30
EL SALVADOR 1.80
GUATEMALA 2.90
HAITI 0.20
HONDURAS 1.10
MEXICO 2.70
NICARAGUA 2.30
PANAMA 2.90
PARAGUAY 2.60
PERU 2.00
URUGUAY 0.70
VENEZUELA 2.70
Source: World Development Report, 1980.

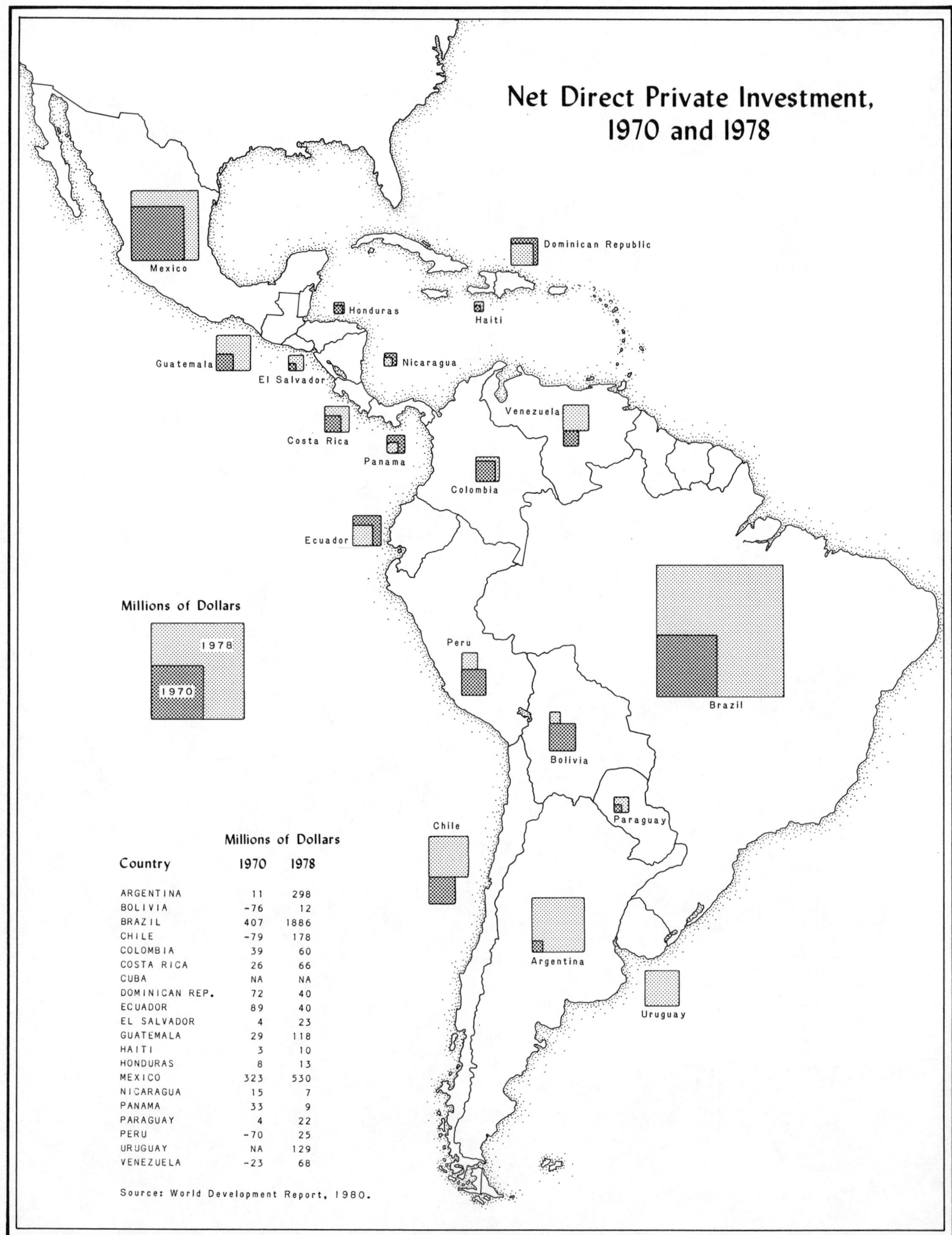

Country	Millions of Dollars 1970	1978
ARGENTINA	11	298
BOLIVIA	-76	12
BRAZIL	407	1886
CHILE	-79	178
COLOMBIA	39	60
COSTA RICA	26	66
CUBA	NA	NA
DOMINICAN REP.	72	40
ECUADOR	89	40
EL SALVADOR	4	23
GUATEMALA	29	118
HAITI	3	10
HONDURAS	8	13
MEXICO	323	530
NICARAGUA	15	7
PANAMA	33	9
PARAGUAY	4	22
PERU	-70	25
URUGUAY	NA	129
VENEZUELA	-23	68

Source: World Development Report, 1980.

Distribution of Gross Domestic Product by Category, 1960 and 1978

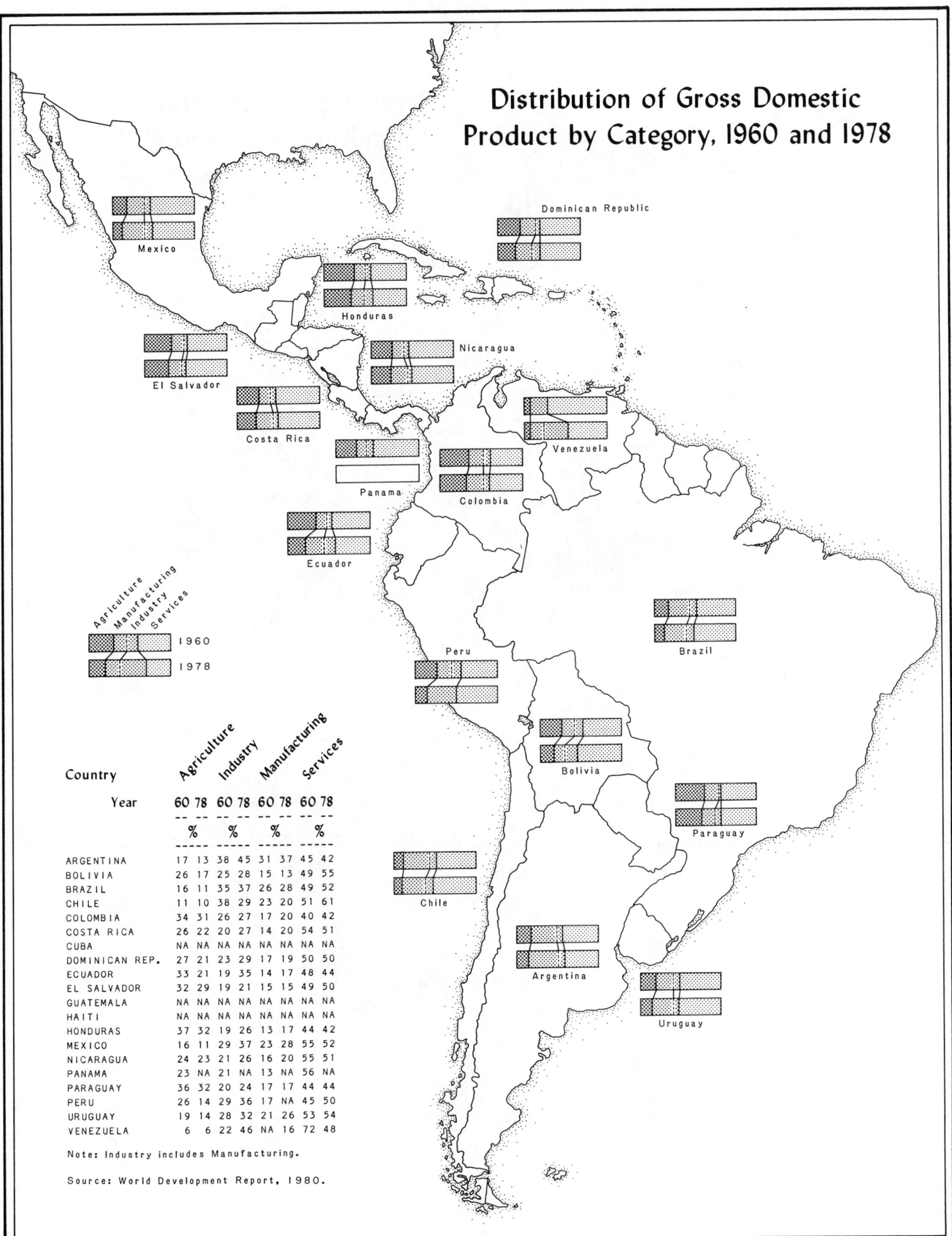

Country	Agriculture		Industry		Manufacturing		Services	
Year	60	78	60	78	60	78	60	78
	%		%		%		%	
ARGENTINA	17	13	38	45	31	37	45	42
BOLIVIA	26	17	25	28	15	13	49	55
BRAZIL	16	11	35	37	26	28	49	52
CHILE	11	10	38	29	23	20	51	61
COLOMBIA	34	31	26	27	17	20	40	42
COSTA RICA	26	22	20	27	14	20	54	51
CUBA	NA	NA	NA	NA	NA	NA	NA	NA
DOMINICAN REP.	27	21	23	29	17	19	50	50
ECUADOR	33	21	19	35	14	17	48	44
EL SALVADOR	32	29	19	21	15	15	49	50
GUATEMALA	NA	NA	NA	NA	NA	NA	NA	NA
HAITI	NA	NA	NA	NA	NA	NA	NA	NA
HONDURAS	37	32	19	26	13	17	44	42
MEXICO	16	11	29	37	23	28	55	52
NICARAGUA	24	23	21	26	16	20	55	51
PANAMA	23	NA	21	NA	13	NA	56	NA
PARAGUAY	36	32	20	24	17	17	44	44
PERU	26	14	29	36	17	NA	45	50
URUGUAY	19	14	28	32	21	26	53	54
VENEZUELA	6	6	22	46	NA	16	72	48

Note: Industry includes Manufacturing.

Source: World Development Report, 1980.

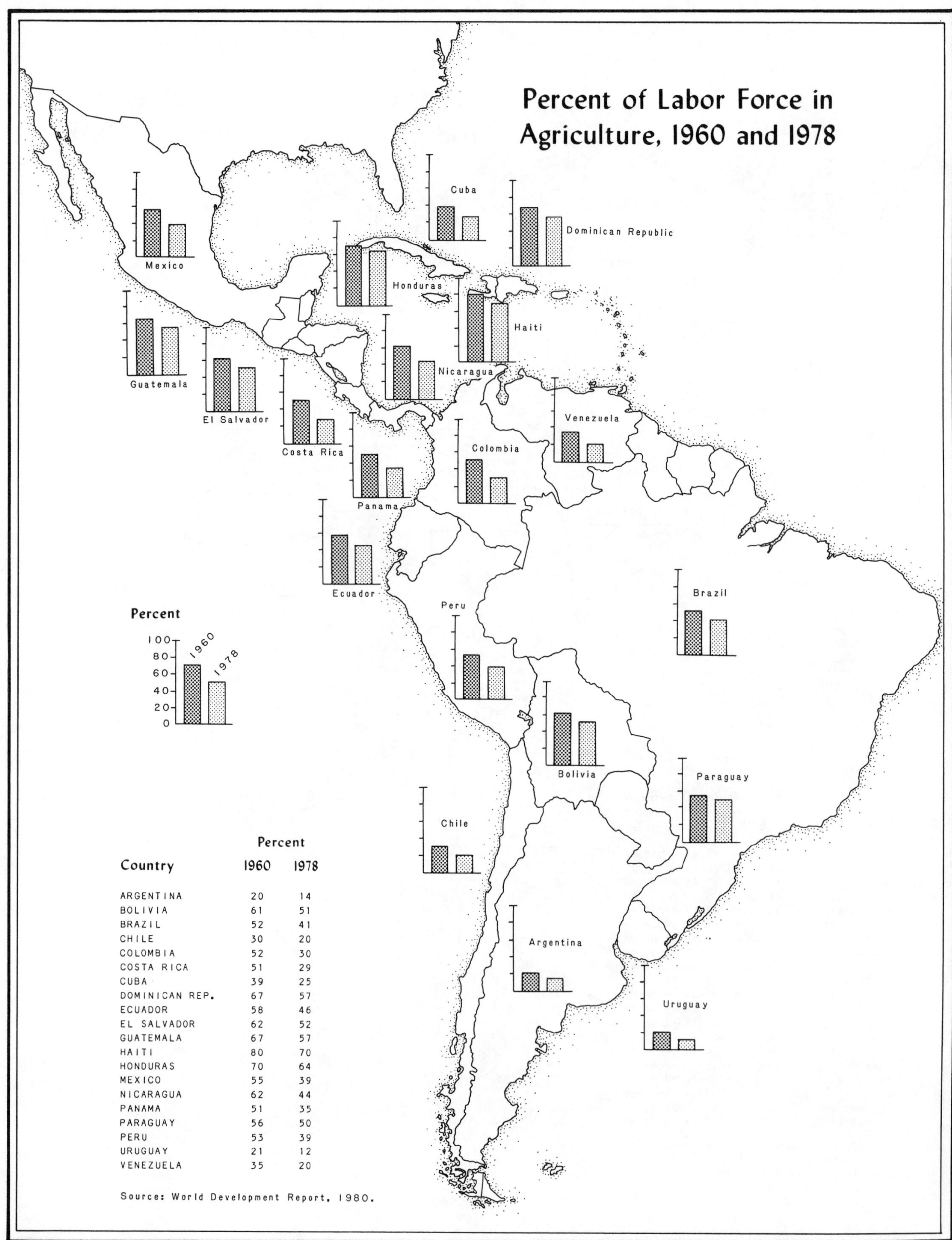

Country	Percent 1960	Percent 1978
ARGENTINA	20	14
BOLIVIA	61	51
BRAZIL	52	41
CHILE	30	20
COLOMBIA	52	30
COSTA RICA	51	29
CUBA	39	25
DOMINICAN REP.	67	57
ECUADOR	58	46
EL SALVADOR	62	52
GUATEMALA	67	57
HAITI	80	70
HONDURAS	70	64
MEXICO	55	39
NICARAGUA	62	44
PANAMA	51	35
PARAGUAY	56	50
PERU	53	39
URUGUAY	21	12
VENEZUELA	35	20

Source: World Development Report, 1980.

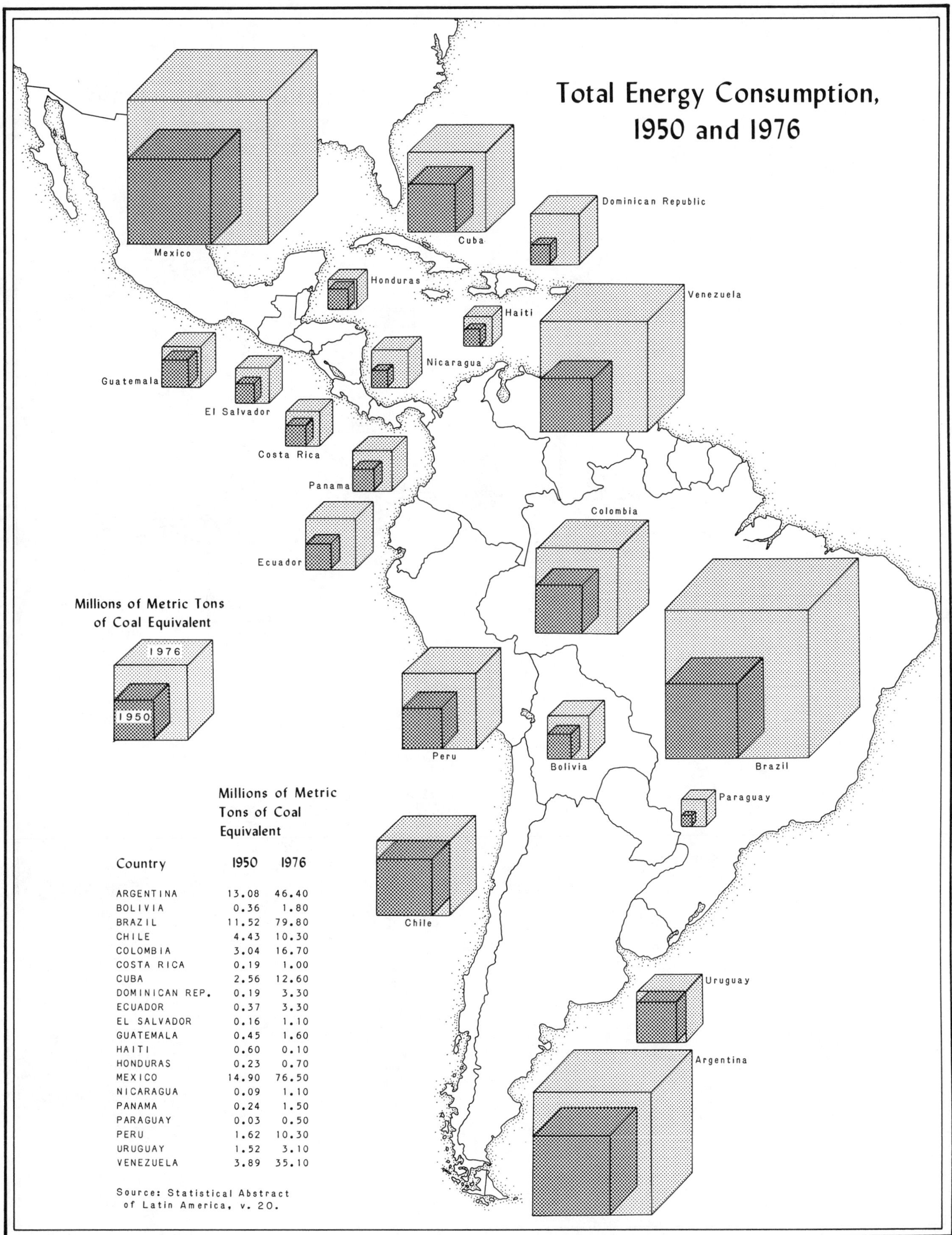

Millions of Metric Tons of Coal Equivalent

Country	1950	1976
ARGENTINA	13.08	46.40
BOLIVIA	0.36	1.80
BRAZIL	11.52	79.80
CHILE	4.43	10.30
COLOMBIA	3.04	16.70
COSTA RICA	0.19	1.00
CUBA	2.56	12.60
DOMINICAN REP.	0.19	3.30
ECUADOR	0.37	3.30
EL SALVADOR	0.16	1.10
GUATEMALA	0.45	1.60
HAITI	0.60	0.10
HONDURAS	0.23	0.70
MEXICO	14.90	76.50
NICARAGUA	0.09	1.10
PANAMA	0.24	1.50
PARAGUAY	0.03	0.50
PERU	1.62	10.30
URUGUAY	1.52	3.10
VENEZUELA	3.89	35.10

Source: Statistical Abstract of Latin America, v. 20.

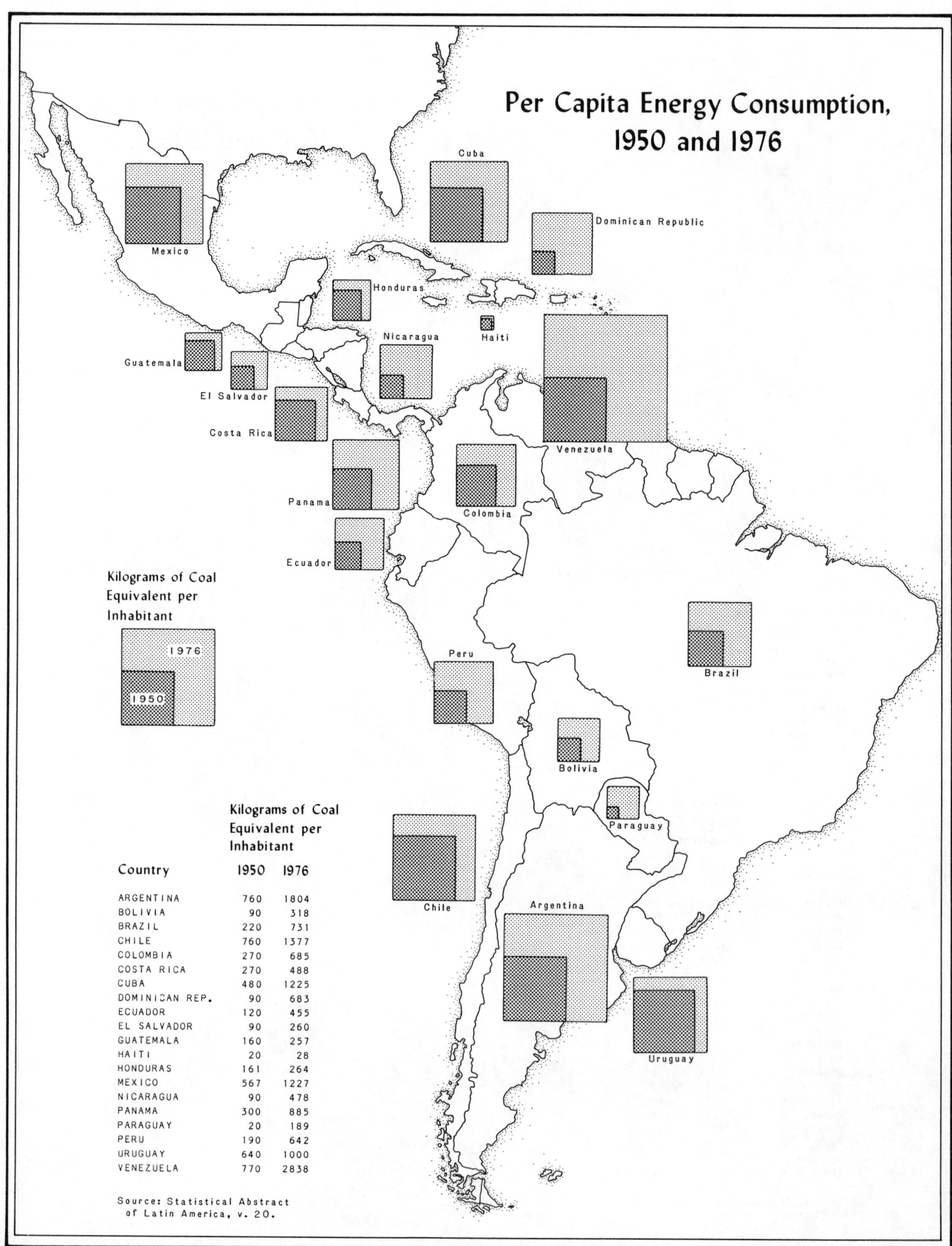

Kilograms of Coal Equivalent per Inhabitant

Country	1950	1976
ARGENTINA	760	1804
BOLIVIA	90	318
BRAZIL	220	731
CHILE	760	1377
COLOMBIA	270	685
COSTA RICA	270	488
CUBA	480	1225
DOMINICAN REP.	90	683
ECUADOR	120	455
EL SALVADOR	90	260
GUATEMALA	160	257
HAITI	20	28
HONDURAS	161	264
MEXICO	567	1227
NICARAGUA	90	478
PANAMA	300	885
PARAGUAY	20	189
PERU	190	642
URUGUAY	640	1000
VENEZUELA	770	2838

Source: Statistical Abstract of Latin America, v. 20.

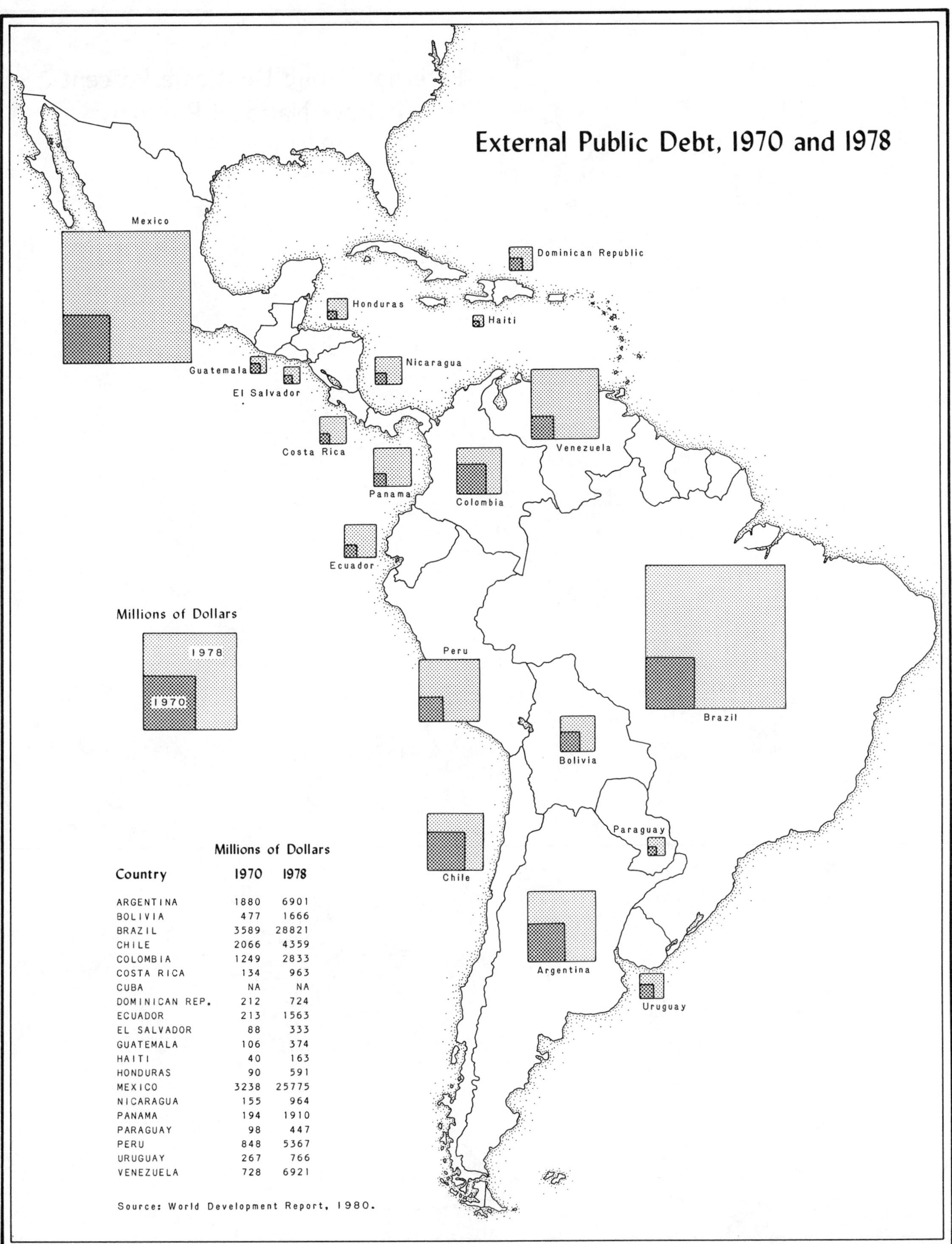

Millions of Dollars

Country	1970	1978
ARGENTINA	1880	6901
BOLIVIA	477	1666
BRAZIL	3589	28821
CHILE	2066	4359
COLOMBIA	1249	2833
COSTA RICA	134	963
CUBA	NA	NA
DOMINICAN REP.	212	724
ECUADOR	213	1563
EL SALVADOR	88	333
GUATEMALA	106	374
HAITI	40	163
HONDURAS	90	591
MEXICO	3238	25775
NICARAGUA	155	964
PANAMA	194	1910
PARAGUAY	98	447
PERU	848	5367
URUGUAY	267	766
VENEZUELA	728	6921

Source: World Development Report, 1980.

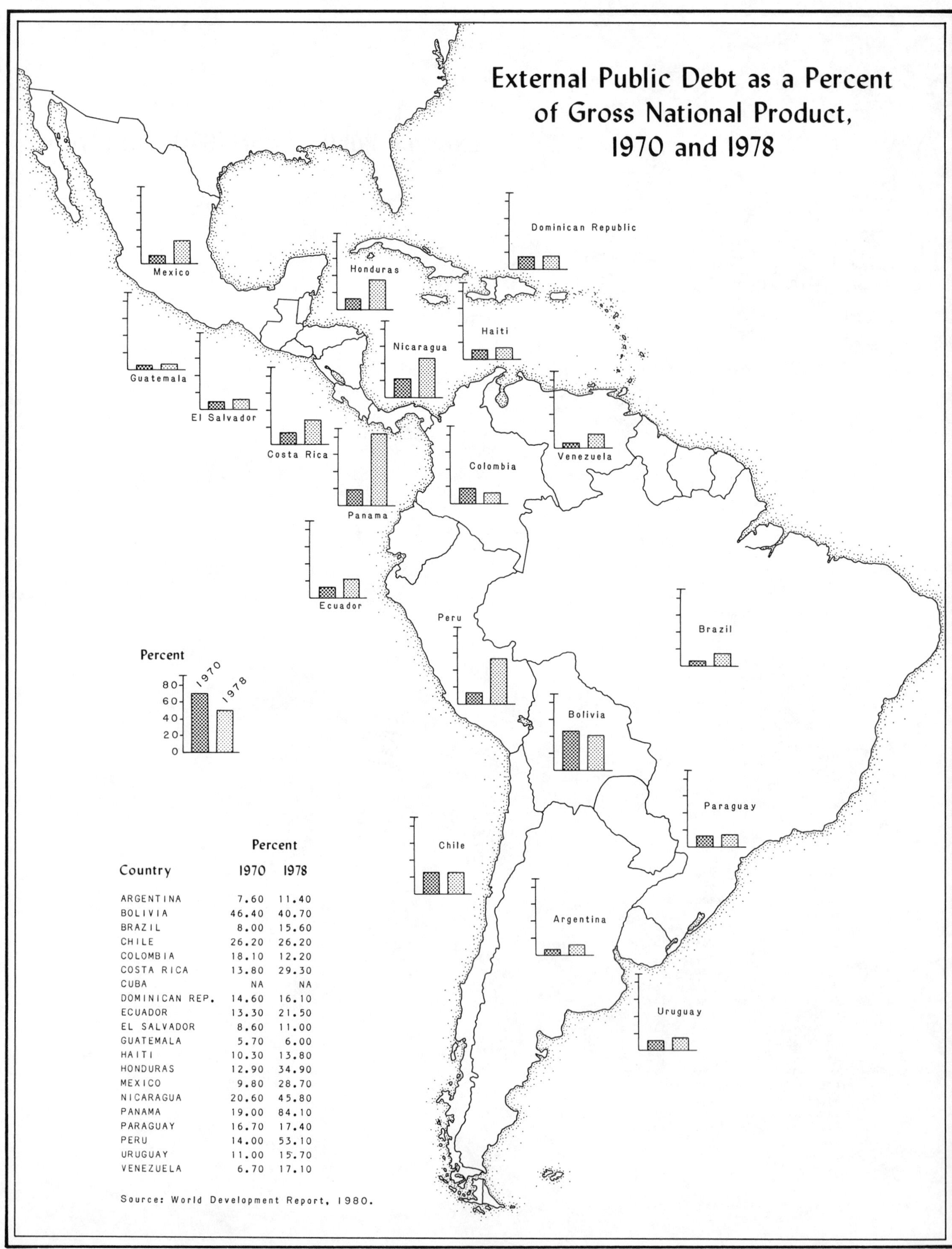

Country	Percent 1970	Percent 1978
ARGENTINA	7.60	11.40
BOLIVIA	46.40	40.70
BRAZIL	8.00	15.60
CHILE	26.20	26.20
COLOMBIA	18.10	12.20
COSTA RICA	13.80	29.30
CUBA	NA	NA
DOMINICAN REP.	14.60	16.10
ECUADOR	13.30	21.50
EL SALVADOR	8.60	11.00
GUATEMALA	5.70	6.00
HAITI	10.30	13.80
HONDURAS	12.90	34.90
MEXICO	9.80	28.70
NICARAGUA	20.60	45.80
PANAMA	19.00	84.10
PARAGUAY	16.70	17.40
PERU	14.00	53.10
URUGUAY	11.00	15.70
VENEZUELA	6.70	17.10

Source: World Development Report, 1980.

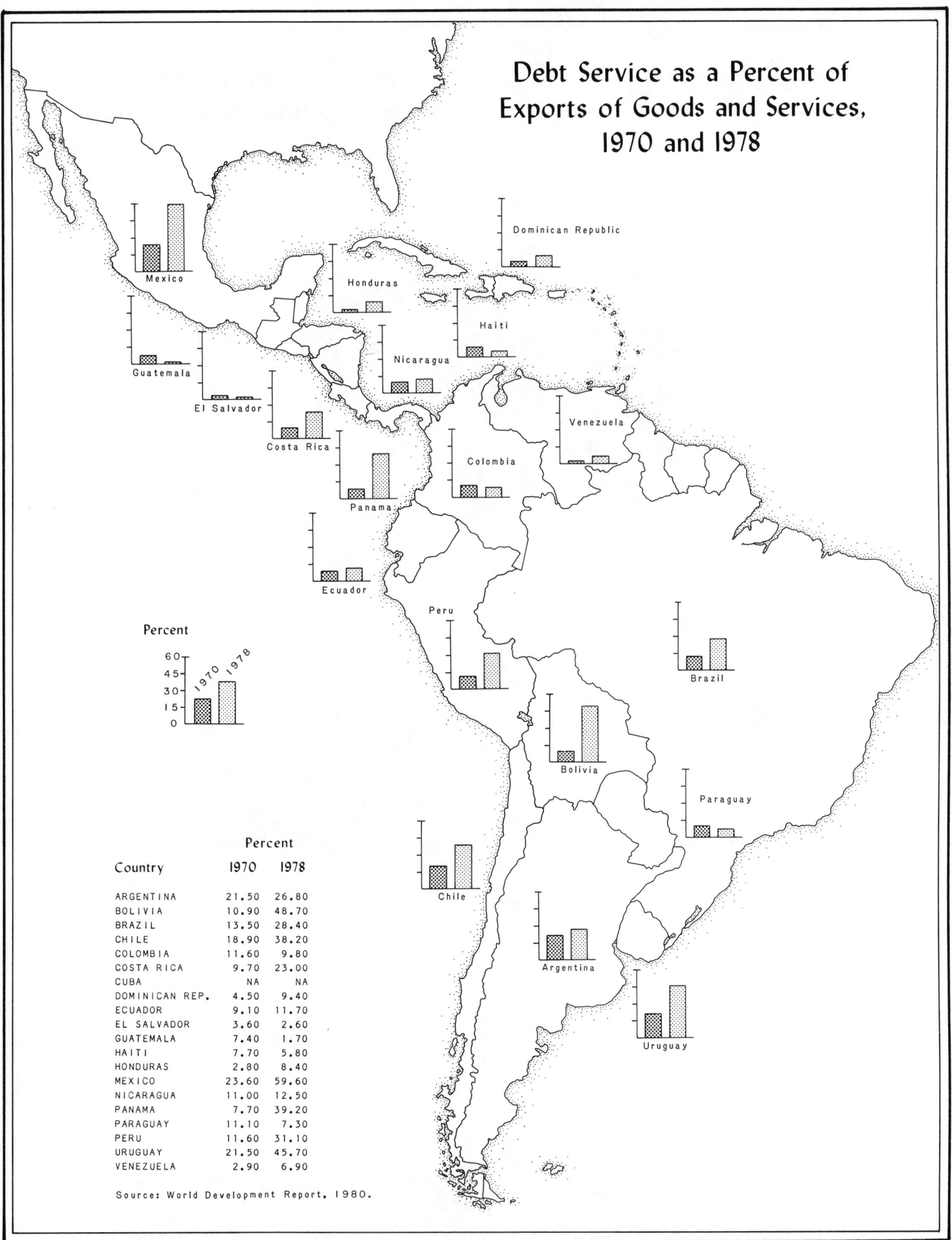

Country	Percent 1970	Percent 1978
ARGENTINA	21.50	26.80
BOLIVIA	10.90	48.70
BRAZIL	13.50	28.40
CHILE	18.90	38.20
COLOMBIA	11.60	9.80
COSTA RICA	9.70	23.00
CUBA	NA	NA
DOMINICAN REP.	4.50	9.40
ECUADOR	9.10	11.70
EL SALVADOR	3.60	2.60
GUATEMALA	7.40	1.70
HAITI	7.70	5.80
HONDURAS	2.80	8.40
MEXICO	23.60	59.60
NICARAGUA	11.00	12.50
PANAMA	7.70	39.20
PARAGUAY	11.10	7.30
PERU	11.60	31.10
URUGUAY	21.50	45.70
VENEZUELA	2.90	6.90

Source: World Development Report, 1980.

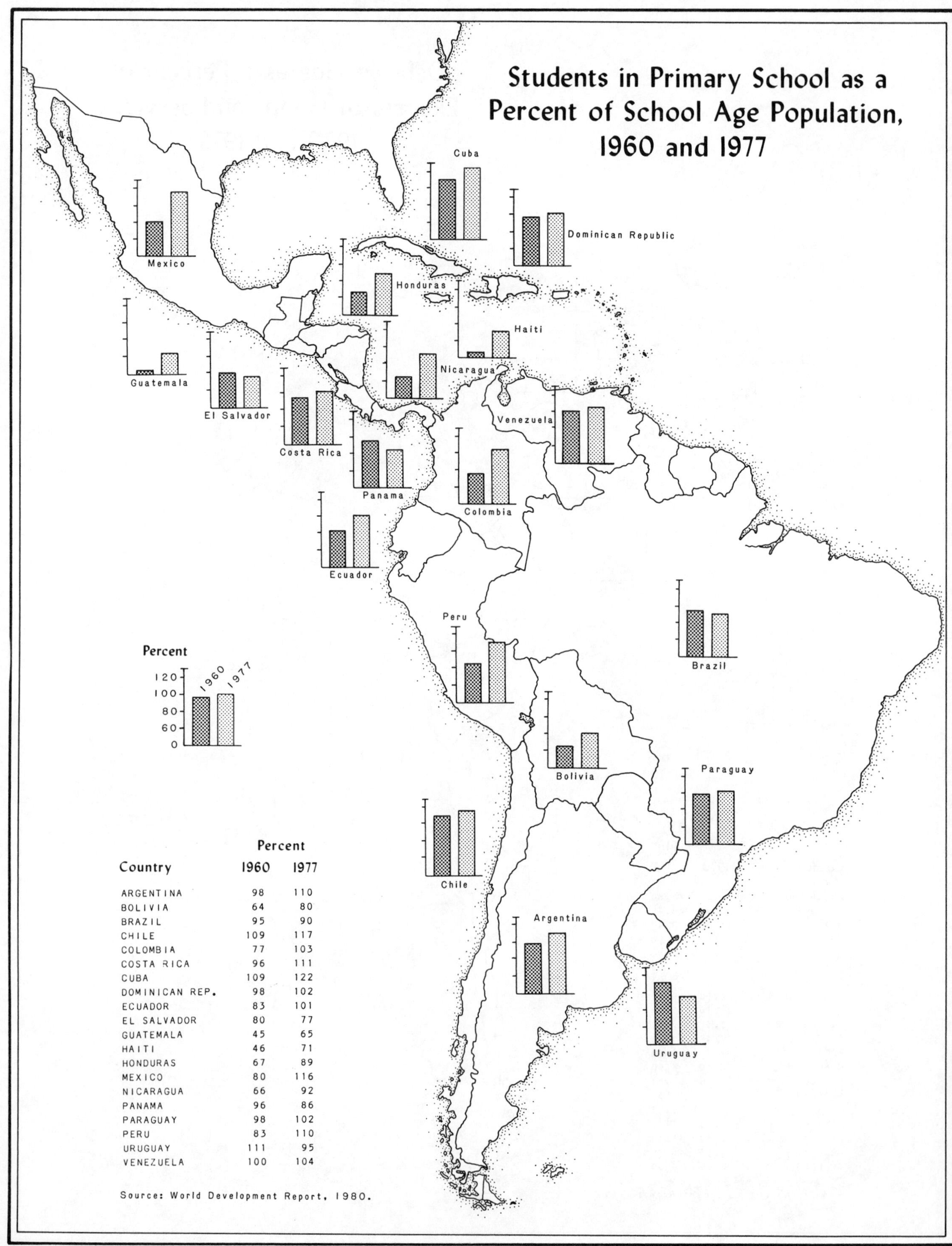

Country	Percent 1960	1977
ARGENTINA	98	110
BOLIVIA	64	80
BRAZIL	95	90
CHILE	109	117
COLOMBIA	77	103
COSTA RICA	96	111
CUBA	109	122
DOMINICAN REP.	98	102
ECUADOR	83	101
EL SALVADOR	80	77
GUATEMALA	45	65
HAITI	46	71
HONDURAS	67	89
MEXICO	80	116
NICARAGUA	66	92
PANAMA	96	86
PARAGUAY	98	102
PERU	83	110
URUGUAY	111	95
VENEZUELA	100	104

Source: World Development Report, 1980.

INDEX

INDEX

INDEX

INDEX

-C-

-D-

-E-

INDEX

-G-

-O-

-S-

-T-

-U-

-V-

-W-